IMAGES
of America

GRAND ISLAND

THE JULIUS LESCHINSKY PHOTOGRAPHS

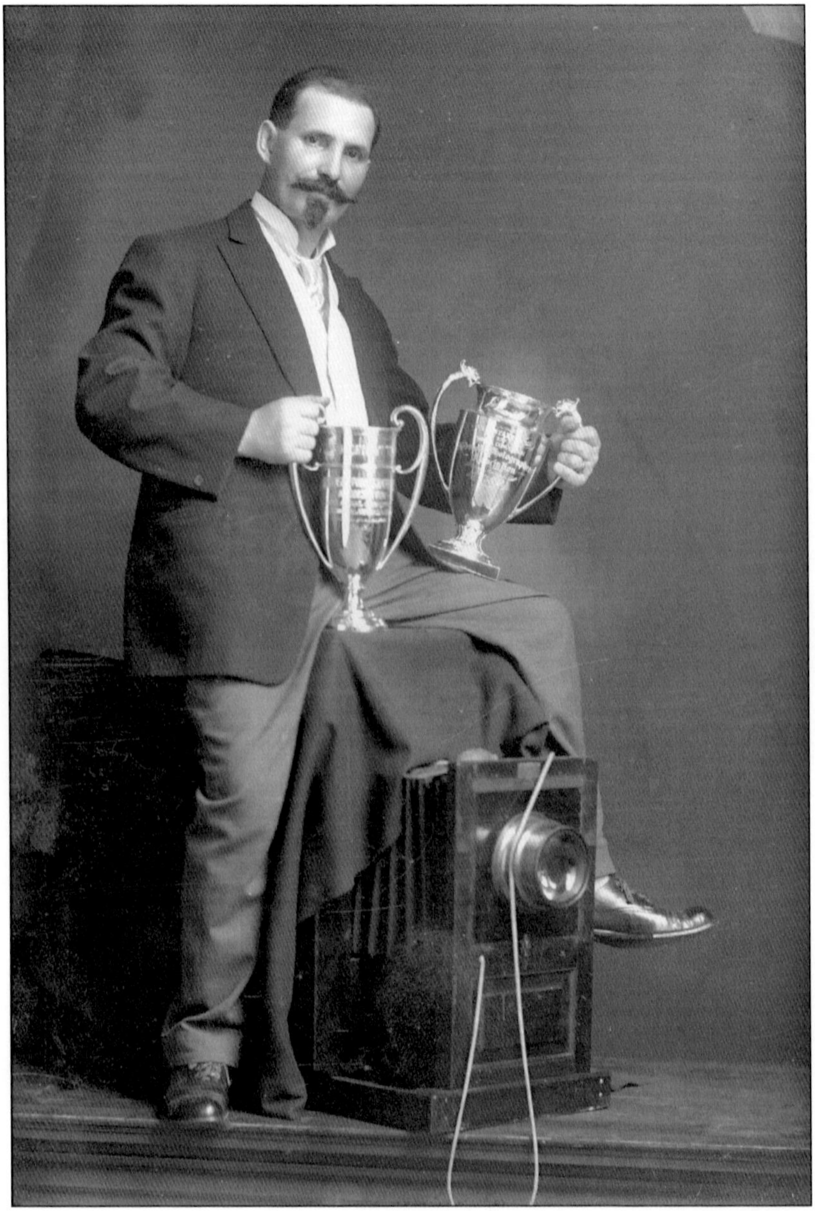

Seated atop an oversized camera, Julius Leschinsky poses with two silver cups, prizes from the 23rd annual Nebraska Photographer Association Convention held in Grand Island on September 24–26, 1912. At the time, Leschinsky was president of the organization. In his opening address, Leschinsky encouraged Nebraska photographers to work together to improve their profession and art form.

On the cover: Taken in July 1915, this patriotic automobile belonged to Grand Island mayor Charles G. Ryan, likely the man driving the automobile. Ryan was mayor from 1911 to 1916 and served as the first president of the chamber of commerce. His wife Evelyn is likely the woman seated in the front passenger seat. She was well known and liked in Grand Island. They had one child, also named Evelyn. (Courtesy of the Lumbard-Leschinsky Studio Collection: Stuhr Museum of the Prairie Pioneer.)

IMAGES
of America

GRAND ISLAND

THE JULIUS LESCHINSKY PHOTOGRAPHS

Stuhr Museum of the Prairie Pioneer

ARCADIA
PUBLISHING

ISBN 978-0-7385-6057-1

Published by Arcadia Publishing
Charleston SC, Chicago IL, Portsmouth NH, San Francisco CA

Printed in the United States of America

Library of Congress Control Number: 2008936321

For all general information contact Arcadia Publishing at:
Telephone 843-853-2070
Fax 843-853-0044
E-mail sales@arcadiapublishing.com
For customer service and orders:
Toll-Free 1-888-313-2665

Visit us on the Internet at www.arcadiapublishing.com

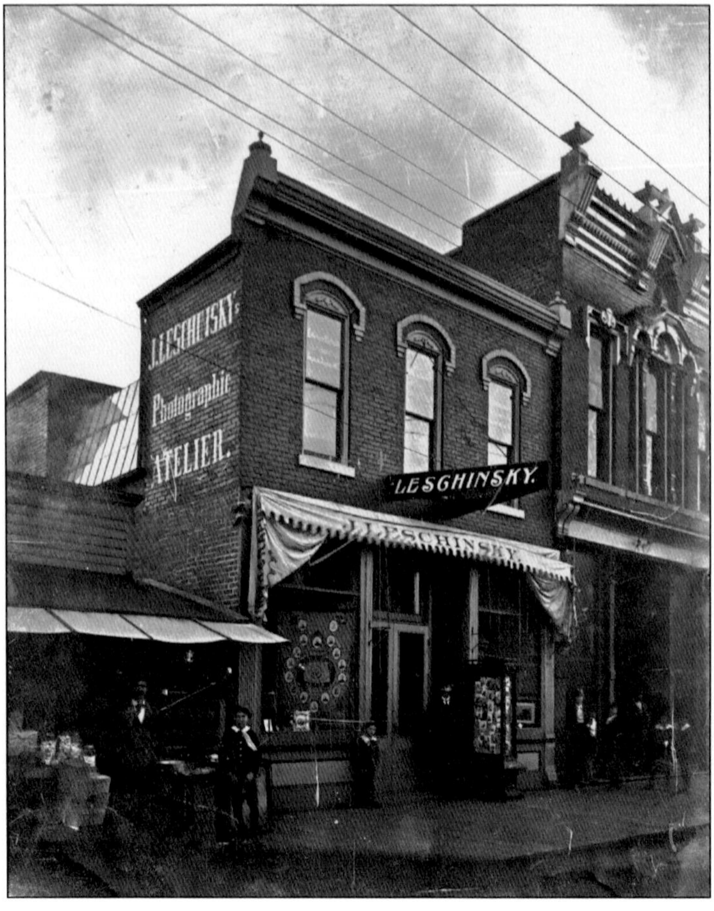

Half brothers Max and Julius Leschinsky opened their first studio in Grand Island in 1886 at 212 East Third Street. In 1890, Max moved to Loup City and Julius purchased the larger, better-equipped studio formerly owned by Michael Murphy at 113 East Third Street. Julius thrived as a businessman and artist. In about 1896, Julius built the new brick studio seen in this photograph at 109 East Third Street.

Contents

Acknowledgments 6

Introduction 7

1. About Town 9

2. Businesses 25

3. Home Sweet Home 37

4. Celebrating Community 51

5. All Dressed Up 67

6. Getting Around 85

7. World War I 101

8. Whimsy, Weird, and Wonderful 113

ACKNOWLEDGMENTS

As curator of the research department, I am often asked if I have a favorite item among the thousands of books, photographs, papers, and maps held in the archives at Stuhr Museum of the Prairie Pioneer. My answer is always the same. I have 28,000 favorites, the number of glass-plate negatives in the Lumbard-Leschinsky Studio Collection. From the moment I walked into the vault where the glass-plate negatives are stored, I was hooked. I wanted to know more about the photographic process, how to care for them, who the people were in the photographs, and how we could share this amazing collection.

When I was approached to compile a follow-up to our 2007 *Grand Island and Hall County* book, I knew instantly what I wanted the focus to be. The Lumbard-Leschinsky Studio Collection is a phenomenal treasure, and I am very excited to share the incredible images contained in these pages.

In writing this book, there are many people who deserve to be thanked. The citizens of Hall County have been a constant source of loyalty and support since they first voted in 1961 to create the Stuhr Museum of the Prairie Pioneer. It is only with their enduring loyalty that we are able to succeed in our mission of preserving and portraying the history of this county.

Stuhr Museum has an amazing staff. We work hard every day to make our events, classes, and exhibits the best they can be. The true heroes of Stuhr Museum, however, are our volunteers, and we can never thank them enough for their hard work and dedication. I would also like to thank the members of our current museum operating board, who offer us endless support, guidance, and vision.

Special thanks must be given to assistant curator Kallie Roberts. Kallie helped me search through hundreds of boxes of negatives for the perfect images and shared my delight as our scans revealed incredible details. She spent untold hours scrolling through microfilm to check and recheck facts. During the writing process, she was my personal thesaurus and sounding board. Thank you, Kallie.

Karen Keehr
Curator, Research Department
Stuhr Museum of the Prairie Pioneer

INTRODUCTION

In 1857, a small band of settlers arrived in the vast and wild prairie of the Nebraska Territory to create a new city. They had been given the task by a group of investors in Davenport, Iowa, who were gambling that the much-talked-about transcontinental railroad would follow the Platte Valley. They believed that if they beat the railroad to the land, they could reap untold economic rewards. Comprised mostly of German immigrants, the settlers envisioned great possibilities for their new city. They chose a strategic spot along the Platte Valley, well known to Native American hunters, French fur trappers, and emigrants headed west along the Oregon, California-Overland, and Mormon Trails. They took their city's name from the French traders' name for the large island that stretched over 50 miles between the north and south channels of the Platte River and named their settlement Grand Island.

The railroad arrived in Grand Island on July 8, 1866, and the city flourished. The railroad brought with it a steady stream of goods, building supplies, and people. Seemingly overnight, Grand Island went from a prairie settlement to an economic center. The population swelled as new businesses and industries thrived. During the 1880s, Grand Island experienced its largest growth as new buildings, businesses, and homes were built. It was during this booming period in Grand Island history that Julius Leschinsky began his photography career.

Born in West Prussia in 1860, Julius Leschinsky came to America at the age of 19 in 1880. He worked several odd jobs across the nation until joining his half brother Max Leschinsky in a Grand Island photography business in 1886. Trusted and well liked, the Leschinsky brothers' business quickly established itself within the community. In 1890, the brothers split the business. Max opened a studio in Loup City, and Julius purchased the larger, better-equipped studio formerly owned by Michael Murphy on East Third Street in Grand Island.

During his career, Julius's business continued to grow and expand, making him Grand Island's premier photographer. He was recognized by the Nebraska State Photographers Association three times with Silver Loving Cups, its highest honor for artistic merit, and served as its president for many years. He was also awarded a silver medal for his entry into the Trans-Mississippi Photographers Convention in 1898.

Julius married Minnie Doll on September 30, 1888, and they had two sons, Oswald and Armand. Julius often took his camera home and captured numerous special family moments as the boys grew to adulthood. Both sons showed talent and interest in their father's profession. Armand enlisted in the U.S. Army during World War I only to contract pneumonia and die in 1918, while serving in France. Oswald demonstrated great promise as a photographer and attended several professional conventions. He married Clara Booth on January 10, 1926.

Tragically, just seven months after his marriage, Oswald died at the age of 37. Julius carried on and continued to take photographs until his death in 1937.

His artist's eye and keen business sense made his studio so successful that his name carried weight even after his death. His nephews Carl, Stanley, and Laurence Lumbard took over the studio under the Leschinsky name. The Lumbards had studied and worked with Julius for a number of years. They continued to expand the business, adding an electronics department in the 1950s. At about this time, they also changed the business's name to the Lumbard-Leschinsky Studio. The Lumbards continued their uncle's tradition of success until the studio finally closed in 1984, just short of its centennial.

In 1980, downtown redevelopment forced the Lumbards to relocate the business. The block where the Leschinsky Studio had stood since the 1890s was torn down to create a parking lot. Seeking a permanent home for their uncle's collection, the Lumbard family donated a large portion of Leschinsky's legacy to Stuhr Museum of the Prairie Pioneer. The collection included 28,000 glass-plate negatives, 4,000 prints, studio equipment, and cameras. Also among the items given were seven business ledgers. The ledgers are a valuable tool that allow for research and identification of the photograph subjects. Identification numbers written on the glass-plate negatives correspond with numbers found in the ledgers and help connect images to names, events, and dates important to Grand Island and Hall County history.

The silver gelatin dry plates of the Lumbard-Leschinsky Studio Collection date mainly from the 1910 to 1919 period. The images captured on these plates form the source for this book. High-resolution scans of the original plates have created images as sharp and crisp as the day Leschinsky captured them. The Leschinsky collection of glass-plate negatives is exclusive to Stuhr Museum. Many of the collection's images have never been published and have not been seen in over 90 years.

The Lumbard-Leschinsky Studio Collection is a vital and important part of Stuhr Museum. Images have been used by all departments of the museum, including marketing, exhibits, education, research, and interpretation. Through the use of digital imaging, new insight has been gained into the history of Grand Island and Hall County. The images are also often published in local and regional newspapers and were heavily featured in several books, including two books published in 2007 coinciding with the 150th anniversary of Hall County. They can also be seen hanging in numerous city and county offices and buildings as well as private homes and businesses. Leschinsky's legacy lives on and continues to inspire new generations of historians and visitors.

Deeply ingrained in the Grand Island community, Leschinsky framed his subjects not as customers, but as friends. From the young men working in the YMCA cafeteria to students studying at the Grand Island Business College, Leschinsky captured the everyday moments of life. The love he felt for his community can be seen in his photographs of the streets, businesses, and people. He was there with his camera as workers built the Yancey Hotel, the Elks building, and the Union Pacific depot. In his photographs, Leschinsky immortalized the pride in the eyes of businessmen, home owners, and new parents. He captured the humor and entertainment he found around the community from dogs doing tricks on the Majestic Theater stage to the costumes at Evelyn Ryan's masquerade ball. Leschinsky was there when young men and women donned their uniforms to fight in World War I, as department stores put up elaborate displays, and as the community rallied to support troops.

The museum takes pride in preserving these images from Hall County's past and sharing them with those who have a passion for Hall County's history. If you would like to learn more about the history of Hall County or plan a visit to Stuhr Museum of the Prairie Pioneer, visit us at www.stuhrmuseum.org.

One

About Town

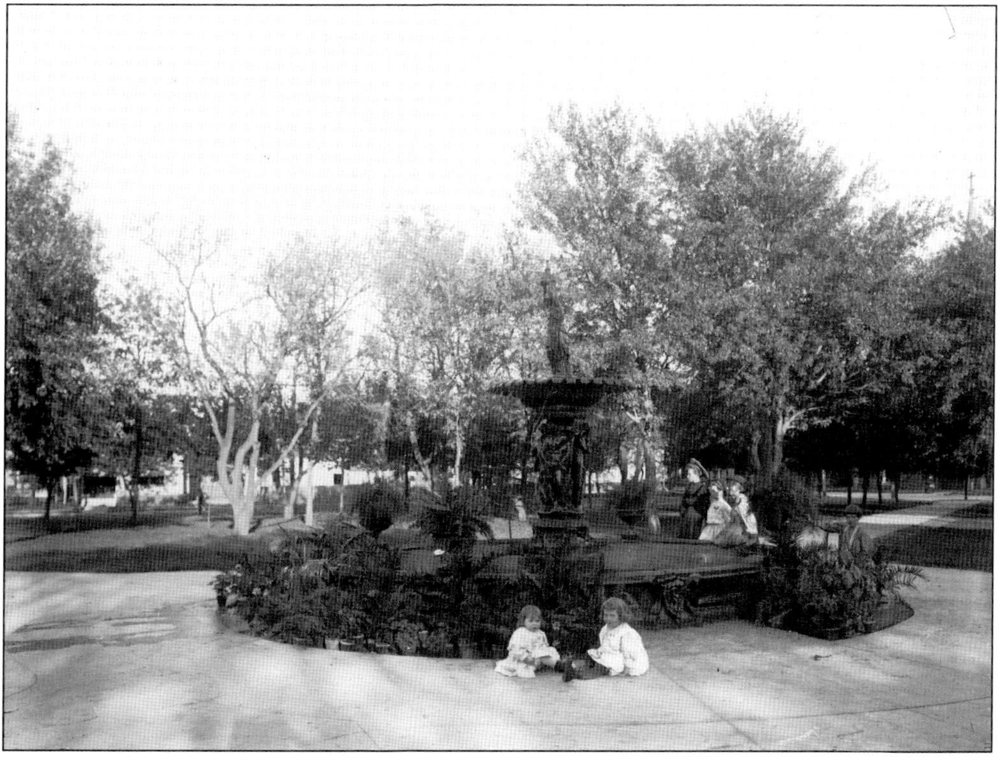

Six unidentified children pose by the fountain in Pioneer Park in 1915. Located in the 600 block of West First and Second Streets, the park was the site of Hall County's first courthouse. When the present courthouse was completed in 1904, the original site was abandoned. In 1906, the former courthouse was razed and the block was landscaped into a park through the fund-raising efforts of the Women's Park Association.

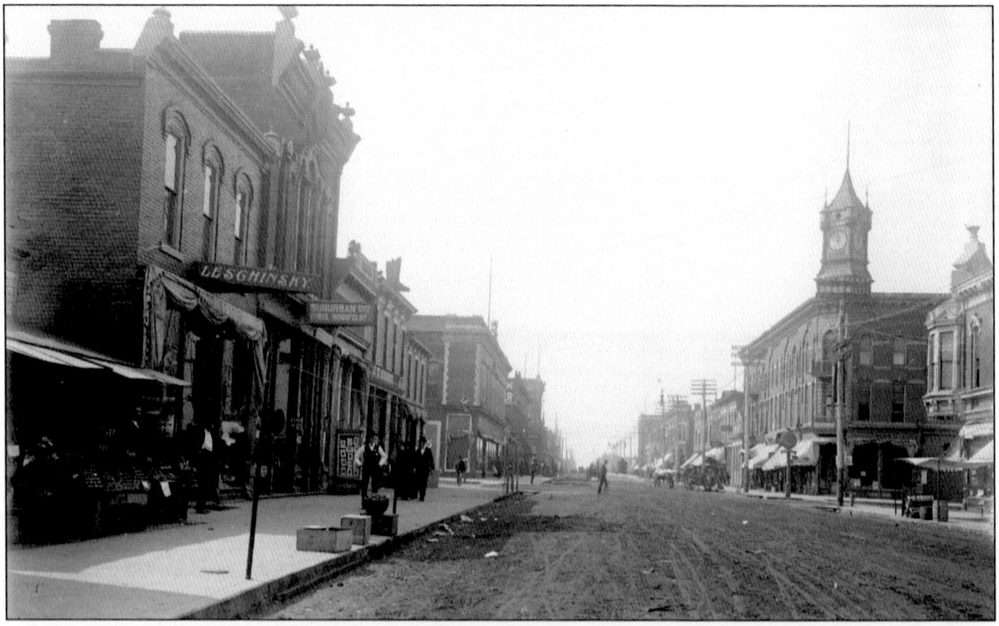

Julius Leschinsky captured this image of Third Street looking west in about 1905. The businesses visible on the left side of the street include a fruit stand, Leschinsky's studio, Chris Ronnfeldt's saloon, Baumann's Photography, and Graber Boot and Shoes. In the distance at the intersection of Third and Pine Streets, Wolbach's Department Store (left) and the Michelson Building (right) can be seen.

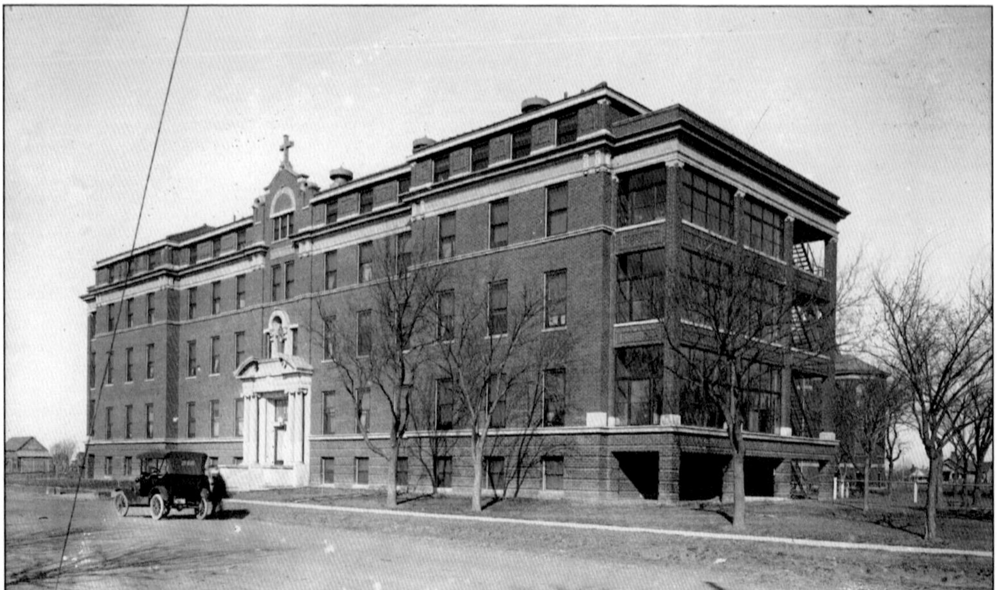

In 1885, the Sisters of St. Francis arrived in Grand Island to build a hospital. They purchased two acres of land between Koenig and Charles Streets and opened their hospital in 1887. Within 10 years, two additions were built to meet public need, with the chapel wing added in 1893 and the Adams Street wing in 1898. Pictured here is the 1912 addition, which changed the hospital's entrance to Charles Street.

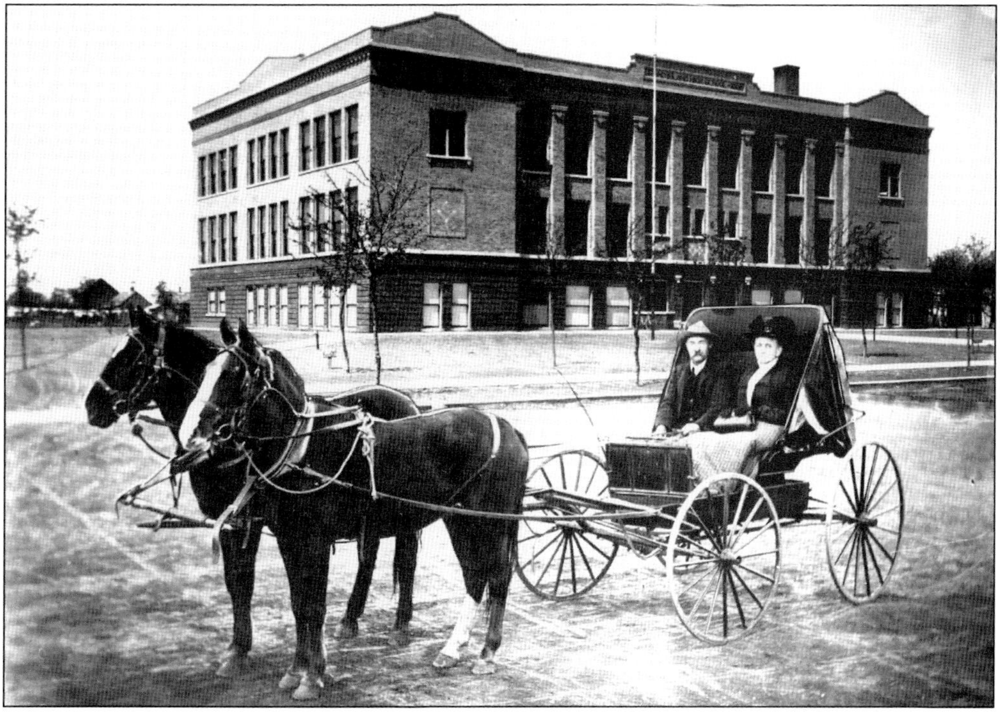

Located on North Walnut Street, the building seen in this photograph served as Grand Island's senior high school from 1908 until 1925. It cost $60,000 to build and was 84 feet wide by 140 feet long. It included the superintendent's office, a gymnasium, chemistry labs, and lecture rooms. It was built with electric and gas lighting and included such amenities as a pneumatic clock and an electric fire-alarm system.

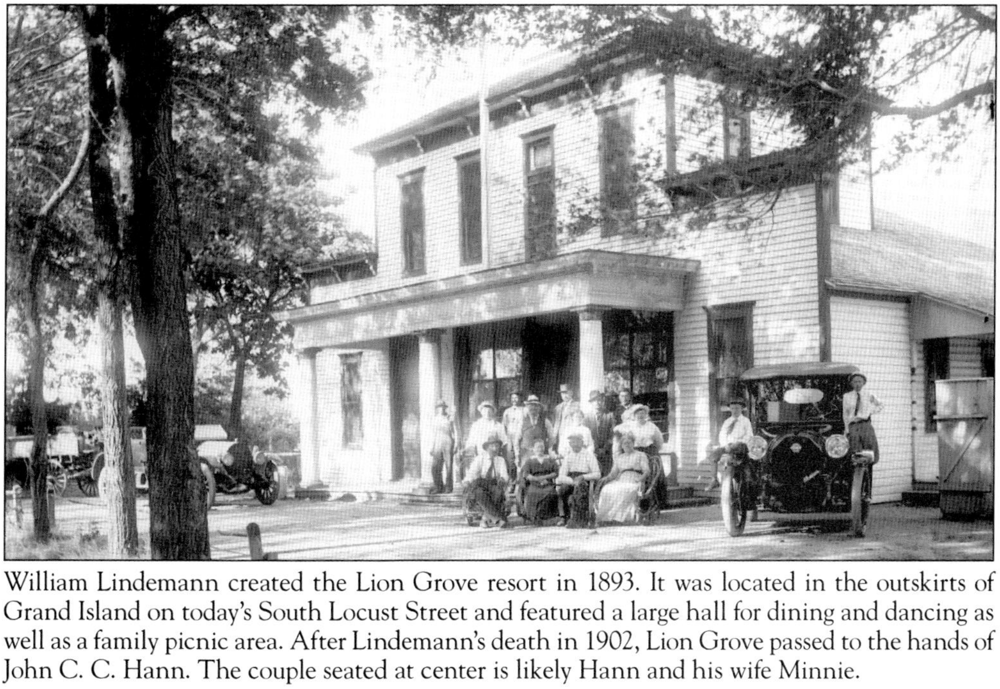

William Lindemann created the Lion Grove resort in 1893. It was located in the outskirts of Grand Island on today's South Locust Street and featured a large hall for dining and dancing as well as a family picnic area. After Lindemann's death in 1902, Lion Grove passed to the hands of John C. C. Hann. The couple seated at center is likely Hann and his wife Minnie.

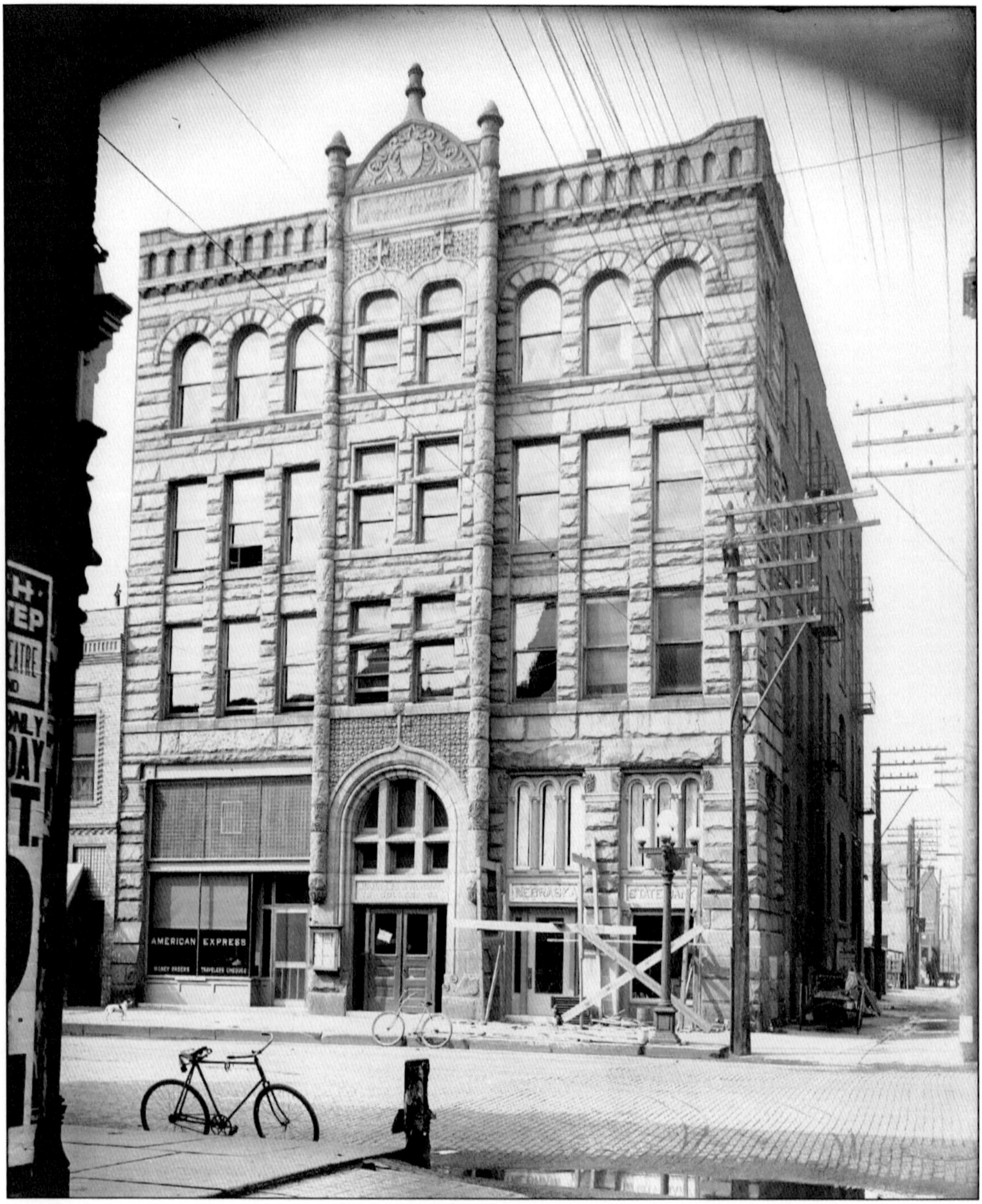

The neo-Gothic sandstone building seen in this photograph was the home of the Grand Island Business College. It was originally built as the Security Building, the home of Security State Bank, and was located in the 200 block of North Locust Street. The bank was a victim of the early-1890s economic crisis and closed in 1893. The business college was started in 1885 by Andrew M. Hargis and H. L. Evans, both of Illinois. They took over the building in 1902 with the college occupying the top three floors. This photograph, taken in September 1917, shows the business space to the left of the college's main entrance occupied by American Express. The space to the right appears to be under construction. The building was razed in 1962.

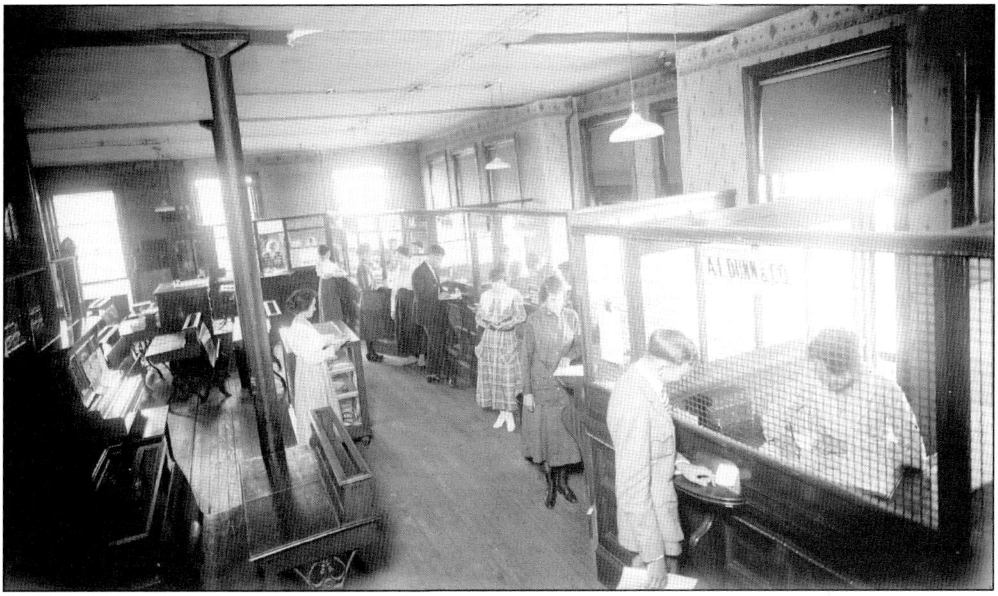

The Grand Island Business College offered students many practical and traditional opportunities for learning. In the photograph above, students practice banking methods in the actual businesses office and bookkeeping department in February 1919. To give students hands-on experience, the college operated a functional bank designed for general banking. In the lower photograph, two unidentified male students study in their college dorm room in October 1913. Postcards and pennants decorate the walls. Students came from all over the Midwest and as far away as Alaska, California, and Canada to study at the Grand Island Business College.

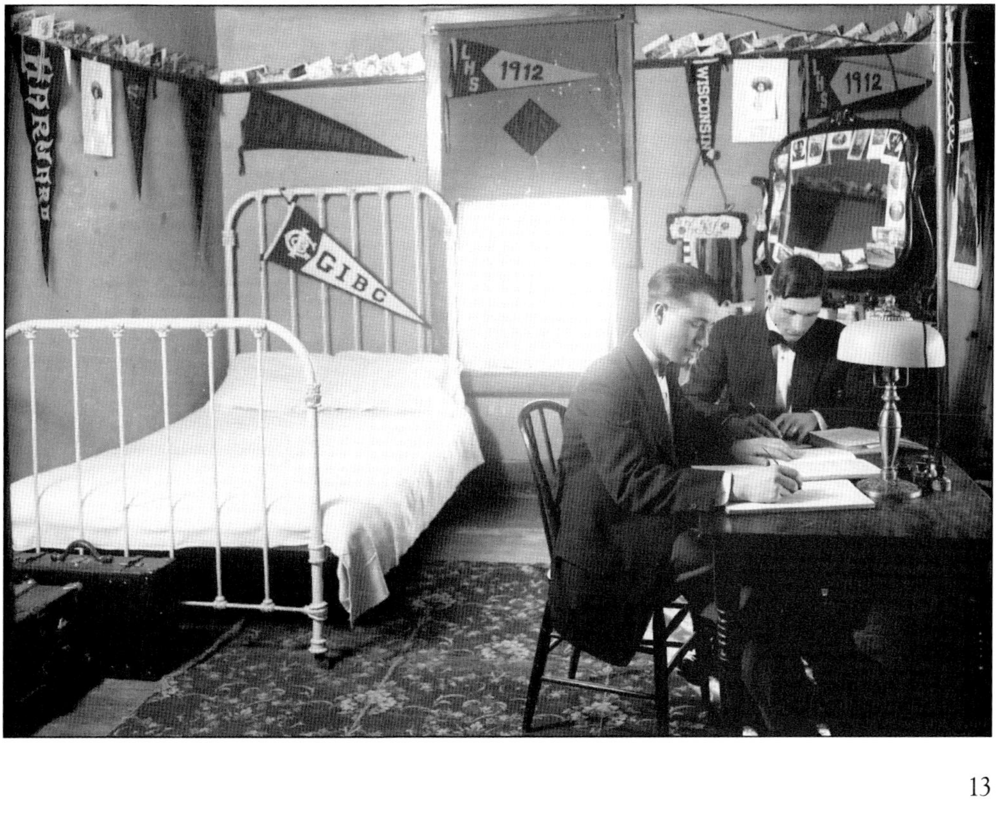

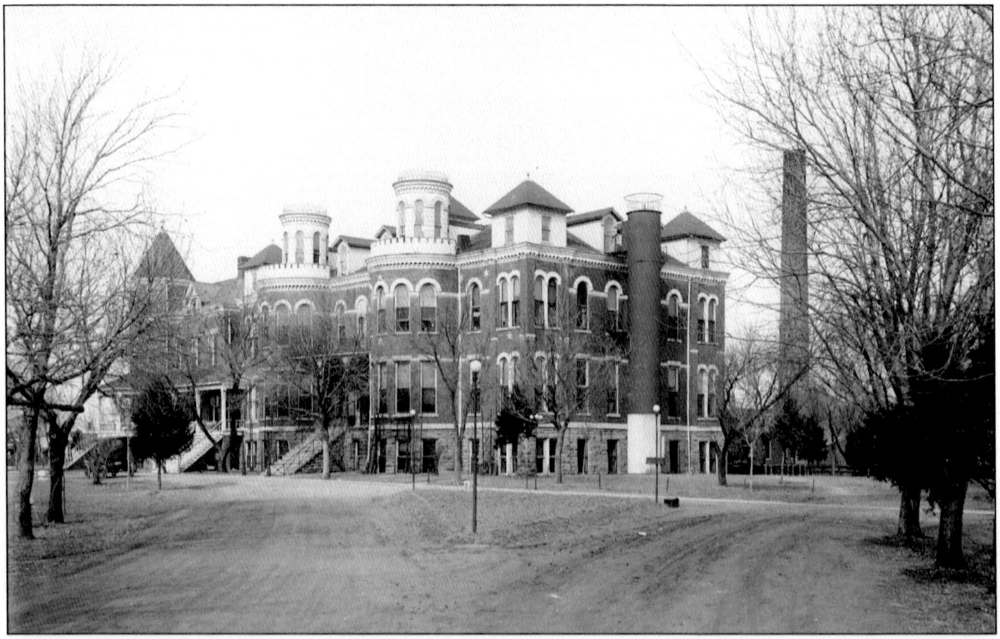

The Grand Island Soldiers' and Sailors' Home offered Civil War veterans and their widows living in Nebraska medical care and a home after retirement. The photograph above, taken in February 1917, shows the Lincoln Building. Built in 1888 and added on to in 1896, the Lincoln Building served as the main building. The basement featured a kitchen and dining room, and the main floor held the headquarters, office, commandant's private consultation room and apartment, a large library, and two elegant parlors. In the 1916 photograph below, several of the residents enjoy the home's library. The library and reading room were a source of great pleasure for the residents. According to an 1895 newspaper, the veterans especially enjoyed reading about the "great rebellion," and nearly two-thirds of the library's holdings were about the Civil War.

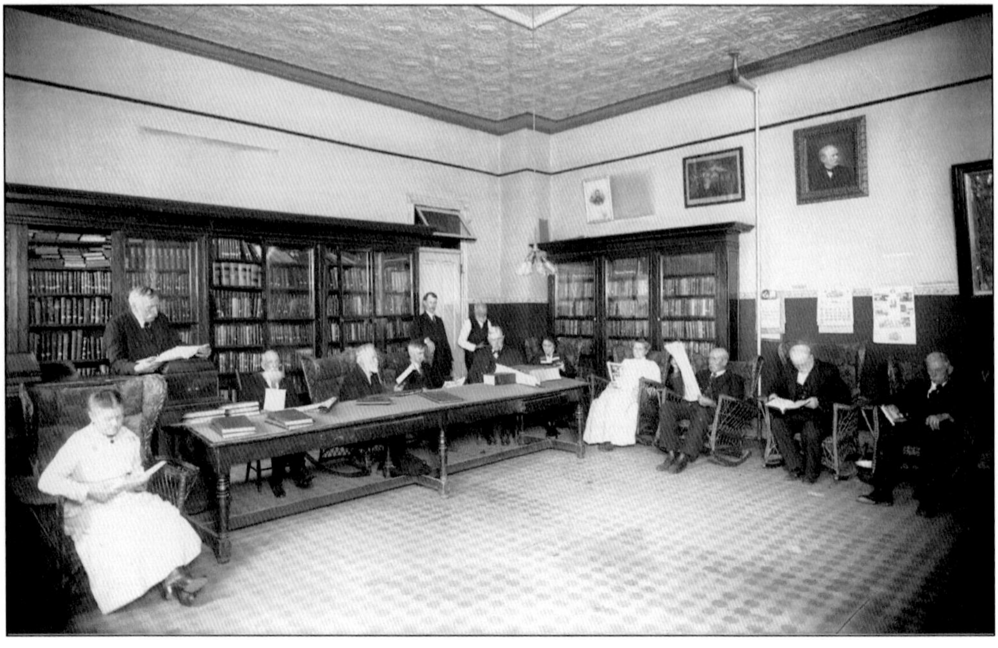

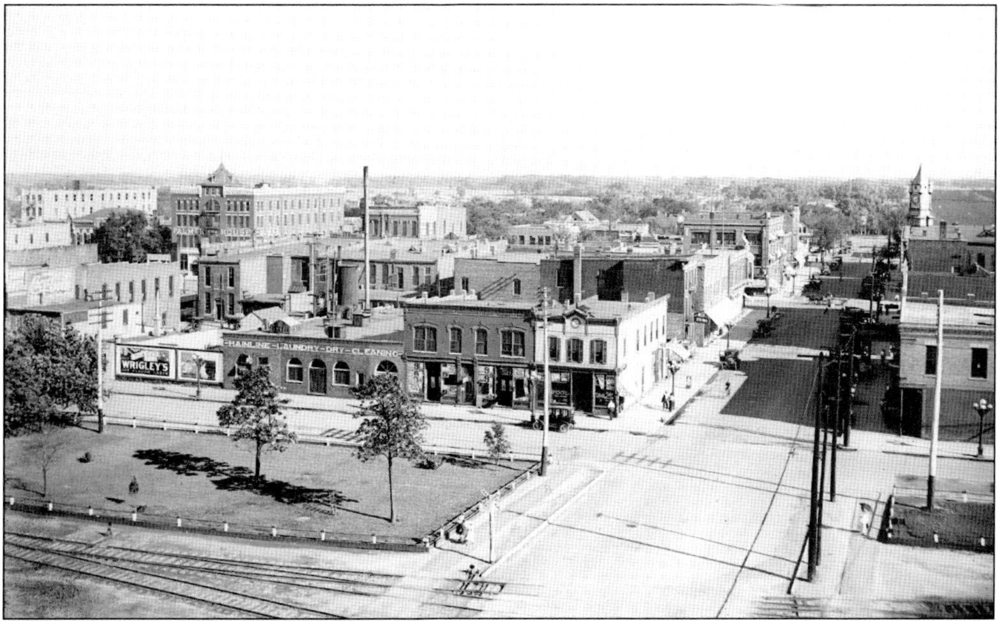

Likely taken from atop the Grand Island Light and Water Department, this aerial view captures downtown's business district from the corner of South Front and Pine Streets. To the far left, the Palmer House Hotel rises above Third Street. At right, the distinctive clock tower of the Michelson Building can be seen. The grassy area along Front Street was part of a park maintained by the Union Pacific Railroad.

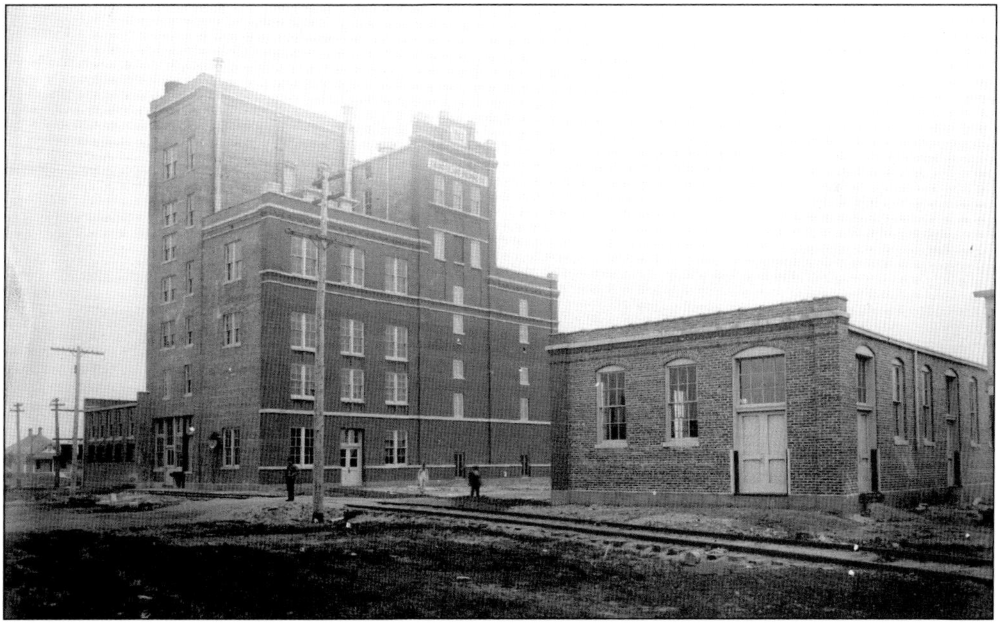

The Grand Island Brewing Company began operation in 1914 in the 1100 block of West North Front Street. In 1917, the Nebraska prohibition law banned the sale and production of alcohol. In 1924, it was discovered that the brewery had made vats with false bottoms and had been producing illegal beer. Forced to close, the building was sold to the city and converted into an ice plant in 1926.

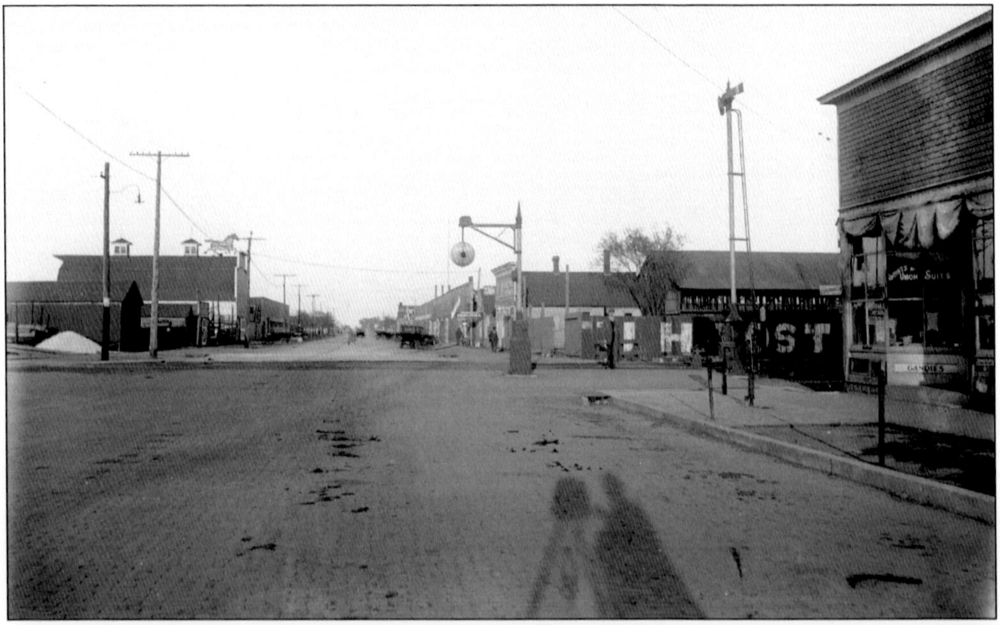

The iconic black stallion sign watches over Grand Island's horse and mule market from atop the North Robinson sale barn at left. Taken in October 1917, this view of East Fourth Street looks east from the Chicago, Burlington and Quincy Railroad tracks. At the time of this photograph, Grand Island boasted the second-largest horse and mule market in the world, shipping animals to many different countries.

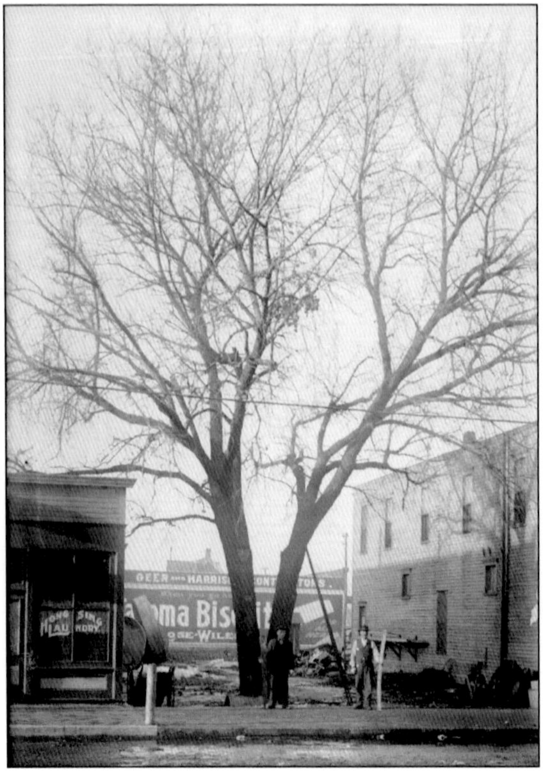

Two men pose next to a large tree in an empty lot on East Third Street. The man at right appears to be holding a saw. Joseph Klinge commissioned this photograph in January 1910. Klinge owned a saloon on West Third Street. The Hong Sing Laundry can be seen at the far left. The building at right was a tin shop located at 224 East Third Street.

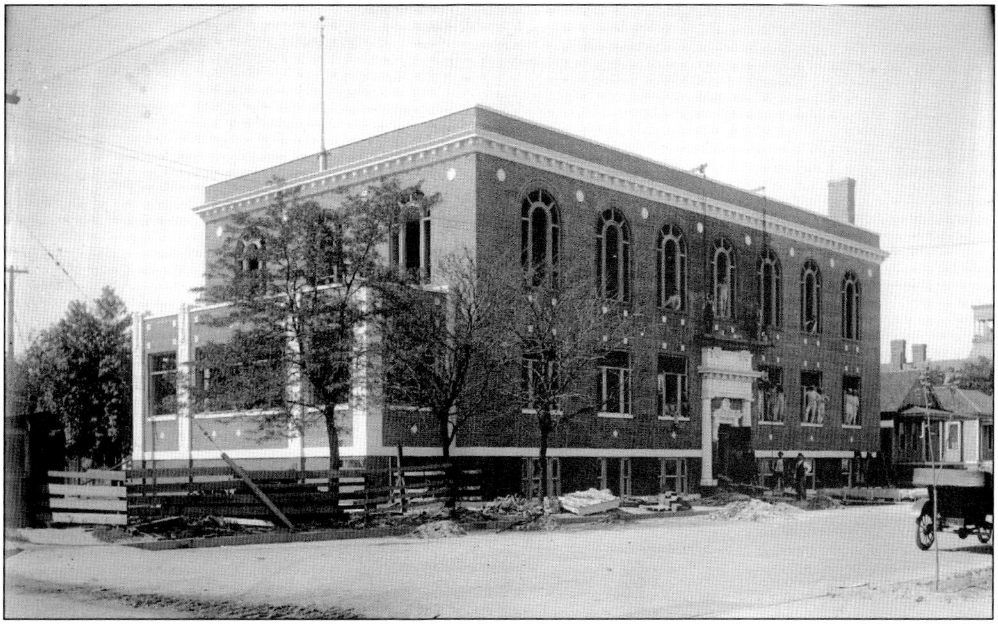

This photograph, taken in July 1917, shows workers posing in the empty window casings of the nearly completed Elks building, located at the corner of First and Locust Streets. Grand Island Lodge No. 604 of the Benevolent and Protective Order of Elks was chartered on July 12, 1900. In 1916, the Elks formed a building committee to raise money and oversee the construction of a permanent home.

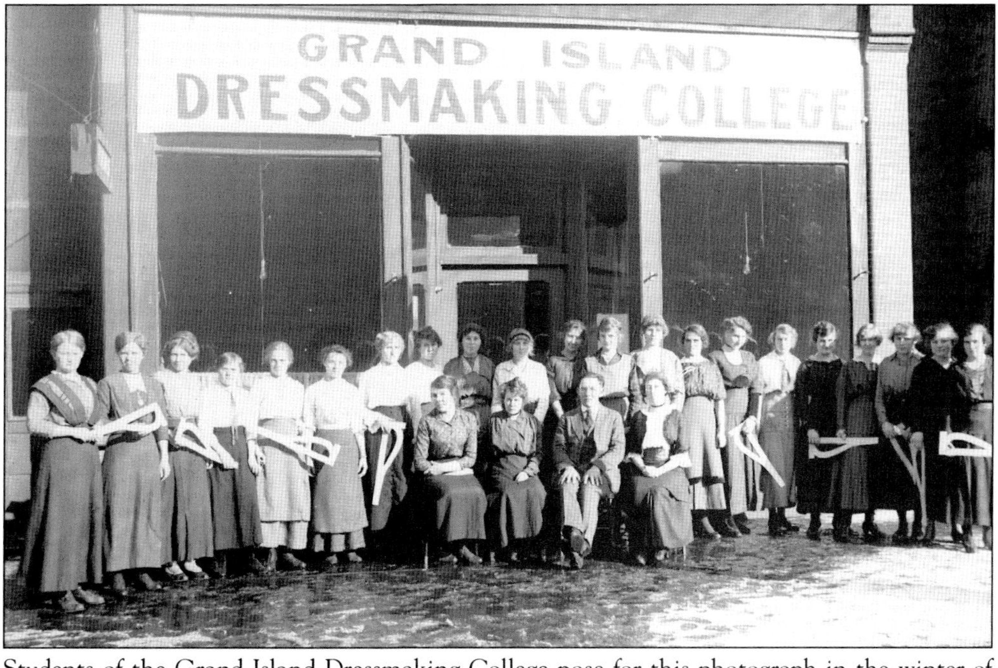

Students of the Grand Island Dressmaking College pose for this photograph in the winter of 1915. The school was likely located at 111 South Pine Street. Several of the women are holding modified French curve dressmaker's squares used in creating patterns for clothing. The four individuals seated in the front row could possibly be the school's instructors.

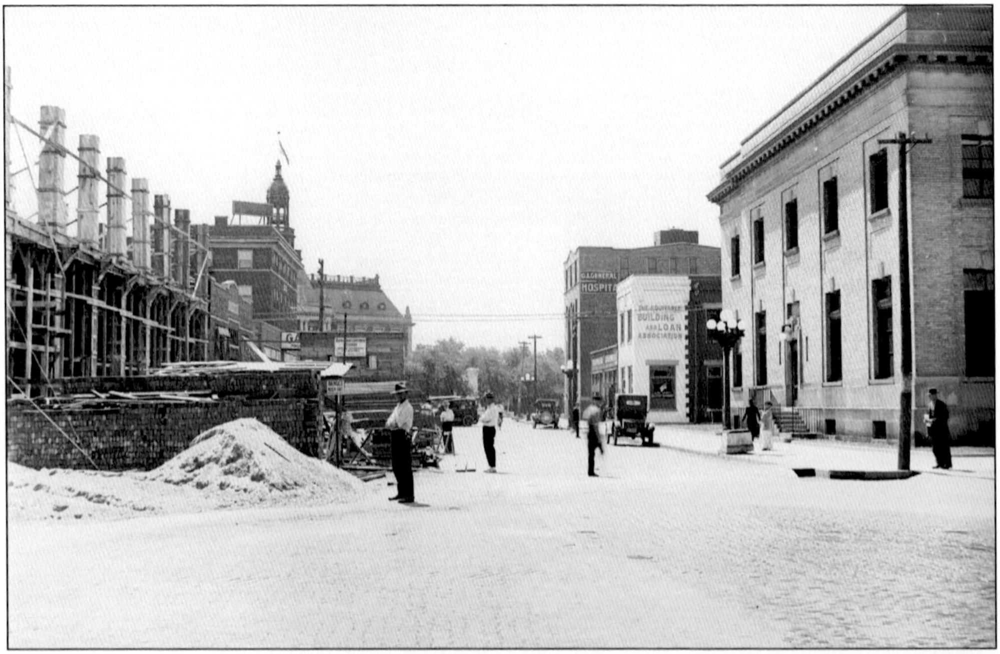

This street view shows construction of the Yancey Hotel from the ground level on August 9, 1917. Note the courthouse visible in the background along with the General Hospital, the Equitable Building and Loan Association, and the Grand Island Post Office. The post office was completed in 1910, with an addition of a west wing in 1935. It is now known as the Federal Building.

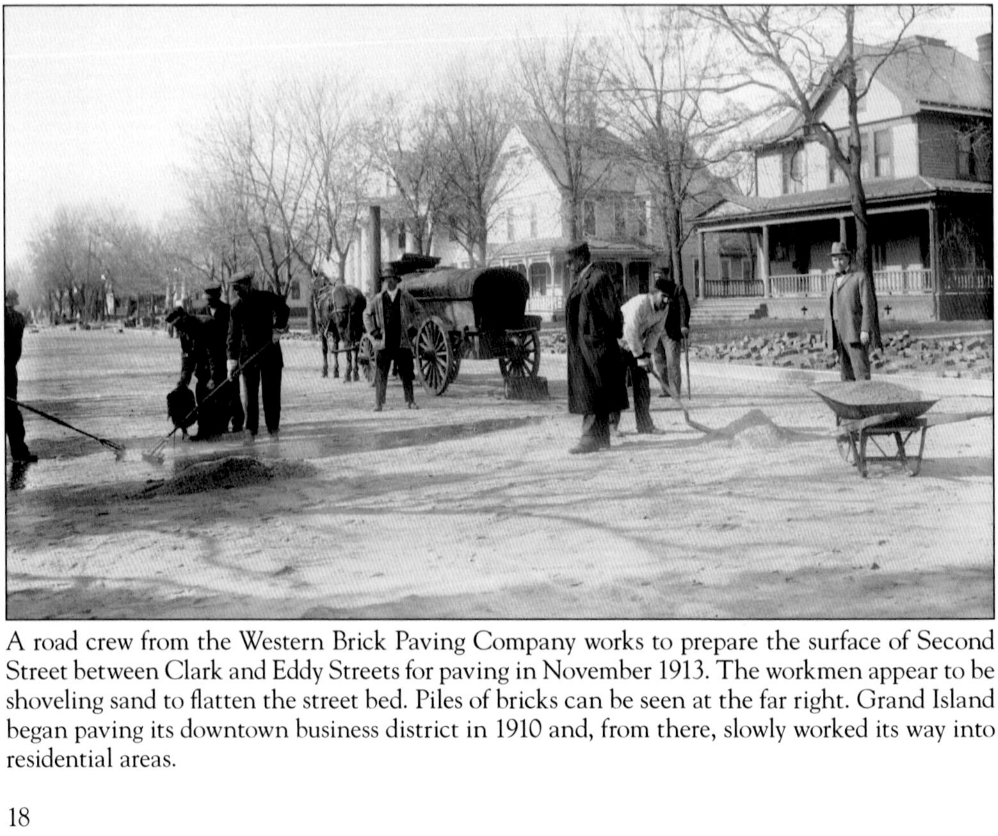

A road crew from the Western Brick Paving Company works to prepare the surface of Second Street between Clark and Eddy Streets for paving in November 1913. The workmen appear to be shoveling sand to flatten the street bed. Piles of bricks can be seen at the far right. Grand Island began paving its downtown business district in 1910 and, from there, slowly worked its way into residential areas.

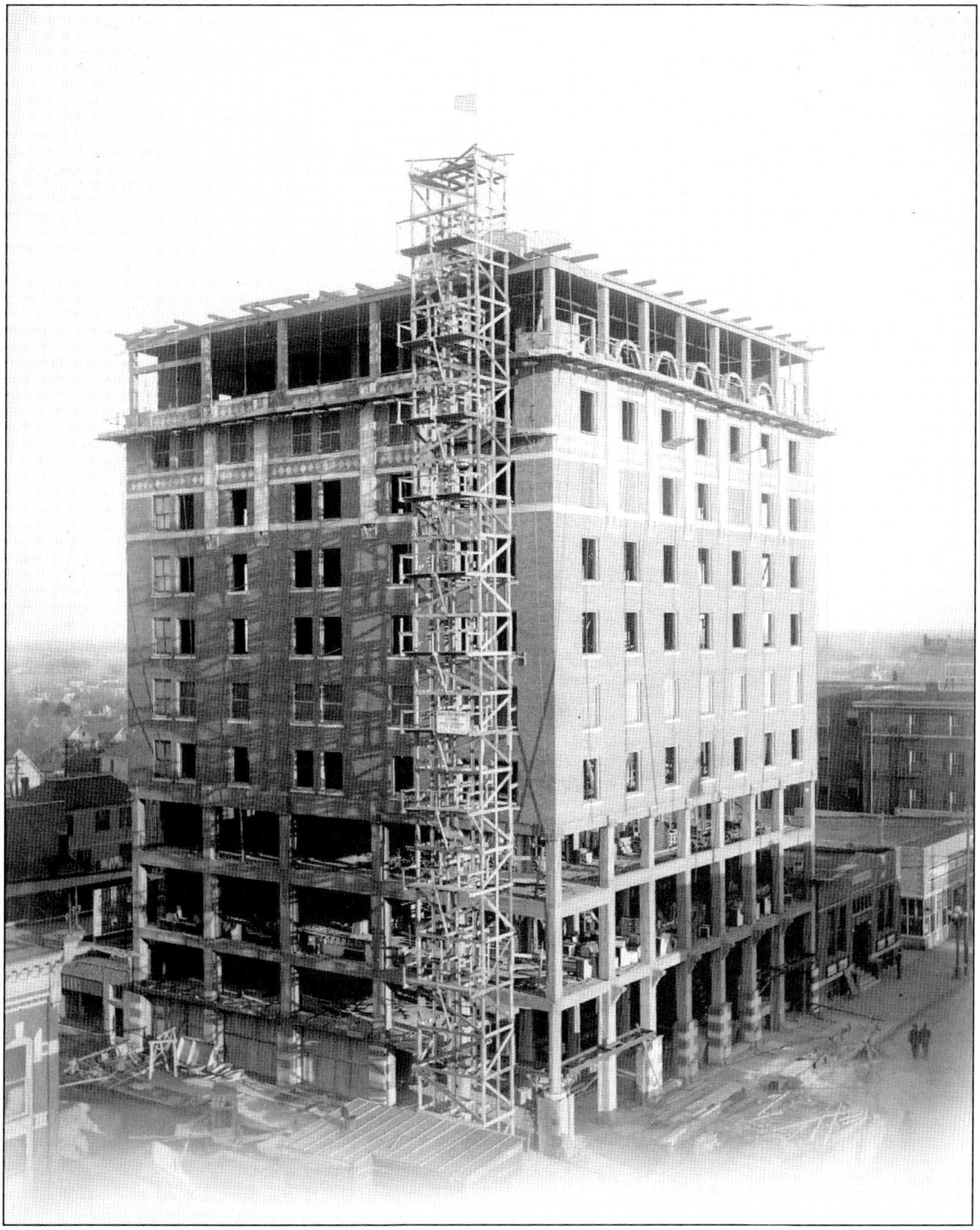

Even in this skeletal state, the Yancey Hotel is recognizable. Work began on the Yancey in April 1917 under the direction of the North American Hotel Company. However, the project ran into financial difficulties and construction stopped shortly after this photograph was taken in the spring of 1918. The hotel stood as a concrete frame until Omaha's Herbert S. Daniel and Associates financed the hotel's completion after World War I. It opened in late October 1923. The hotel was named for William L. Yancey, who leased it from Daniel's group. The 10-story building went through several other ownerships before closing in December 1982. In 1984 and 1985, it was remodeled into an office-apartment-condominium complex.

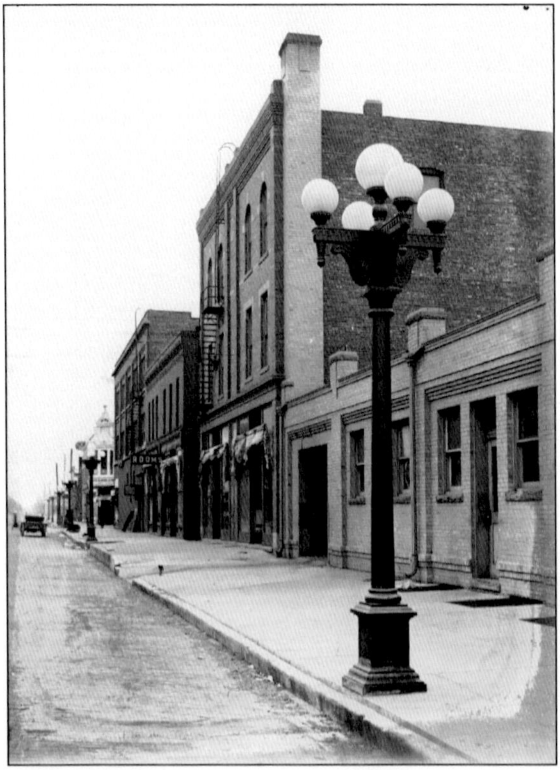

Taken from the Second Street intersection, this view of Grand Island's business district looks north along the 100 block of South Pine Street. The Hastings Foundry and Iron Works Company commissioned this photograph in November 1913. The company likely created the five-globe streetlight featured prominently in this photograph. The three-story brick building at center was the Independent Order of Odd Fellows building.

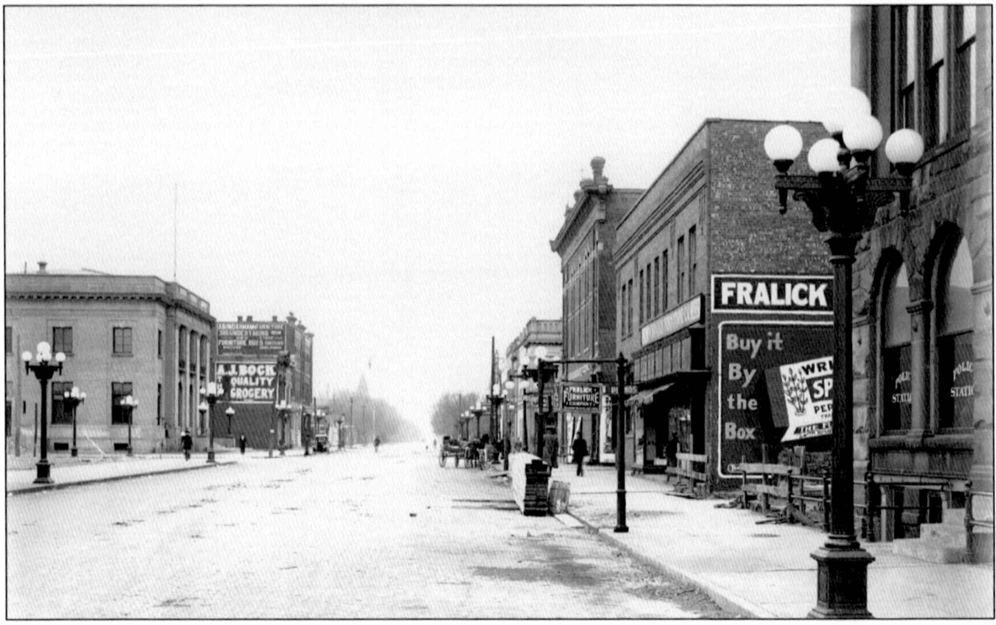

This 1913 photograph looks west down Second Street from the Pine Street intersection. A Wrigley's spearmint chewing gum advertisement is painted on the side of Fralick's Furniture Company, 101–105 West Second Street. Next to Fralick's is the Bartenbach Building, which still stands today on Second and Locust Streets. The Grand Island Police Department can be seen at right in the old city hall. At left, the former post office is visible.

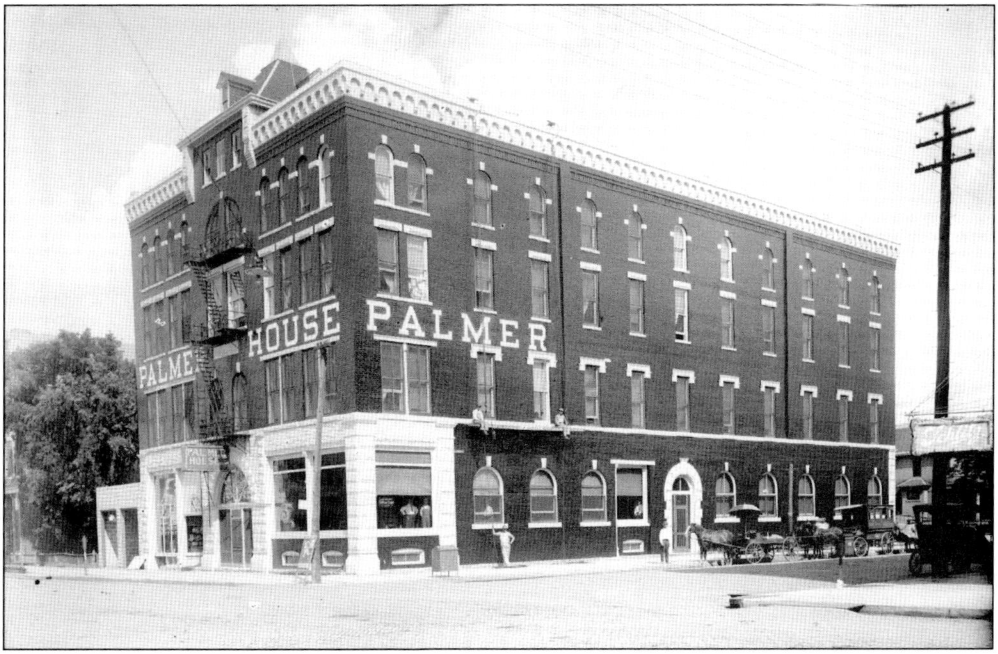

Located on the southeast corner of Third and Sycamore Streets, the Palmer House Hotel opened in 1888 and cost $100,000 to build. This photograph was taken in the summer of 1913 when Henry Schuff served as proprietor. He purchased the Palmer in 1909, and it remained in the Schuff family for more than 30 years. The hotel closed in 1977 and was razed in 1979.

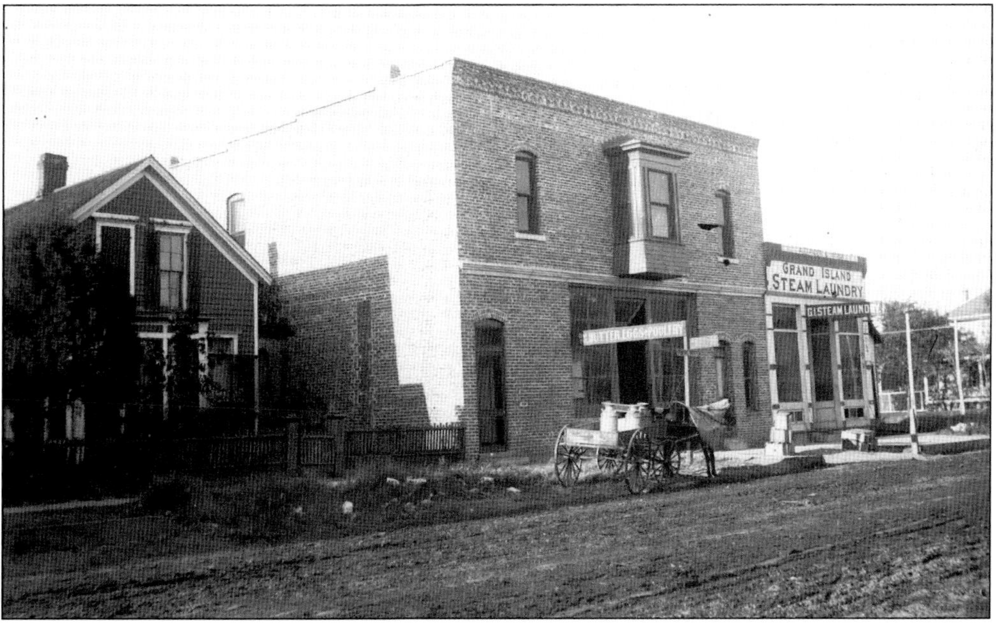

R. R. Watson's butter, eggs, and poultry business was located at 114–116 East Second Street. In this photograph taken in about 1910, a horse-drawn delivery wagon is parked in front of Watson's. A canvas cover protects the horse from flies and other biting insects. Numerous wooden crates are stacked in front of the business. At the far right is the Grand Island Steam Laundry (118 East Second Street).

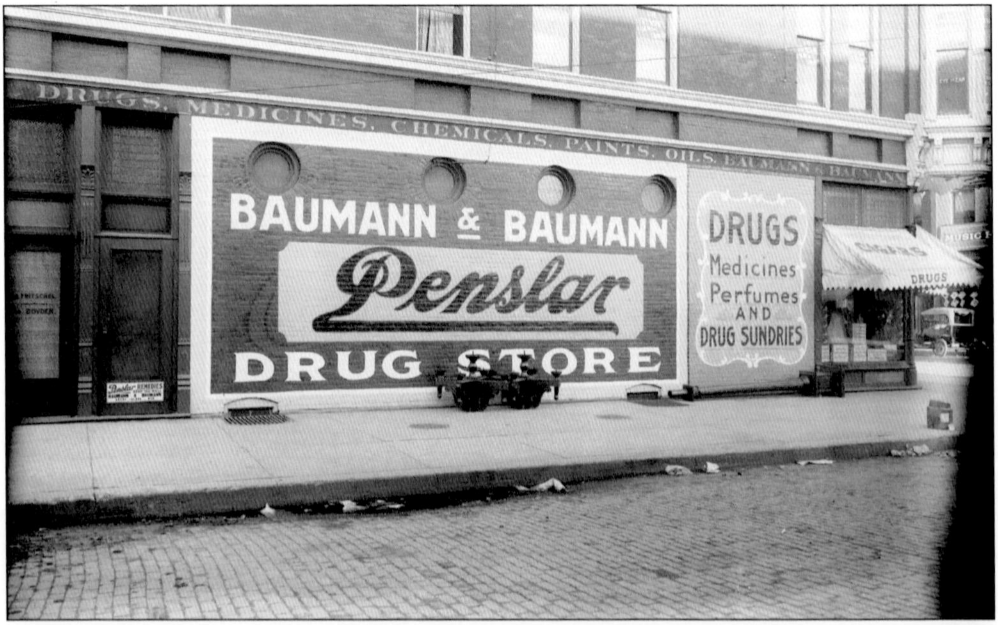

A freshly painted sign adorns the Pine Street side of Baumann and Baumann Drug Store at 102 East Third Street. The sign was likely painted by George Losey. A well-known sign painter, Losey commissioned this photograph in September 1913. Twin brothers Herman and Oscar Baumann operated this drugstore at this location from 1900 until 1914. Note the signpost and light fixtures lying next to the building awaiting installation.

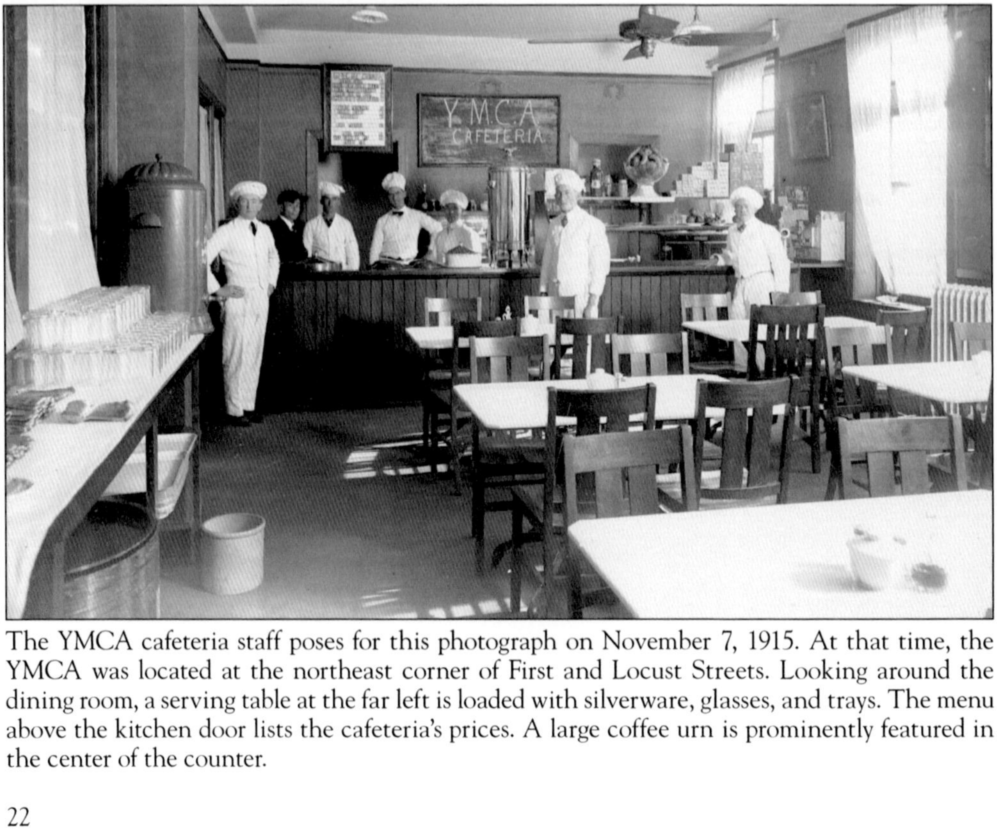

The YMCA cafeteria staff poses for this photograph on November 7, 1915. At that time, the YMCA was located at the northeast corner of First and Locust Streets. Looking around the dining room, a serving table at the far left is loaded with silverware, glasses, and trays. The menu above the kitchen door lists the cafeteria's prices. A large coffee urn is prominently featured in the center of the counter.

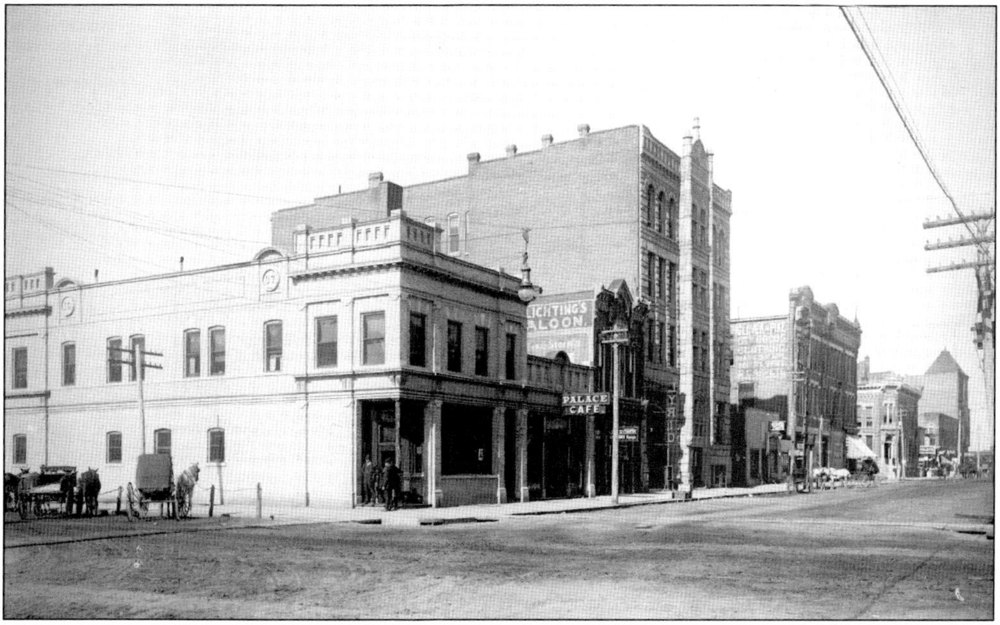

This view of Grand Island was taken at the northwest corner of Locust and Second Streets. The H. A. Sievers Saloon, the two-story brick building on the corner, was completed in 1907. Next door is the Palace Café, operated by Japanese businessman Saburo Shindo. The tall building at center is the Grand Island Business College. On the first floor of the college was the Lyric Theater, which entertained audiences from 1907 to 1915.

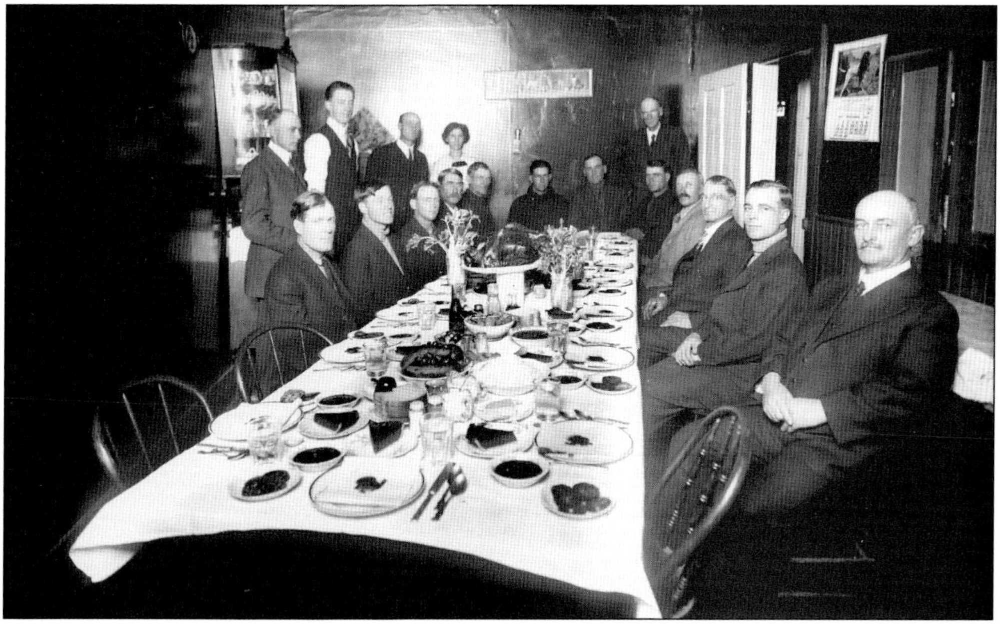

The Gold Cure Institute, founded in 1892 by George H. Thummel and George B. Bell, was a hospital for the treatment of drug and alcohol addictions. Located in the former Estes House, a 30-room hotel at 201 Kimball Avenue, they used Dr. Leslie E. Keeley's gold cure injections to treat substance addictions. Gathered around the table are 17 people ready to enjoy a Thanksgiving feast. The institute closed in 1918.

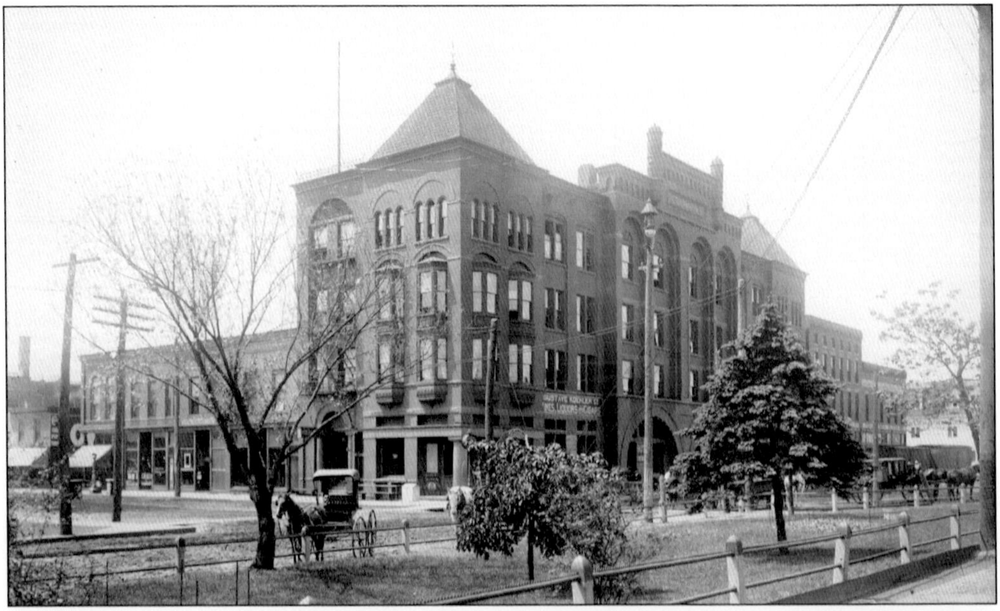

The Koehler Hotel once stood on the southwest corner of North Locust and West South Front Streets, directly across from the Union Pacific Railroad depot. The 95-room hotel was built at a cost of nearly $100,000 by Gustav Koehler and opened in October 1893. Grand Island architect Julius Fuehrman designed the hotel. Fuehrman worked closely with Omaha interior designer Mr. Lemann to insure the hotel's furnishings were as grand as the exterior. The photograph of the hotel's lobby, with its marble desk and intricately patterned floor, clearly shows Fuehrman's attention to detail. Seen at the far right is the entrance to the Koehler's lunchroom that was added in 1914, around the time of this photograph.

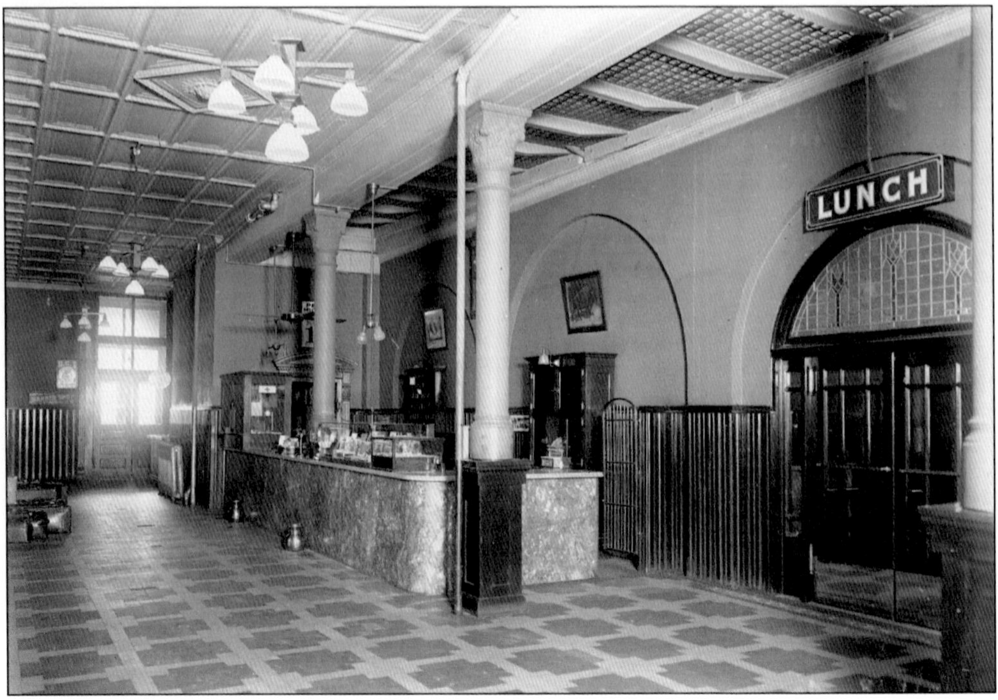

Two

BUSINESSES

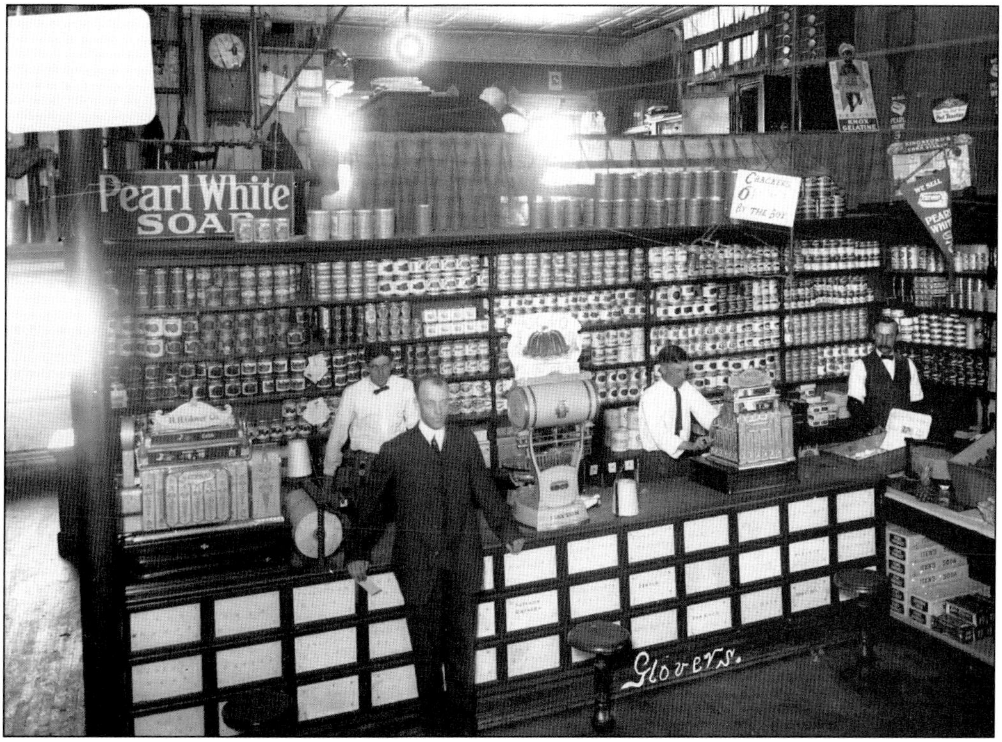

Taken in 1913, this photograph shows the dry goods counter of H. H. Glover's department store at 302–304 West Third Street. Glover was born in 1854 in Massachusetts. In 1879, he opened a dry goods store in Grand Island. By 1882, he employed 12 men and carried a stock of $30,000. Glover had three sons, Edward (likely the man in front of the counter), George, and Herbert F. Glover.

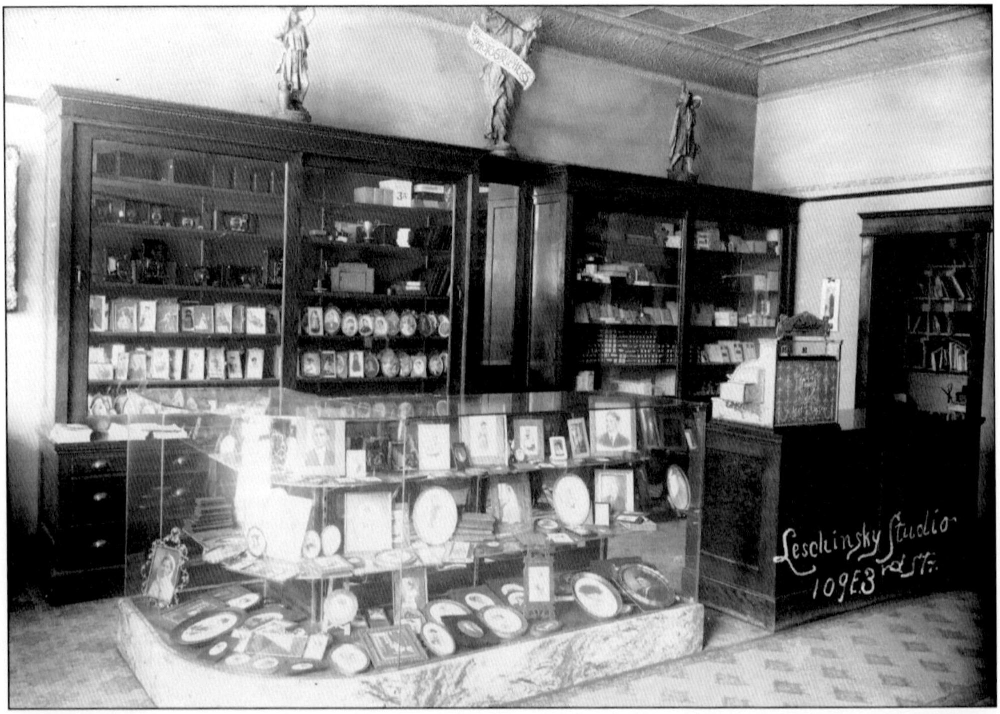

Samples of Julius Leschinsky's work are on display in the lobby of his studio at 109 East Third Street in July 1913. In the display case behind the counter are several styles and models of Kodak cameras. His ornate National brand cash register is visible at the far right. Through the doorway, cubbies filled with orders waiting for pickup can be seen.

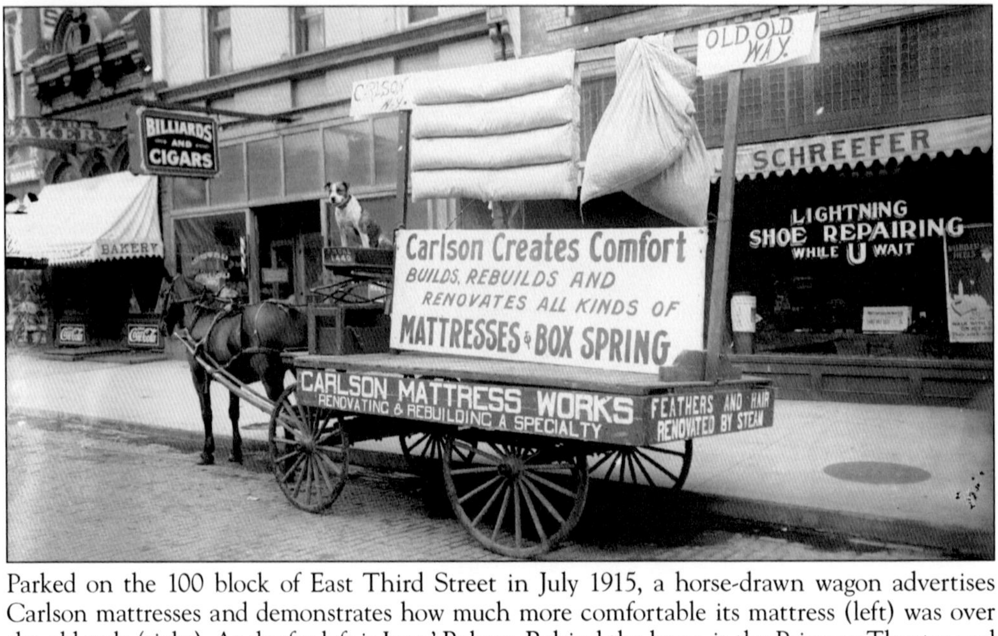

Parked on the 100 block of East Third Street in July 1915, a horse-drawn wagon advertises Carlson mattresses and demonstrates how much more comfortable its mattress (left) was over the old style (right). At the far left is Ivers' Bakery. Behind the horse is the Princess Theater and George J. Schreefer's Shoe Shop. Carlson Mattress Works was operated by L. M. Carlson and located on Lincoln Avenue.

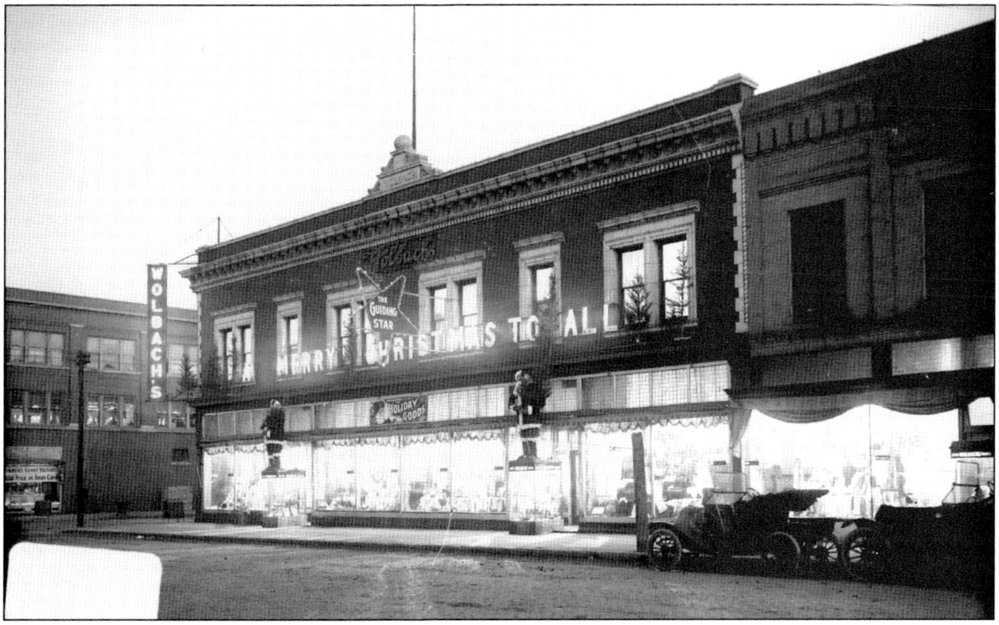

Wolbach's Department Store's front, located on West Third Street, is merrily decorated for the 1912 Christmas season. Decorations include a large electric sign proclaiming, "A Merry Christmas To All," and a large guiding light star outlined with Christmas lights. The top of the overhang is decorated with pine trees. The window display advertises Christmas items for sale, including toys, pictures, china, Christmas cards, clothes, satchels, and jewelry.

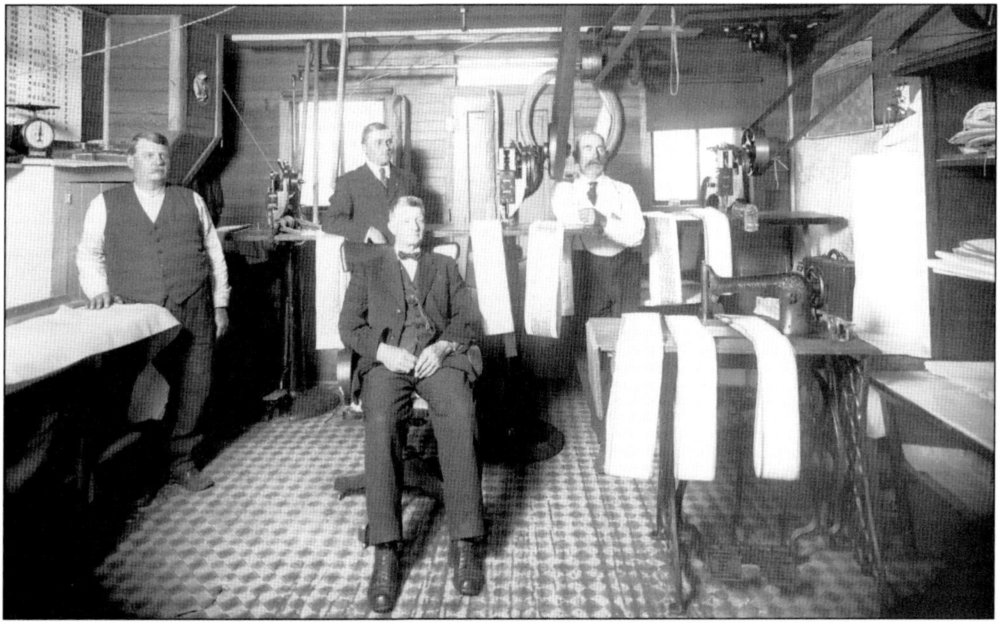
In 1910, William Sampson received a patent for his puncture-proof tire protector. Sampson's invention was designed to act as a defensive barrier between a pneumatic tire's outer rubber tread and the soft, easily punctured inner tube. His idea was that closely spaced, metal rivets secured to a continuous piece of material would help prevent flat tires. This photograph, taken in April 1915, shows Sampson's invention in production.

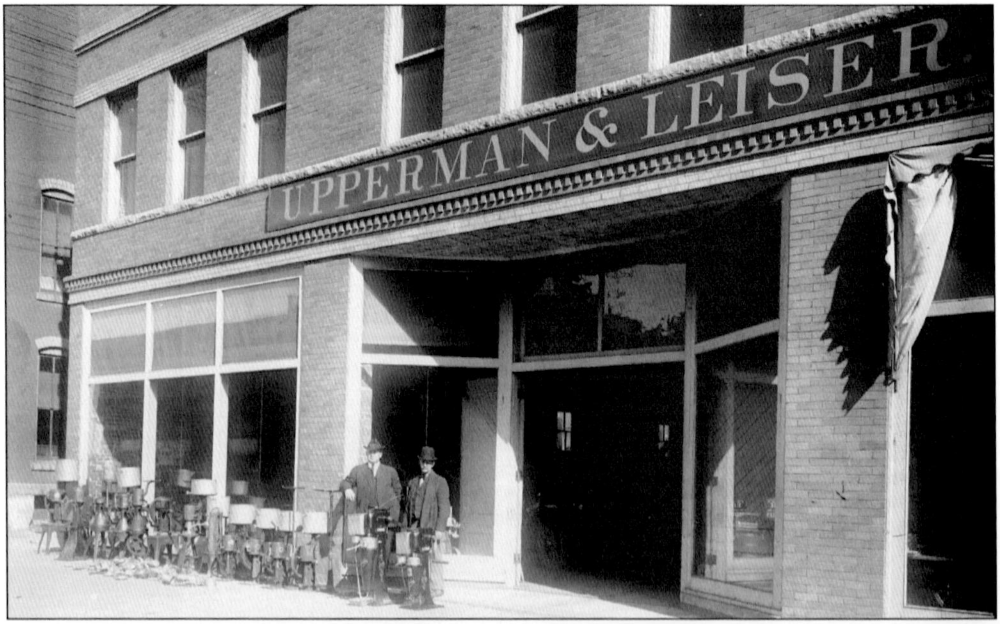

Located at 109–111 North Pine Street, Upperman and Leiser owned one of the largest agricultural implement stores in the area selling buggies, windmills, pumps, and hydraulic wells. Pictured here are two unidentified men with the store's supply of cream separators in October 1911. Louis E. Upperman and George A. Leiser first opened the store in 1891 at a location on Locust Street. Upperman retired in 1919, and the business changed its name to G. A. Leiser and Company.

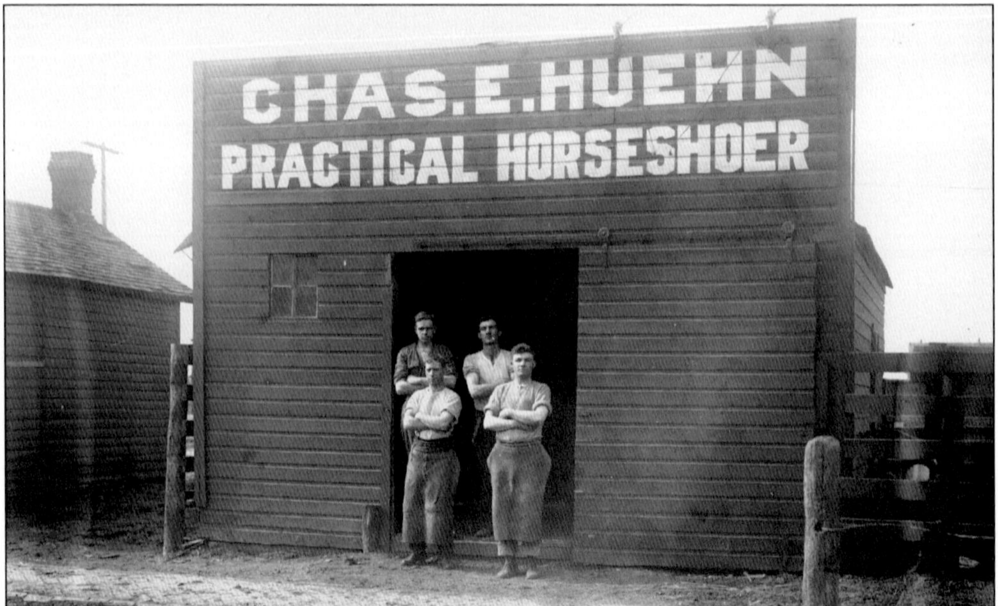

Four unidentified men pose in the doorway of Charles E. Huehn's blacksmith shop. Huehn apparently specialized in horseshoeing. Note that the two men standing in front are wearing leather work aprons. Huehn's business was located on East Fourth Street in Grand Island's horse and mule market.

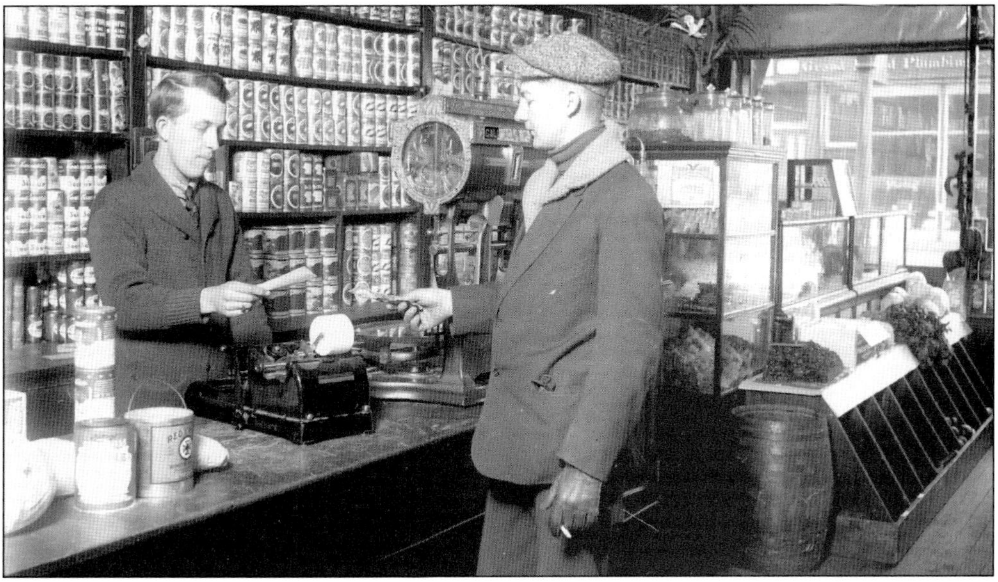

Two unidentified men conduct a business transaction inside the grocery store of William Veit in 1915. William Veit's grocery was located at 224 West Second Street. He was the son of grocer Louis Veit, who opened the original Veit's Grocery in about 1886 on East Third Street. Goods on the shelves include Campbell's Soup, Van Camp's Pork and Beans, Carnation Milk, Rumford Baking Powder, and countless varieties of canned vegetables.

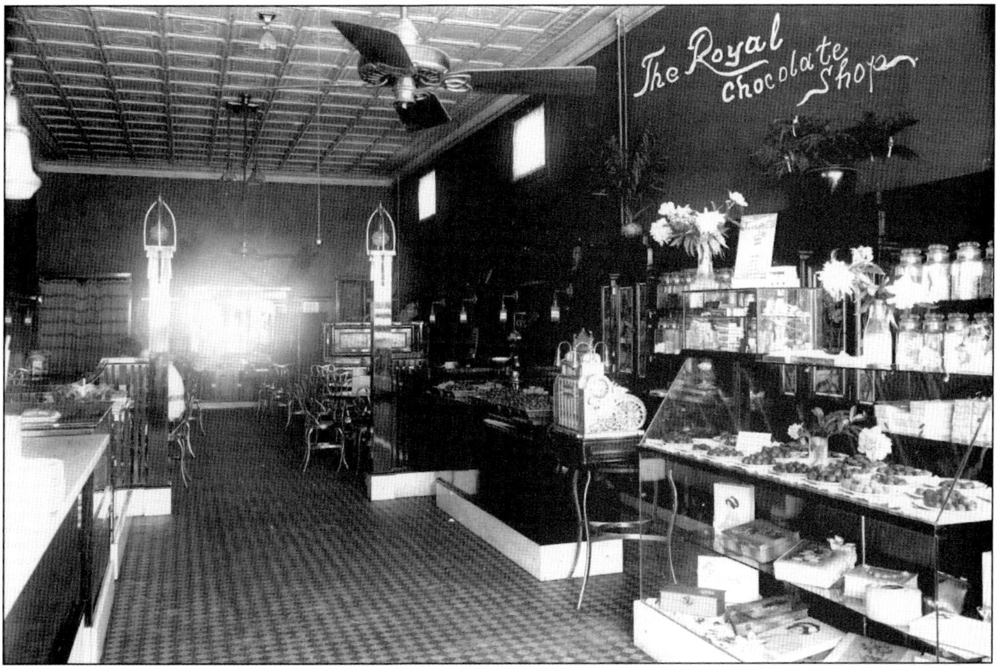

This 1913 photograph features the Royal Chocolate Shop at 217 West Third Street. It is one of several images commissioned by the National Cash Register Company highlighting local businesses using the company's cash registers. A large, ornate cash register can be seen in the center of the image. The glass case at right is filled with decadent, hand-made chocolates and fancy candy boxes.

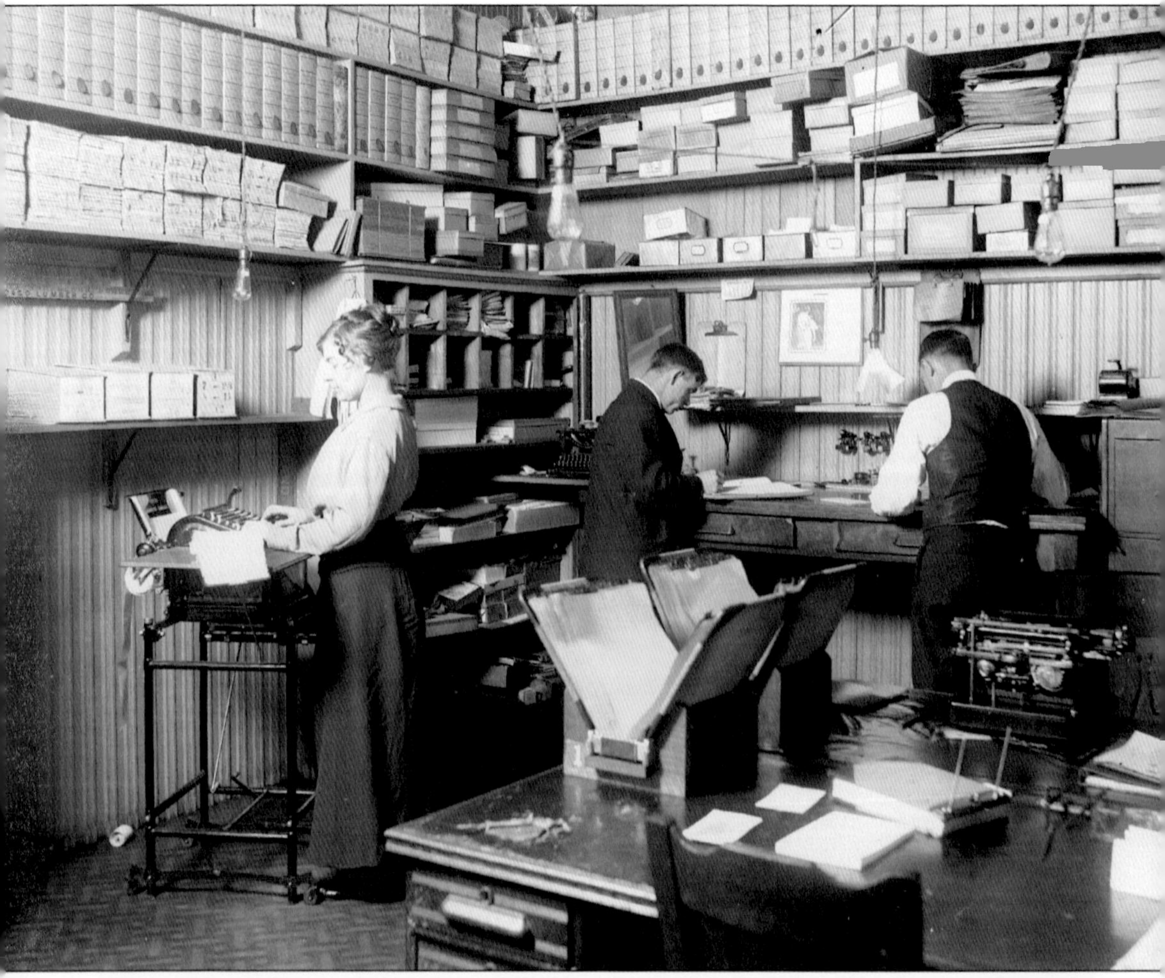

Two unidentified men and one unidentified woman work in the office of the Dolan Fruit Company. The Dolan Fruit Company was located at the southwest corner of Front and Wheeler Streets. Born in Ireland, Michael L. Dolan opened a grocery business in Grand Island in about 1883. In March 1894, he organized the Dolan Fruit Company, which offered wholesale fruits, vegetables, nuts, candies, and other products. Its location along the main line of the Union Pacific Railroad allowed it to import and export its goods easily from coast to coast. Among the wholesale goods Dolan offered were apples, oranges, lemons, bananas, vinegars, ciders, cheeses, crackers, tobacco, and cigars. The Burrough's Adding Machine Company commissioned this image in October 1915. The lovely young lady at left is using a Burrough's brand adding machine. In the center of the image, account books lie open and ready atop a large wooden desk.

Two unidentified workers weigh a large bunch of bananas at Brown Fruit Company in September 1917. The wholesale fruit company was started in 1914 by E. L. Brown, C. C. Kelso, J. D. Webster, and B. B. Farrell. The two-story brick warehouse and office was built in 1916 at 355 North Pine Street along the main line of the Union Pacific Railway. Bananas were among the many non-Nebraska fruits and vegetables distributed by the Brown Fruit Company.

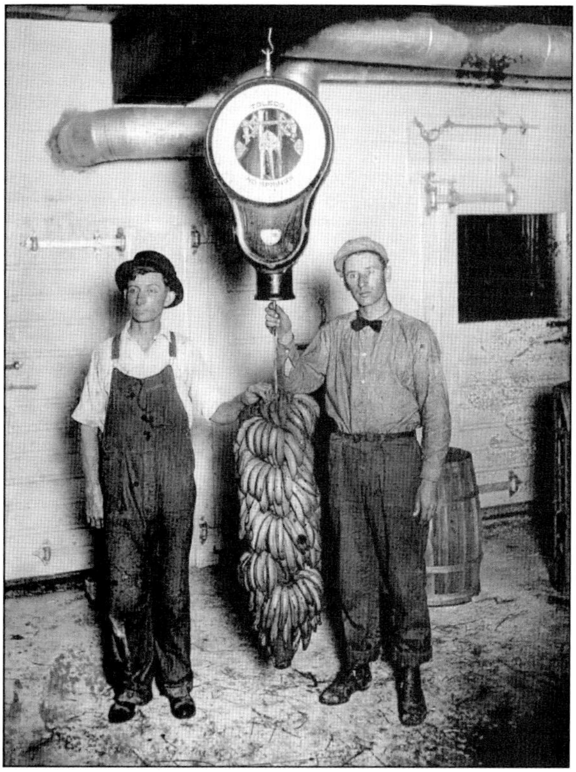

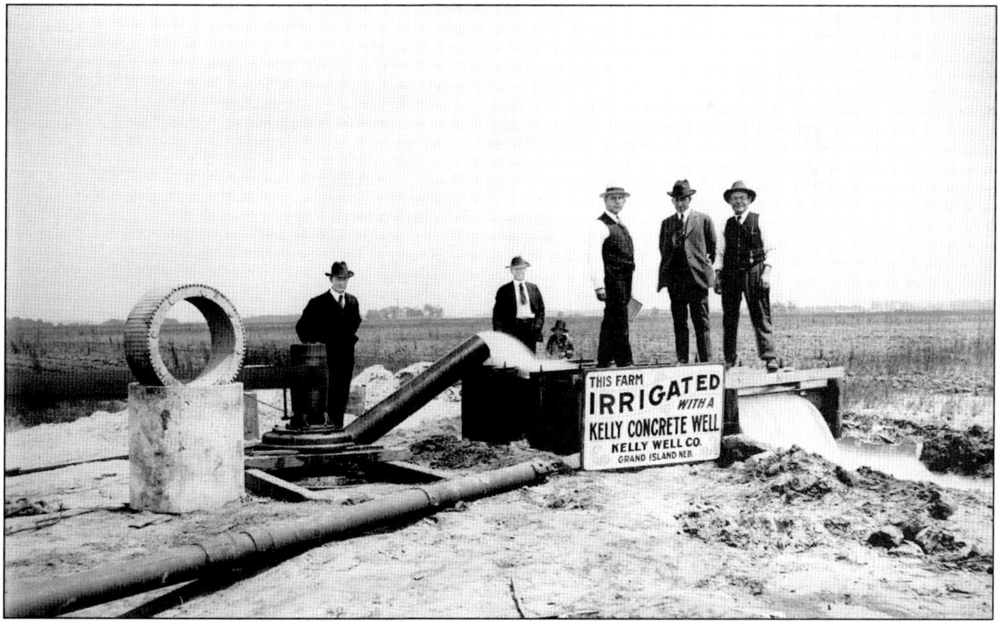

Grand Island plumber and businessman William Kelly designed and patented a process of building concrete wells used in installing power and irrigation systems. By 1917, the Kelly Well Company was marketing, manufacturing, and installing its system throughout the area. Seen here, five unidentified men and one small child pose for a promotional photograph that proudly proclaims, "This farm irrigated with a Kelly Concrete Well."

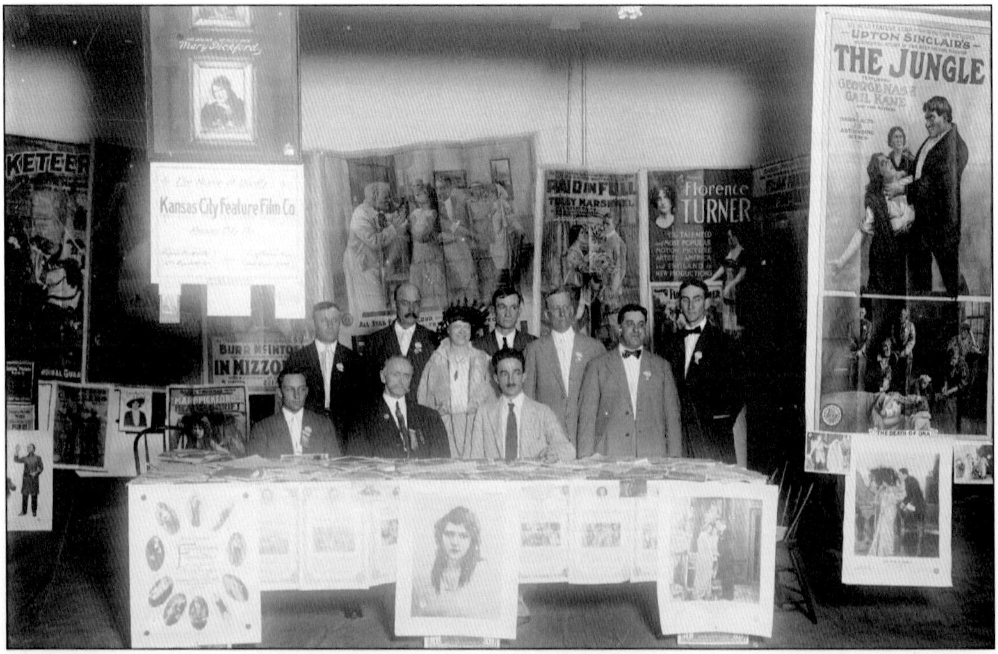

Members and delegates of the Nebraska Moving Picture Association gather at the Liederkranz building for a conference held on June 2 and 3, 1914. This photograph shows an exhibit from the Kansas City Feature Film Company about the films the company distributed. A large movie poster at the right advertises Upton Sinclair's *The Jungle*, released on May 25, 1914.

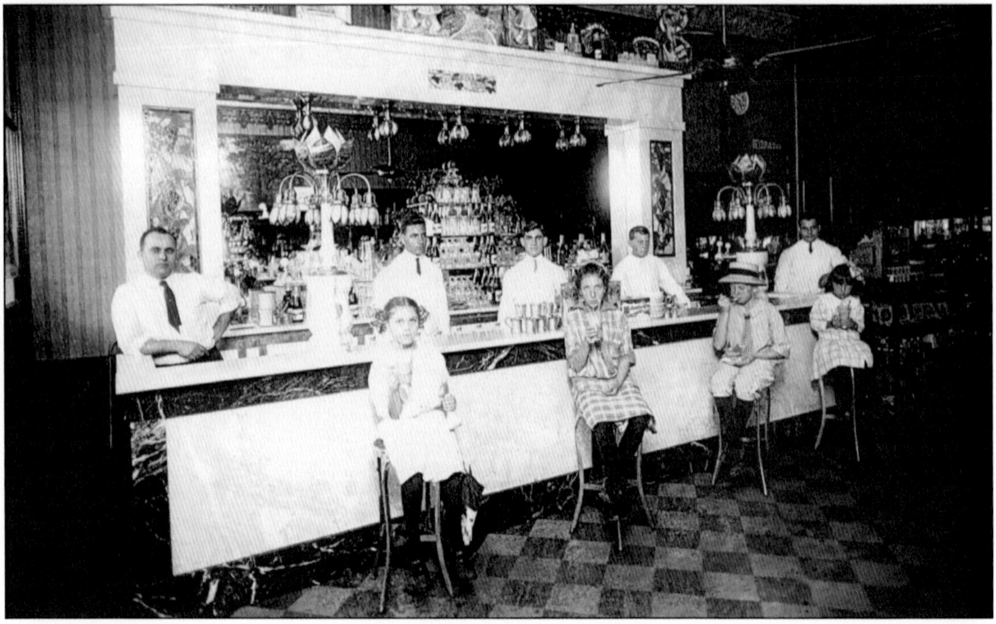

Seated at the soda fountain of the Grand Island Candy Kitchen, four youths enjoy sweet treats around 1915. Located at 318 West Third Street, the Candy Kitchen was owned at this time by Gus Valonis. Valonis was born in Greece and immigrated to the United States in 1901. Valonis came to Grand Island in about 1904 and soon established a confectionery business. The business had many locations over the years.

The R. H. McAllister Company hardware store was opened in 1883 by R. H. McAllister. Located at 118 West Third Street, the store was owned and operated by McAllister family members for two generations. R. H. McAllister passed away in July 1917, three months before this photograph was taken. Upon his death, his sons Robert and Charles and his wife Mary owned the business.

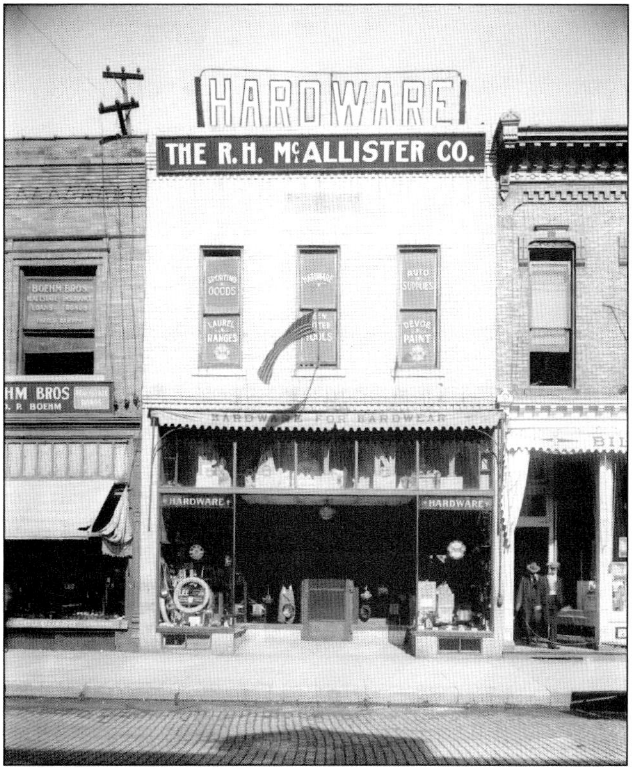

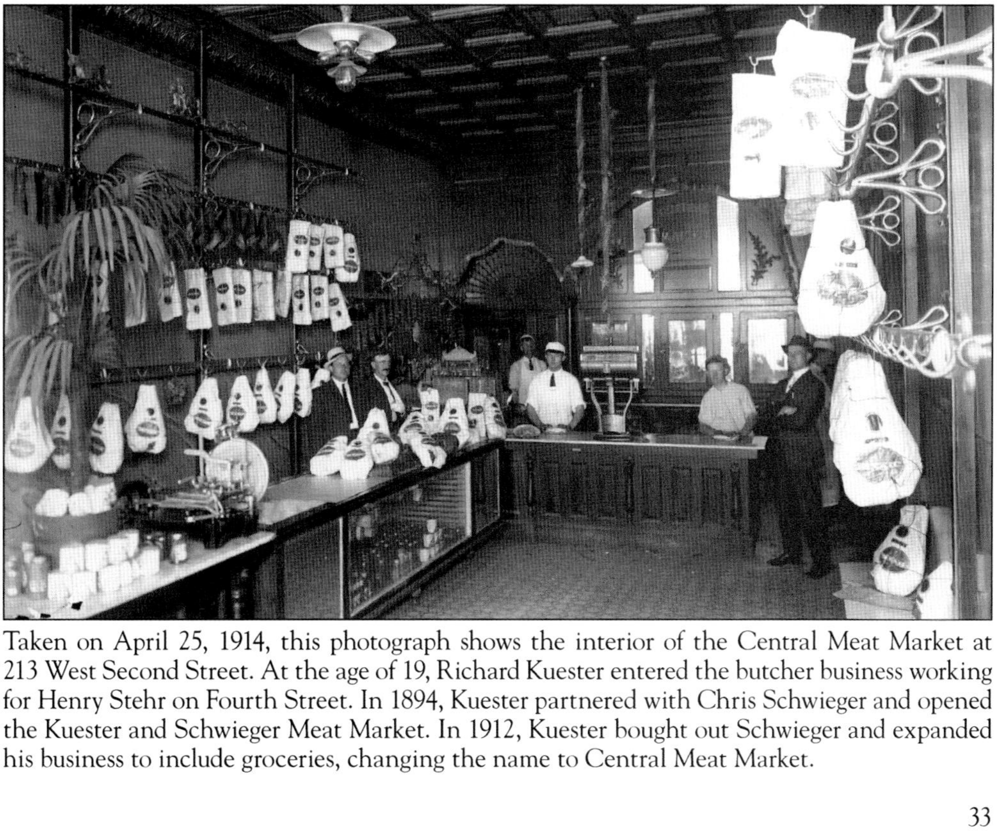

Taken on April 25, 1914, this photograph shows the interior of the Central Meat Market at 213 West Second Street. At the age of 19, Richard Kuester entered the butcher business working for Henry Stehr on Fourth Street. In 1894, Kuester partnered with Chris Schwieger and opened the Kuester and Schwieger Meat Market. In 1912, Kuester bought out Schwieger and expanded his business to include groceries, changing the name to Central Meat Market.

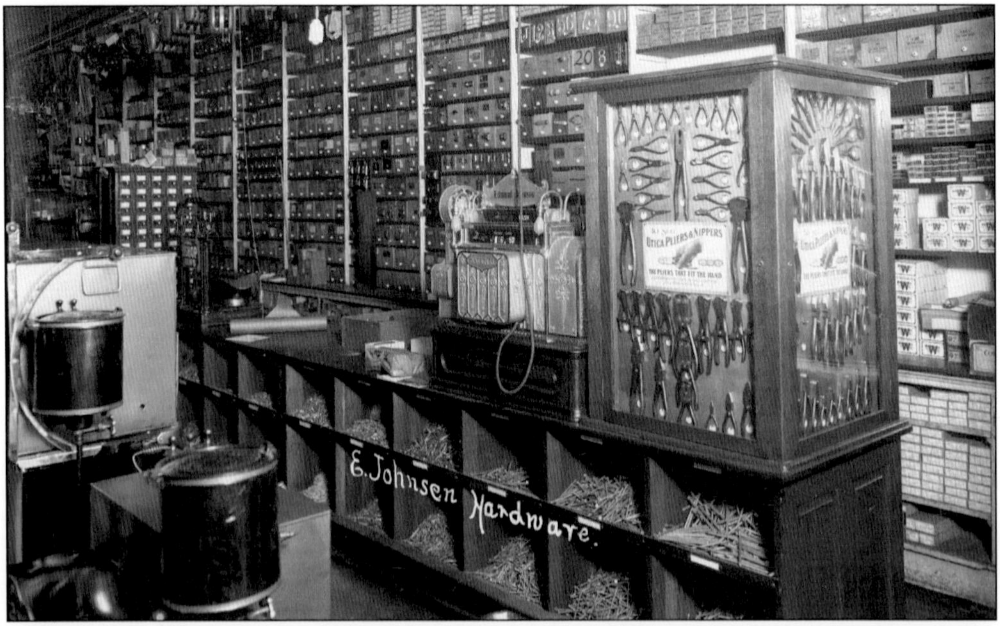

Bins of nails of every size and shape form the counter of Edmund Johnsen's hardware store, 211 West Third Street, in July 1913. A case atop the counter artfully displays Utica Pliers and Nippers. The store is filled from floor to ceiling with knobs, latches, house numbers, pulleys, padlocks, nuts, and bolts. In addition to all the hardware bits and pieces, Johnsen's sold garden and field seeds.

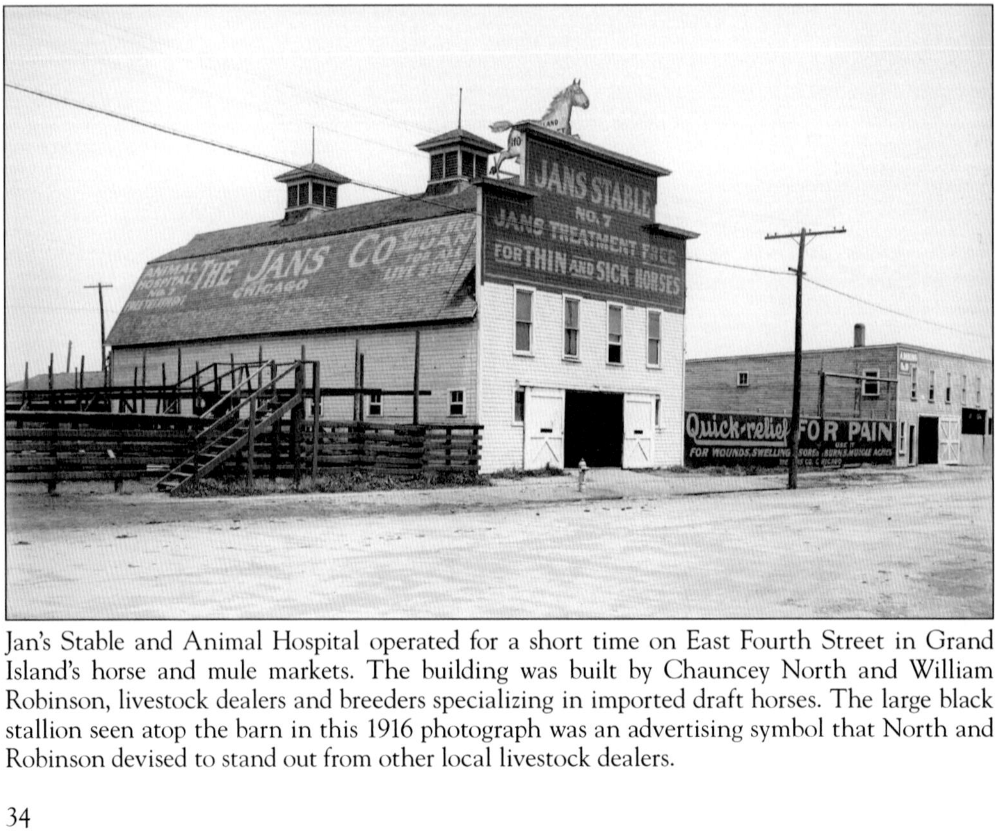

Jan's Stable and Animal Hospital operated for a short time on East Fourth Street in Grand Island's horse and mule markets. The building was built by Chauncey North and William Robinson, livestock dealers and breeders specializing in imported draft horses. The large black stallion seen atop the barn in this 1916 photograph was an advertising symbol that North and Robinson devised to stand out from other local livestock dealers.

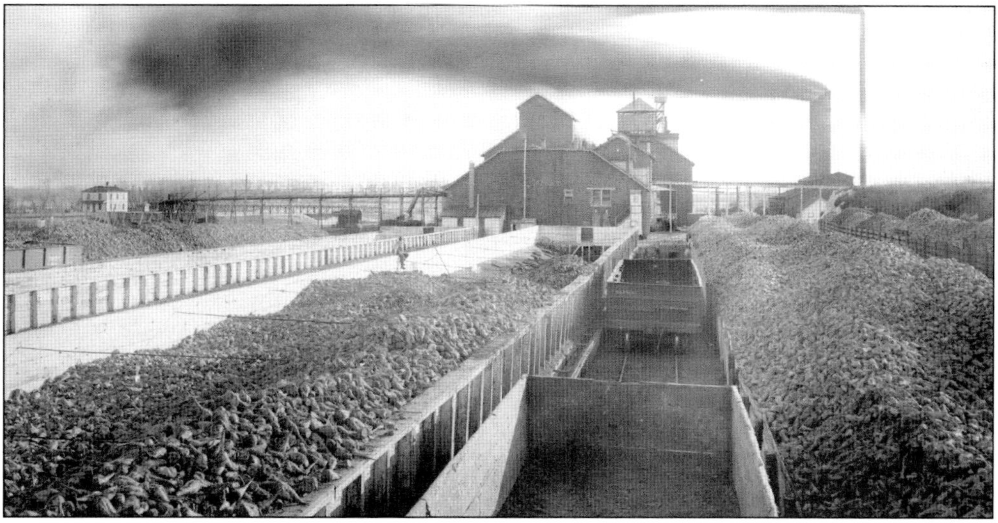

In the photograph above, mountains of sugar beets await processing at the American Beet Sugar Company factory in October 1913. On December 9, 1889, the Oxnard Beet Sugar Company broke ground for its factory, located on West Koenig Street. The building was 595 feet in length, 85 feet wide, and equal to a four-story building in height. When it opened, the factory was capable of producing 70,000 pounds of refined sugar per day and employed about 200 men. By 1903, the factory was reported to have consumed 29,000 tons of beets and to have manufactured 6,500,000 pounds of sugar. From early on, the company and the community joined forces to promote the growing of sugar beets by area farmers. The photograph below, taken in April 1913, captures a display set up in a local music store showing the various stages of sugar refinement.

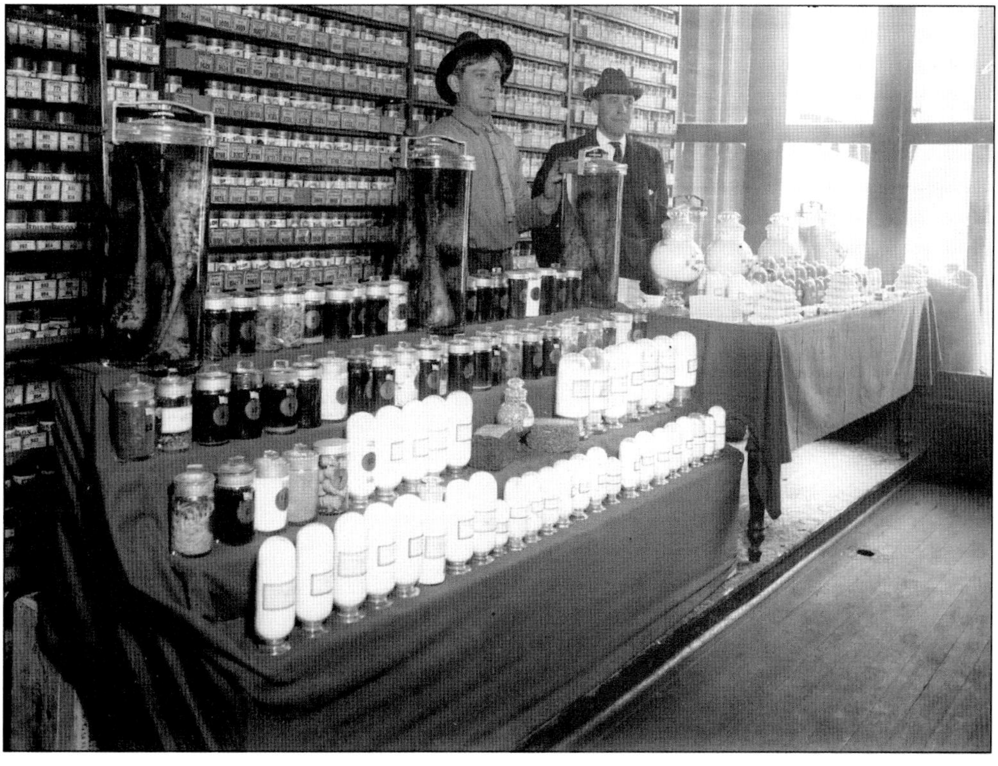

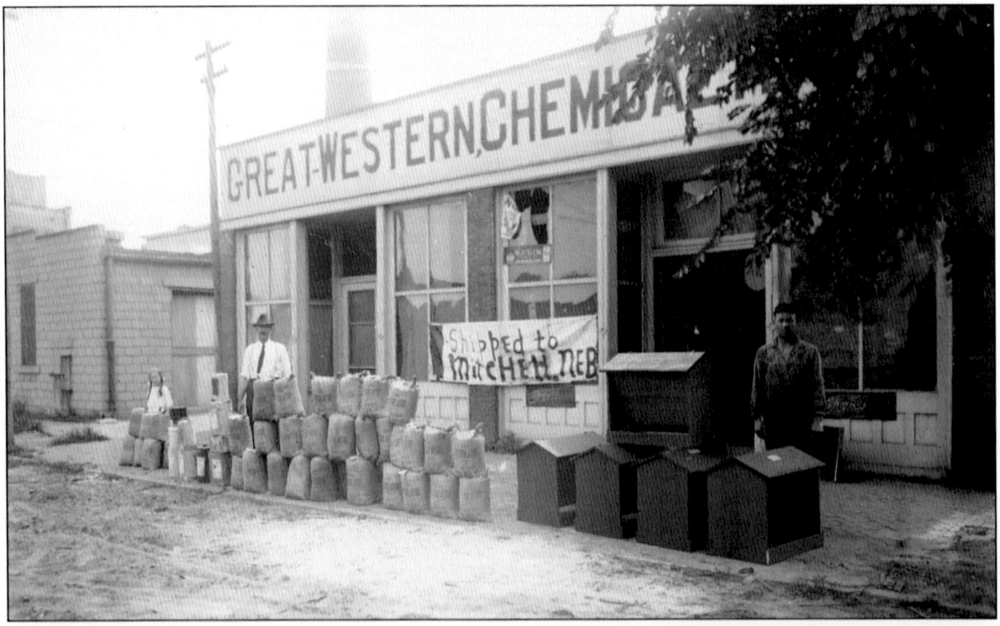

Two unidentified men and a young girl are pictured in front of the Great Western Chemical Company, 114–116 North Kimball Avenue, in August 1915. Lining the boardwalk are 50-pound feed sacks with the words "hog regulator" printed on them. The chemical company's feed was likely formulated to help combat the highly contagious disease of hog cholera. To the right of the feed sacks are hog feeders.

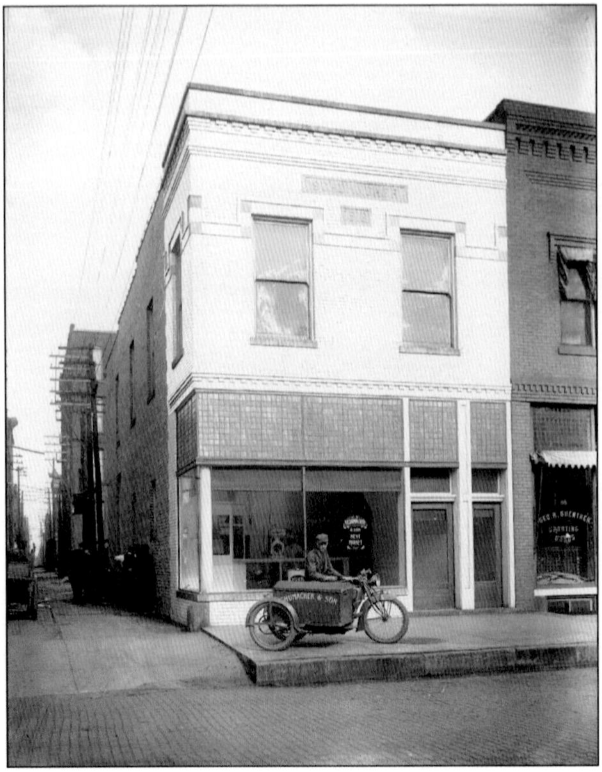

Taken in May 1917, an unidentified man poses on a motorcycle in front of the Schumacher and Sons Meat Market at 113 South Wheeler Street. Modified to make deliveries, a large metal icebox takes the place of a sidecar on the motorcycle. Born in Germany, Henry Schumacher moved to Grand Island in 1897. In 1916, he built the two-story brick building seen in this photograph and opened a meat market.

Three

Home Sweet Home

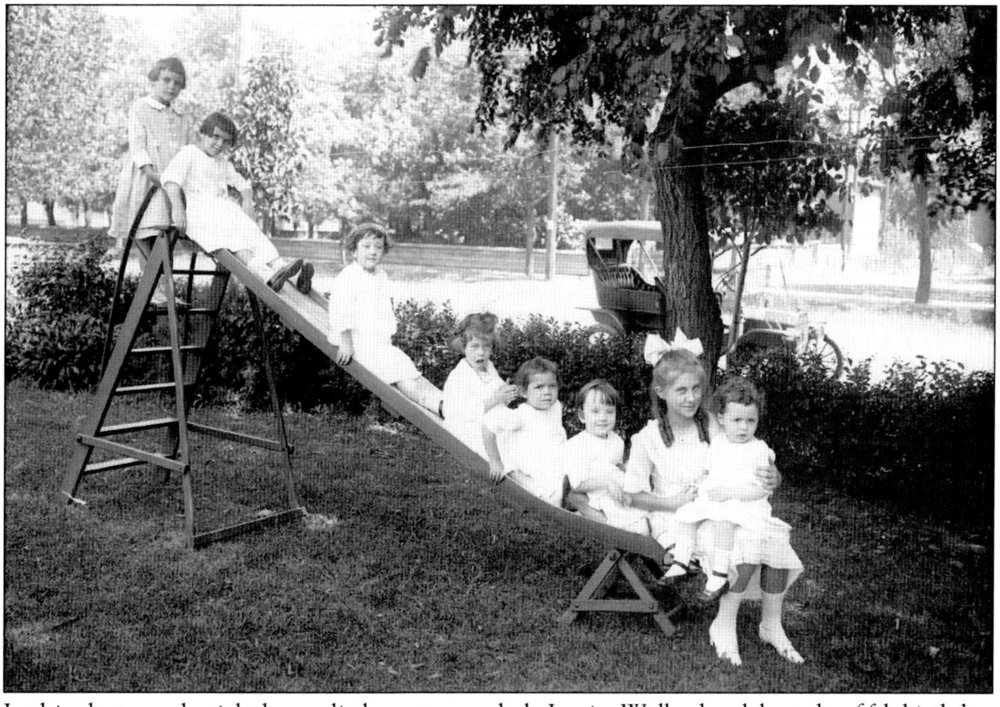

In this photograph, eight happy little partygoers help Louise Wolbach celebrate her fifth birthday. Born on July 21, 1911, Louise was the daughter of Edwin and Jeannette Wolbach. Jeannette hosted her daughter's birthday party at the family home at 804 West Division Street. Louise is likely the little girl with the big bow and bigger look of surprise in the middle of the slide.

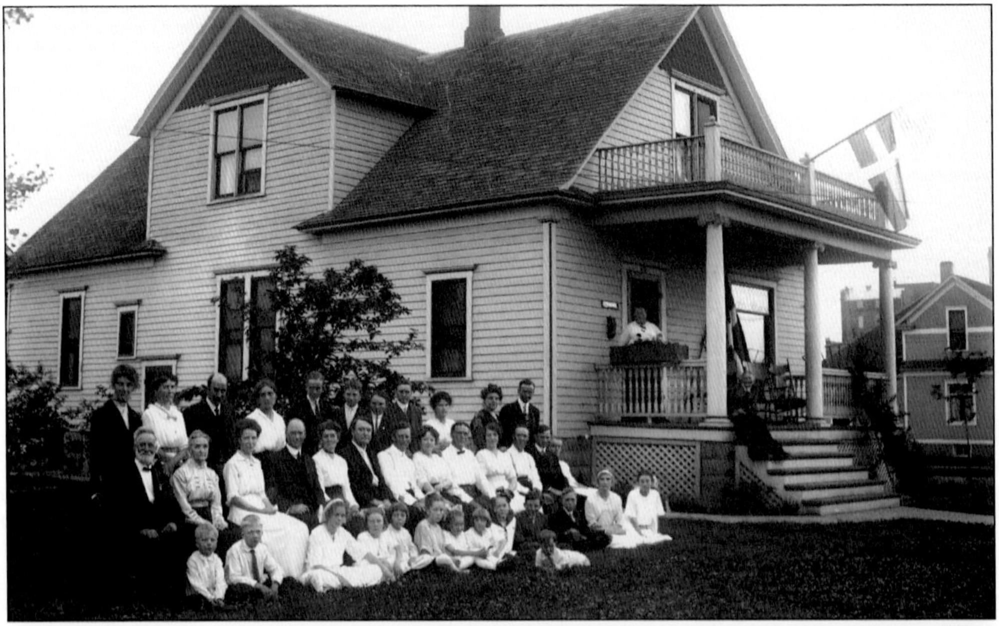

The family of Jens and Anna Eriksen gathered in May 1915 to celebrate their 50th wedding anniversary. A Danish and an American flag fly proudly from the family home at 921 West Fourth Street. Jens and Anna were married on May 25, 1865, in Denmark. Jens, a contractor by trade, brought his family to America in 1887. Of their 13 children, only the youngest, Ernest, was born in America.

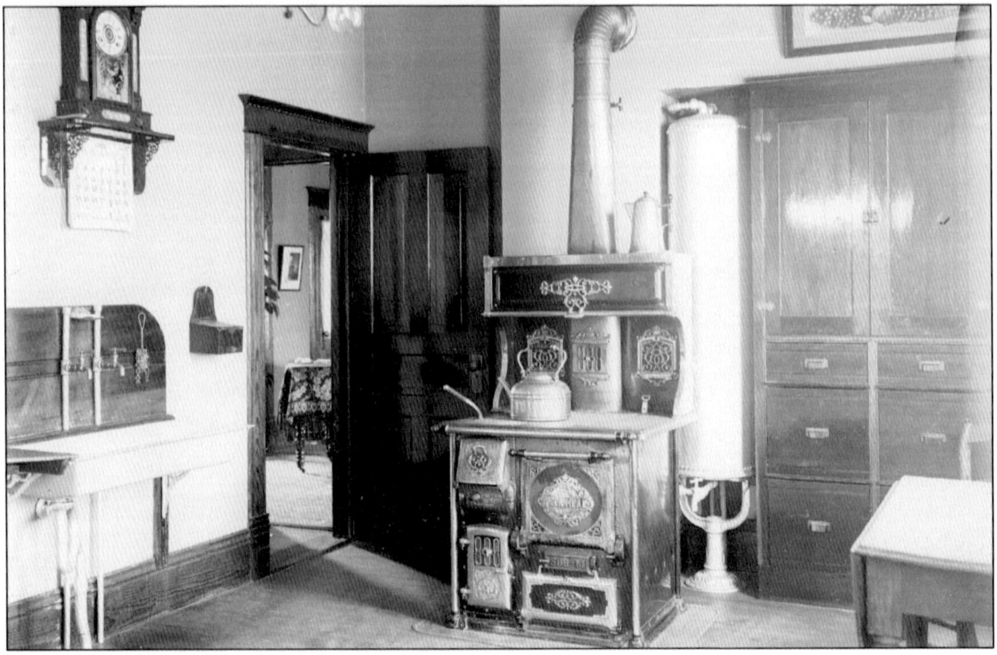

This simple yet elegant kitchen belonged to Minnie Leschinsky. In April 1904, the Leschinskys were living at 522 West Koenig Street. At the far left, a shallow sink features running hot and cold water. The tall, slender white water heater is neatly tucked away behind the stove in the center of the photograph. The woodstove was made by the Quick Meal Stove Company of St. Louis, Missouri.

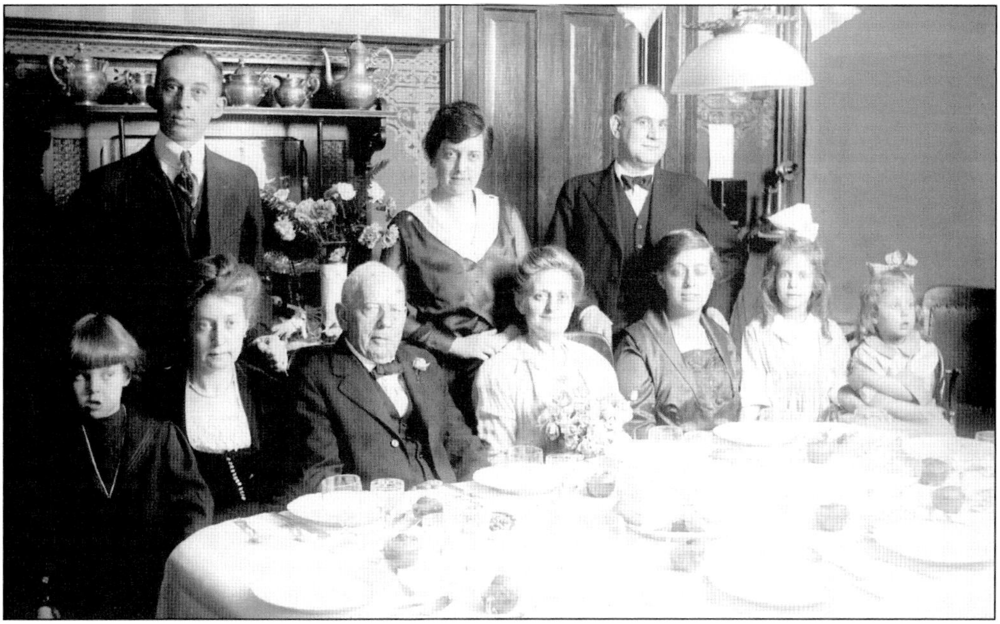

This unidentified family is seated at a beautifully set dinner table. Cups of frozen sorbet have been placed at each table setting. In the center of the table, an elaborately decorated, round cake indicates this is a celebration. Note the rose boutonniere on the older gentleman's lapel and the bouquet of flowers held by the woman seated to his right. Could this be a special anniversary for the couple?

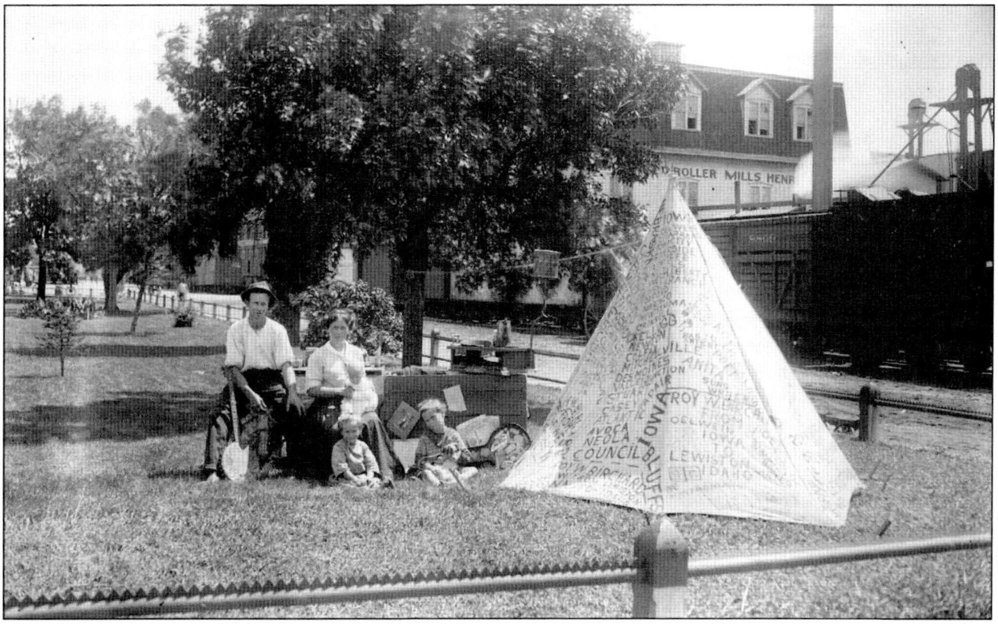

In July 1913, the Roy W. Birchard family of traveling musicians camped on the lawn of the Union Pacific Railroad depot, located on Front Street. According to the writing on the family's tent, the Birchards were traveling from Iowa to Ohio and everywhere in between. Roy W. Birchard described himself as a poet, songwriter, and musician. Note the wooden trunk that had to hold all their possessions while traveling.

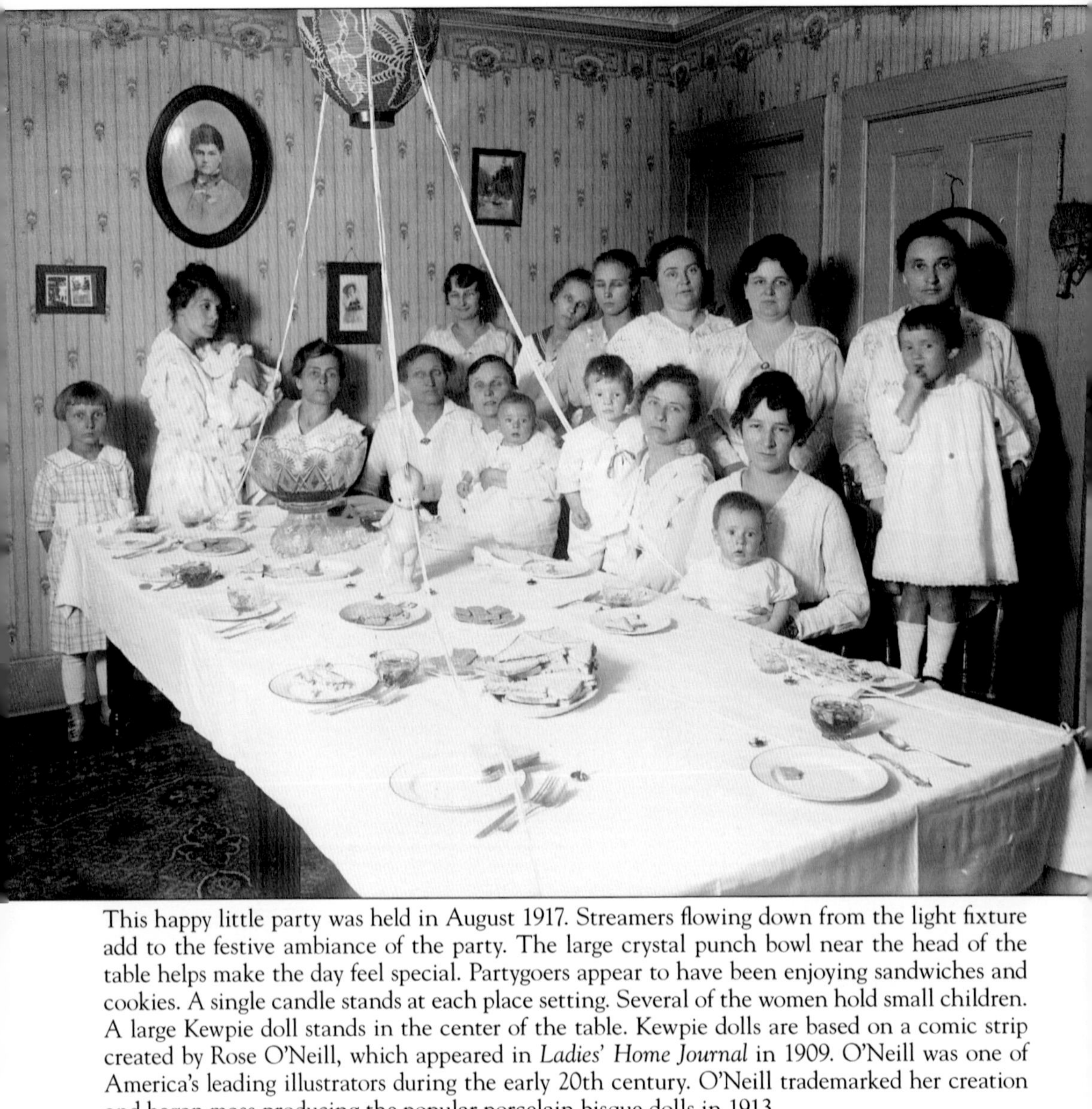

This happy little party was held in August 1917. Streamers flowing down from the light fixture add to the festive ambiance of the party. The large crystal punch bowl near the head of the table helps make the day feel special. Partygoers appear to have been enjoying sandwiches and cookies. A single candle stands at each place setting. Several of the women hold small children. A large Kewpie doll stands in the center of the table. Kewpie dolls are based on a comic strip created by Rose O'Neill, which appeared in *Ladies' Home Journal* in 1909. O'Neill was one of America's leading illustrators during the early 20th century. O'Neill trademarked her creation and began mass-producing the popular porcelain bisque dolls in 1913.

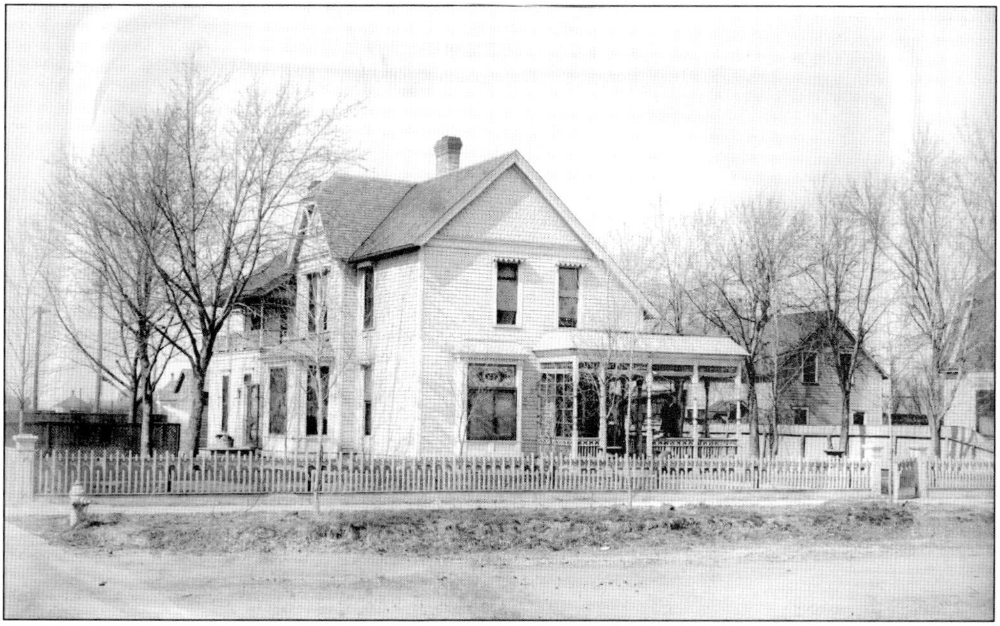

Located at 120 West Tenth Street, Julius Leschinsky photographed this large two-story frame house in March 1910. Many of the architectural details of this home mark the transition between the Victorian and craftsman styles. Visible are elaborate and ornate details typical of a Victorian home with the gingerbread-style trim and fish scale siding near the roofline. However, this home also combines the cleaner, simpler lines of the craftsman-style homes.

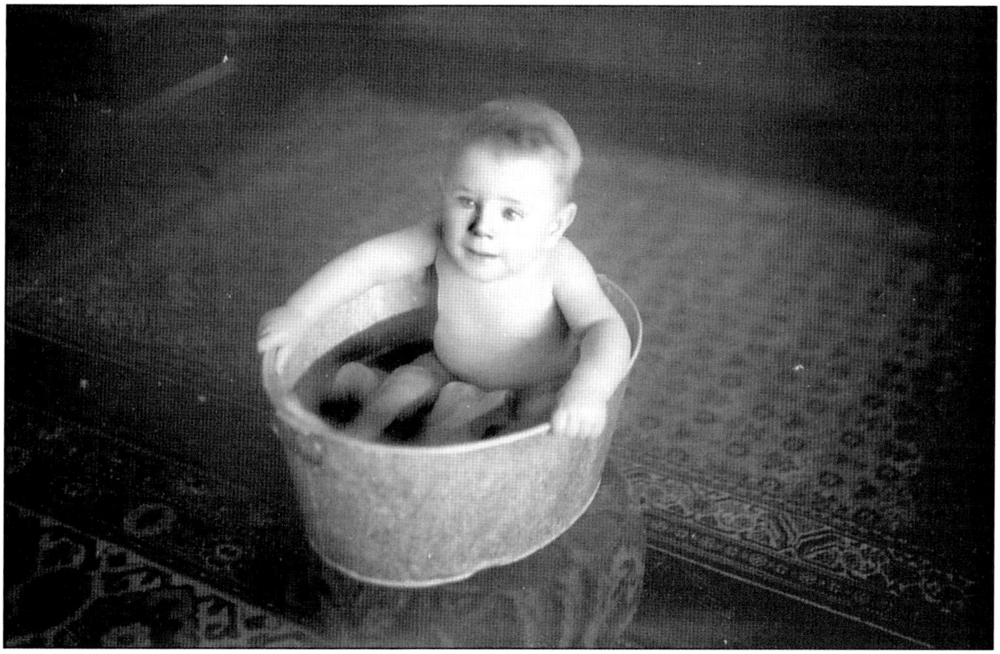

This little cutie laughingly poses for the camera while taking a bath in a metal washtub. Frank Kunze commissioned this photograph in January 1911. Kunze operated a hardware store located at 303 West Third Street. Kunze and his wife Louisa had two children, Clayton and Hazel. Clayton, who was born on June 10, 1910, is likely the baby in the bathtub.

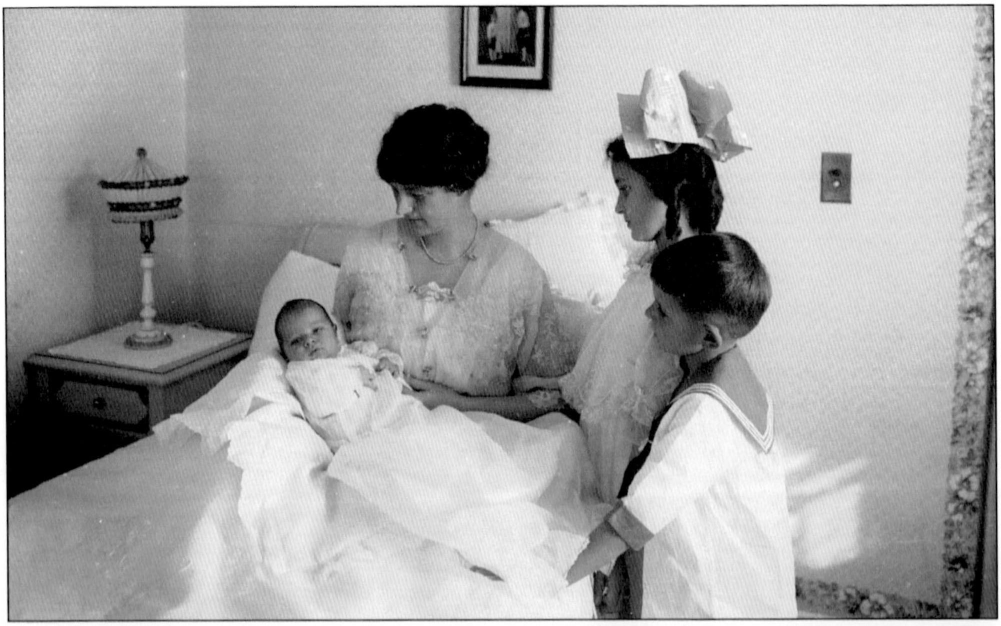

Callie Farnsworth, wife of Dr. Albert H. Farnsworth, holds newborn Albert Henry in this photograph taken in December 1917. Big sister Elizabeth and brother Frederick look on with interest. The photograph appears to have been taken in the family home located at 1319 West Second Street. Dr. Farnsworth opened his Grand Island office in February 1902 and practiced general medicine and surgery.

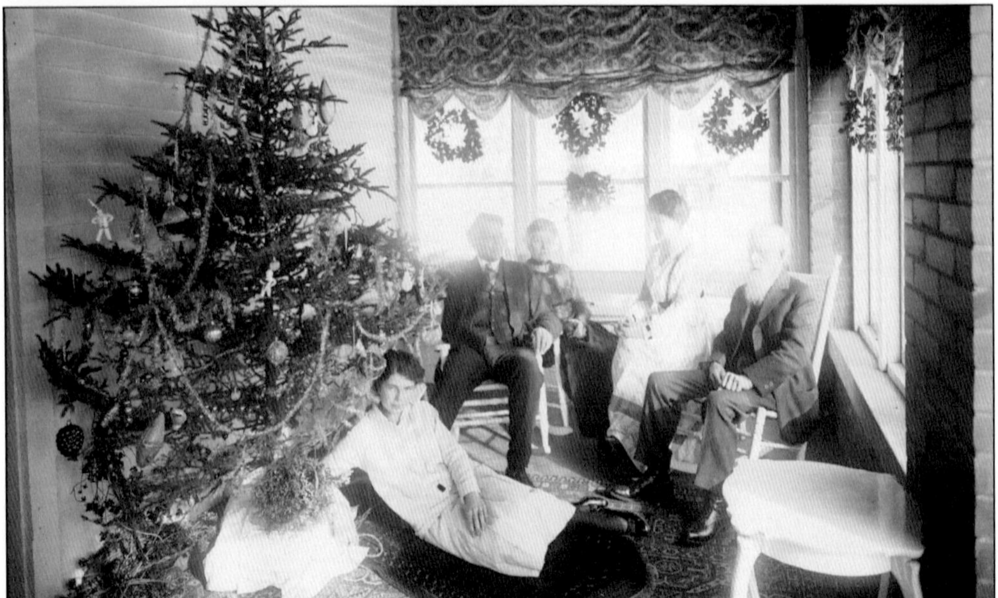

Grand Island mayor Charles G. Ryan and his family pose around a Christmas tree while holly wreaths hang in the windows of their home at 406 South Lincoln Street in 1915. Photographed are likely (from left to right) Evelyn Ryan (seated on the floor), Charles Ryan, Eliza (Humphrey) Murphy, Evelyn (Murphy) Ryan, and Michael Murphy. Christmas in the Ryan home was an extra-special time. Charles married Evelyn on Christmas Eve 1896.

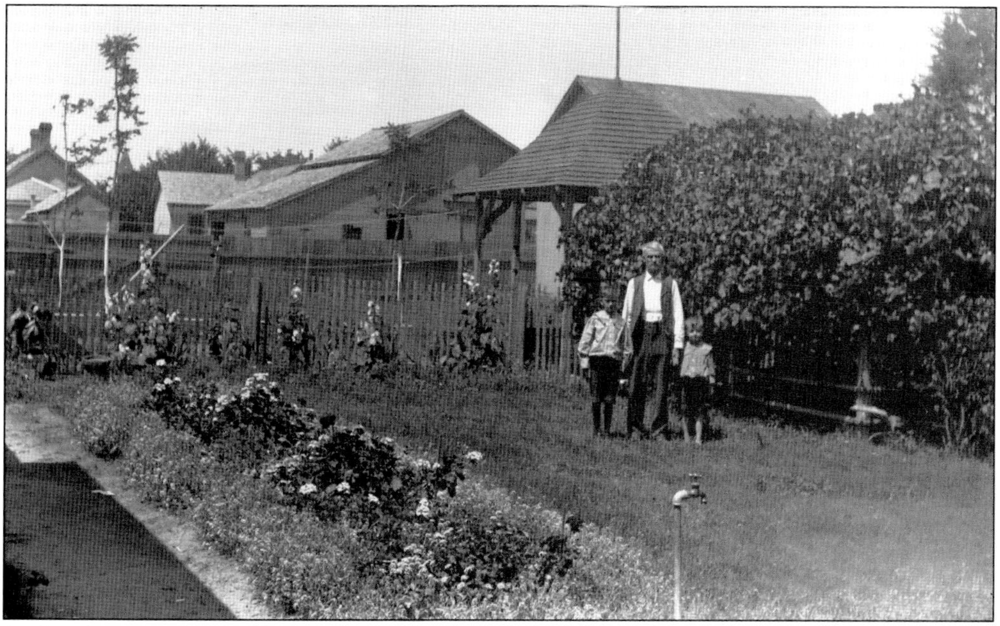

In this photograph, an older gentleman holds the hands of two small boys in a well-kept backyard garden in about 1900. Delicate white blossoms of alyssum border larger geranium plants in the foreground flower bed. In the background, hollyhocks and irises grow along the fence. A wooden pagoda-style gazebo can be seen in the far corner. Note the water spigot in the foreground of the photograph.

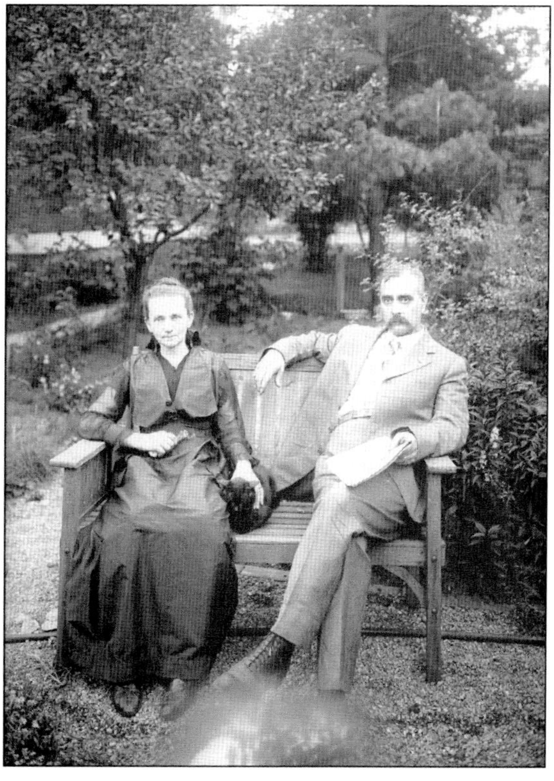

Max and Margaretha Leschinsky are seated in the backyard of Julius Leschinsky's home at 518 West Koenig Street. Max and Julius were half brothers. In 1886, Max and Julius opened their first photography studio together on East Third Street. In 1890, Max and his family moved to Loup City, where he worked briefly as a photographer until opening a general merchandise store.

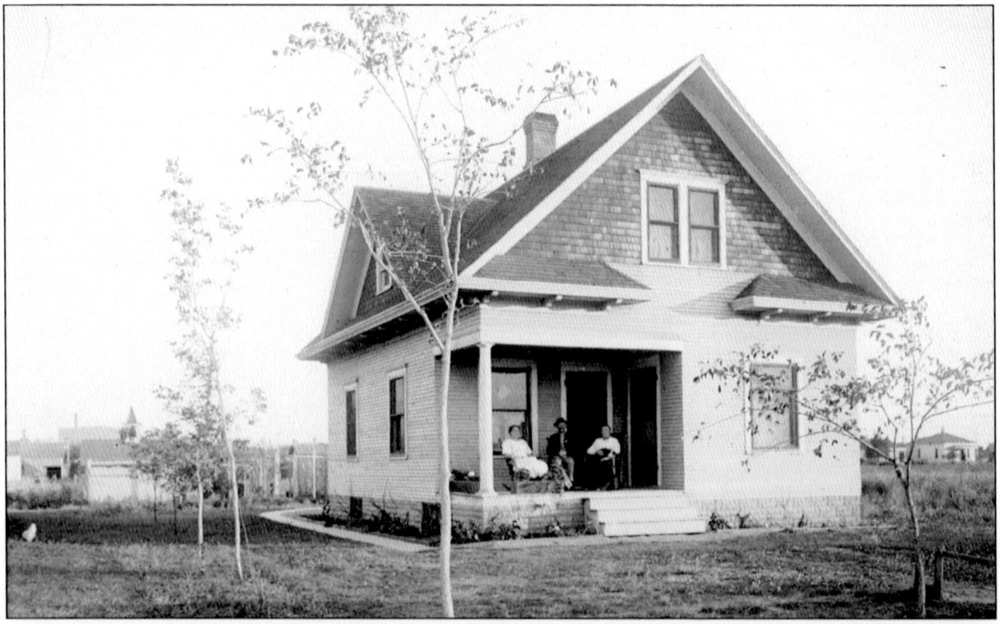

This attractive house was likely located at 409 West Thirteenth Street. It was owned by Fred and Marie Bartels, probably the older couple seen sitting on the porch. Their daughter Sophia Bartels commissioned this photograph in September 1918 and may be the woman seated at the far left on the porch. From about 1910 through the 1920s, Sophia worked at the Donald Company and later the Nebraska Telephone Company.

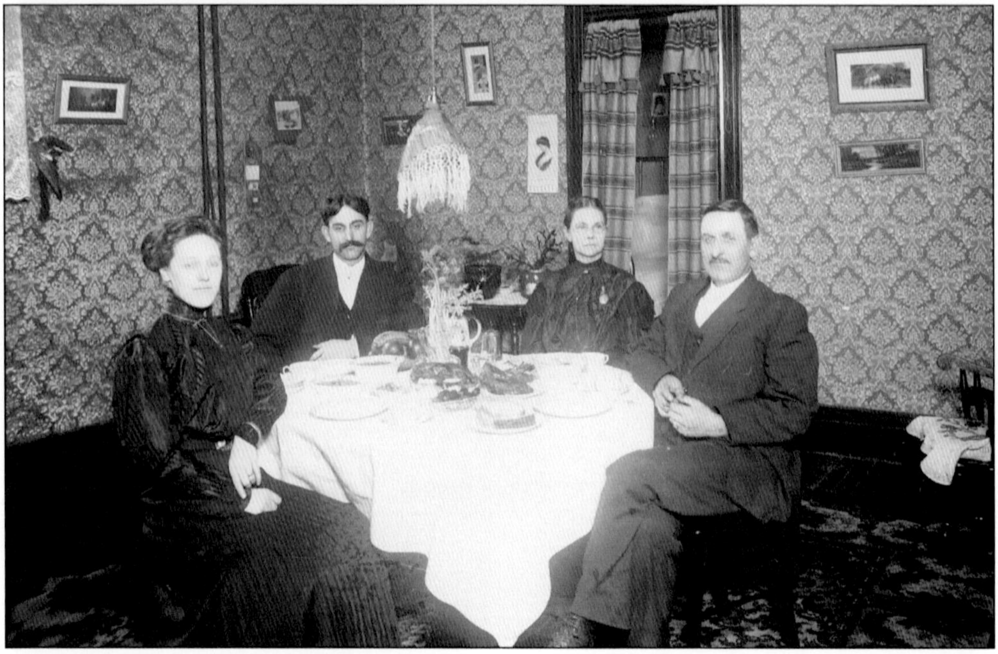

Two couples share a meal at the home of Grant Watkins. Served on fine china, a meal of roast duck, boiled potatoes, sliced bread, and pickles graced the table. Stalks of celery have been artfully arranged in a celery vase to serve as the centerpiece. A bowl of apples and bananas can also be seen on the table. Hanging on the wall is a calendar displaying November 1910.

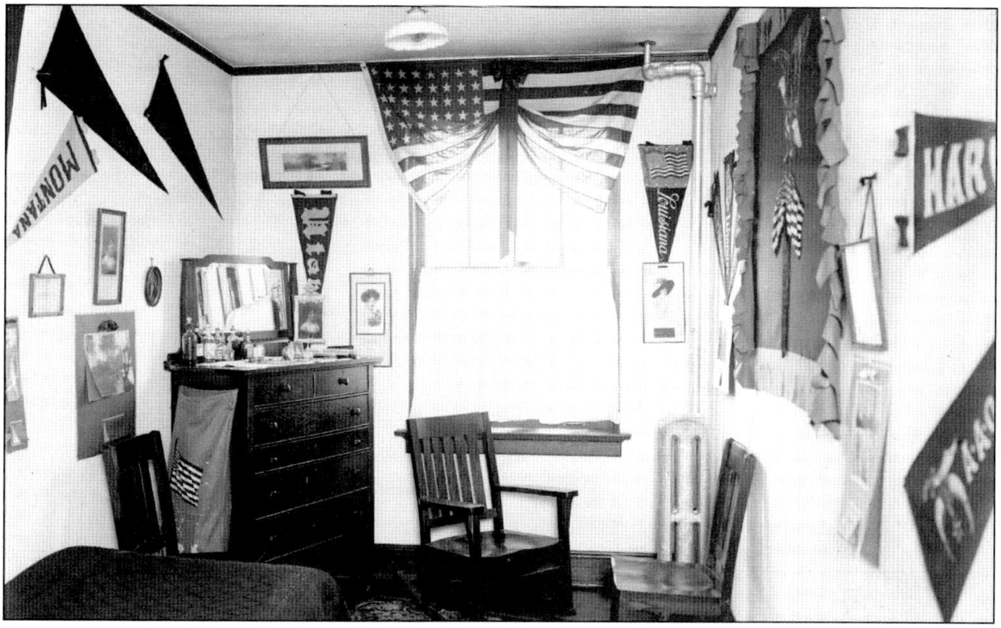

This photograph shows the interior of one of the rooms of Grand Island's YMCA. The calendar hanging on the wall between the dresser and the window indicates the date to be March 1915. Located at the northeast corner of First and Locust Streets, the four-story redbrick structure was known as "the City and Railroad YMCA." It opened in 1914 and featured an indoor swimming pool and gymnasium.

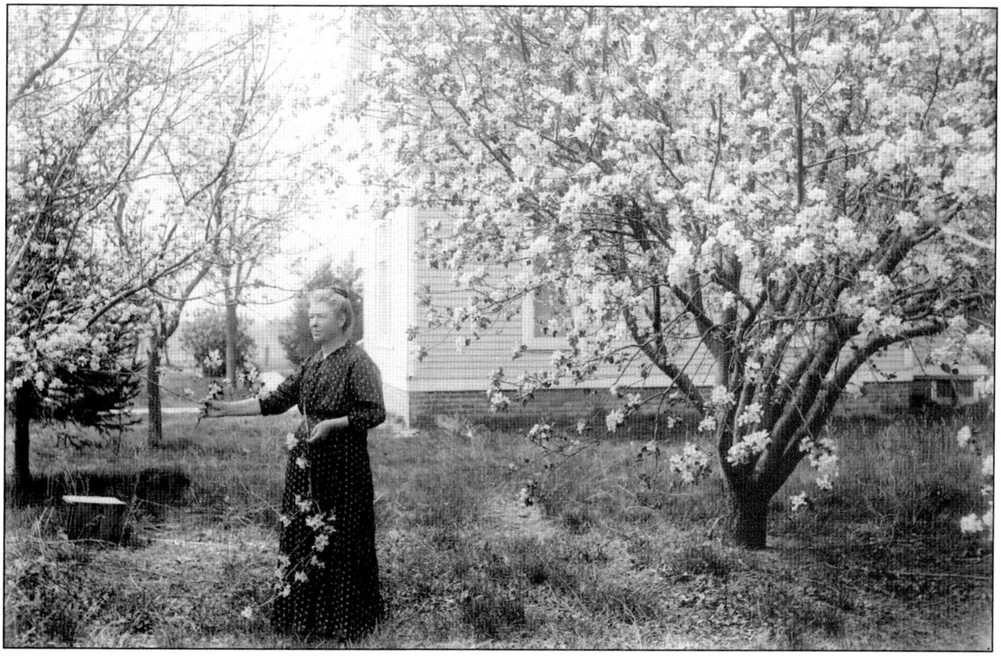

An unidentified woman examines the blossoms of several large apple trees in about 1915. A two-story frame house can be seen through the trees. The first apple trees in Hall County were successfully grown by pioneer settler William Stolley in 1872. Stolley also experimented with several other varieties of fruit-bearing trees, including pear, peach, and cherry.

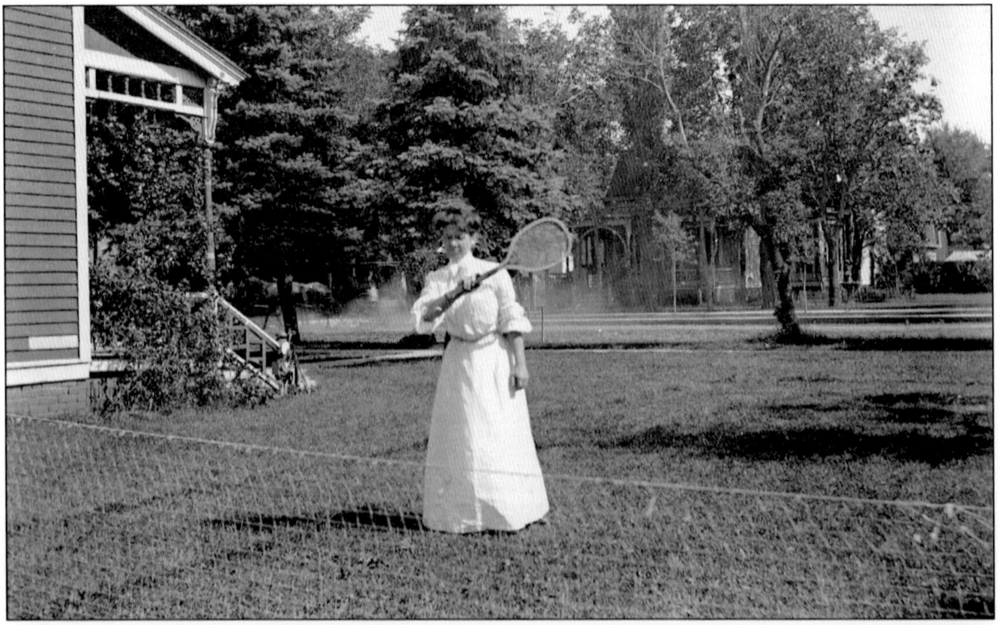

This unidentified woman prepares to hit a backhand shot while playing lawn tennis at a Grand Island home around 1910. She is using a wooden racket, and a net has been stretched tight across the lawn. A popular sport for both men and women at the time of this photograph, lawn tennis credits its invention to around 1865.

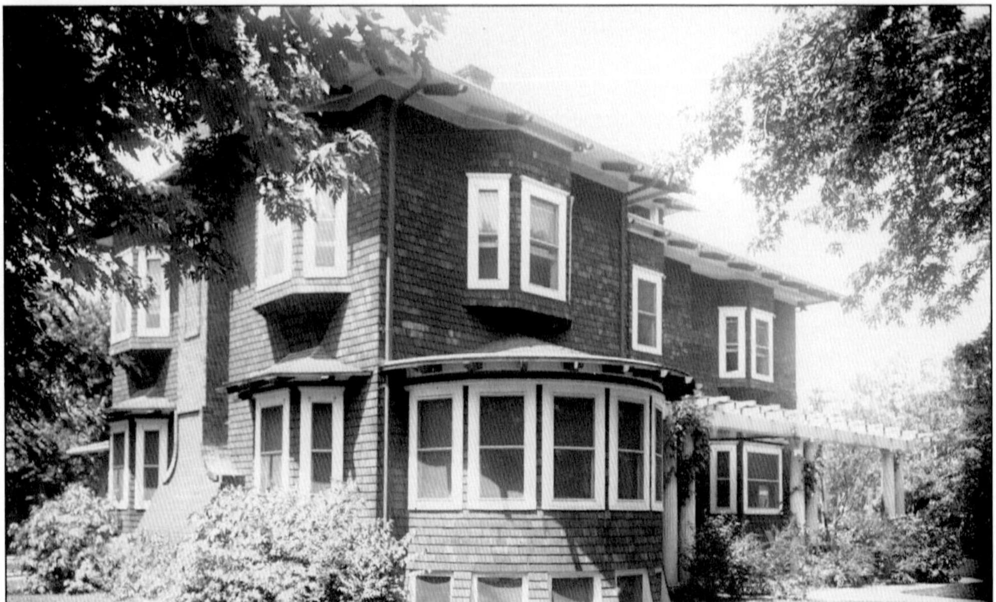

Located at 1004 West Division Street, this two-story home was originally built by Henry Glade in 1905. Born in Germany, Glade owned a successful flour mill in Grand Island. After his death in 1910, the house was purchased by Lawrence Donald, who operated a wholesale fruit company with his brother John. A stellar example of shingle-style architecture, this house has earned a spot on the National Register of Historic Places.

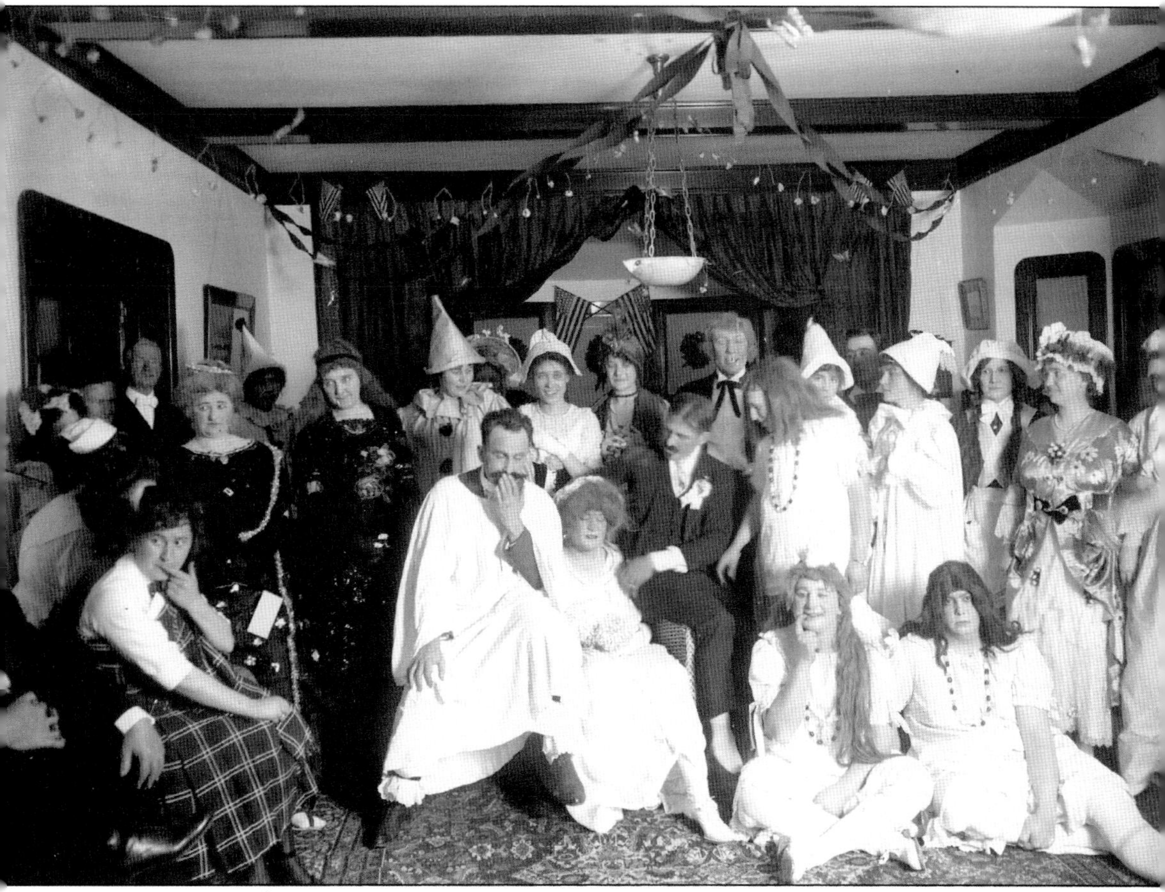

On February 3, 1914, Lawrence and Dorothy Donald held a masquerade ball at their home at 1004 West Division Street. According to details published in the newspaper the next morning, nearly 100 of Grand Island's elite attended the ball. As can be seen in this photograph, costumes ranged from the refined to burlesque and otherwise. A stage was set up in the spacious home where many of the guests showcased their special talents and "stunts." Dorothy's sisters, visiting from Denver, Colorado, performed well-received vocal solos. The hit of the evening was the "bridal party," claiming the prize for best burlesque show. The all-male bridal party consisted of some of Grand Island's most respected businessmen and leaders. Perhaps the best costumes of the night belonged to Evelyn Ryan and Mary Conner, who were able to keep their identities a mystery until masks were removed. Ryan attended as an East Indian prince and Conner as a Hungarian. Partygoers danced the night away to a six-piece orchestra. The ball lasted until well after midnight.

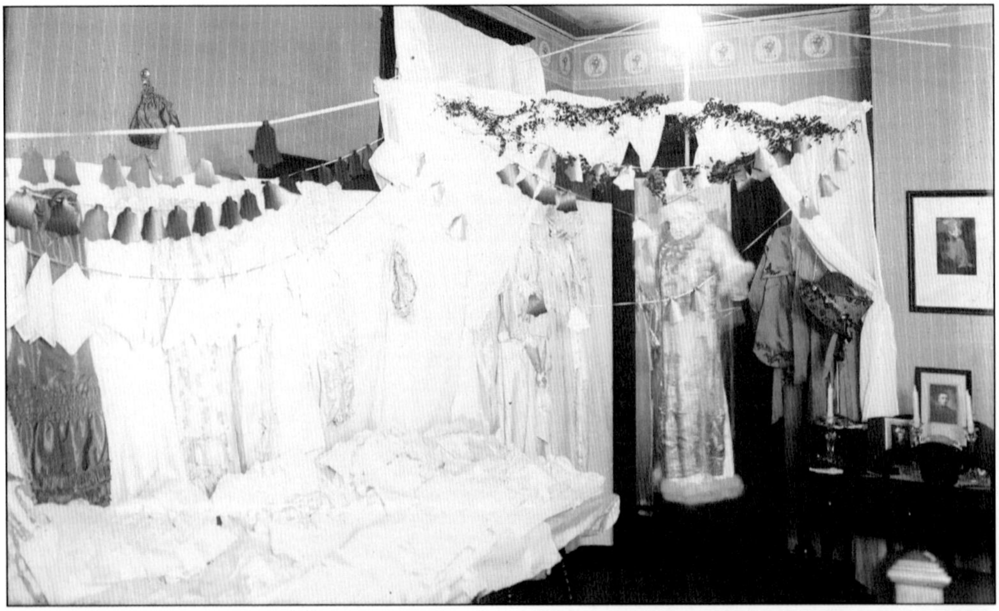

The wedding trousseau and decorations for the intimate wedding of Hazel Prince to Addison Bolton shows richness and taste. The wedding occurred on the evening of March 14, 1918, in the Prince family home. In the photograph above, Hazel's wedding clothing is displayed, including the wedding gown designed by the House of Worth, a famous designer of the late 19th and early 20th century. This dress was also worn by the bride's cousin, Mrs. Chester H. Aldrich, for her husband's inaugural reception as governor of Nebraska. A wedding trousseau included the wedding clothing as well as clothes and undergarments the bride wore on the honeymoon. According to a local newspaper article, a two-course dinner was served on tables decorated with pink and white bride's roses, sweat peas, and festoons of smilax, like the one seen below.

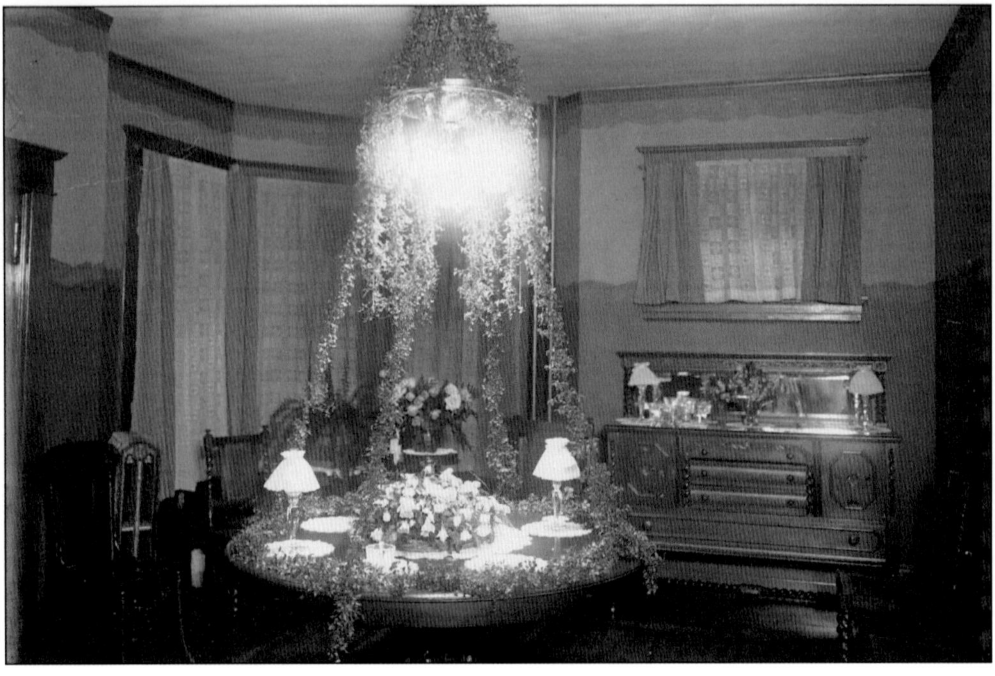

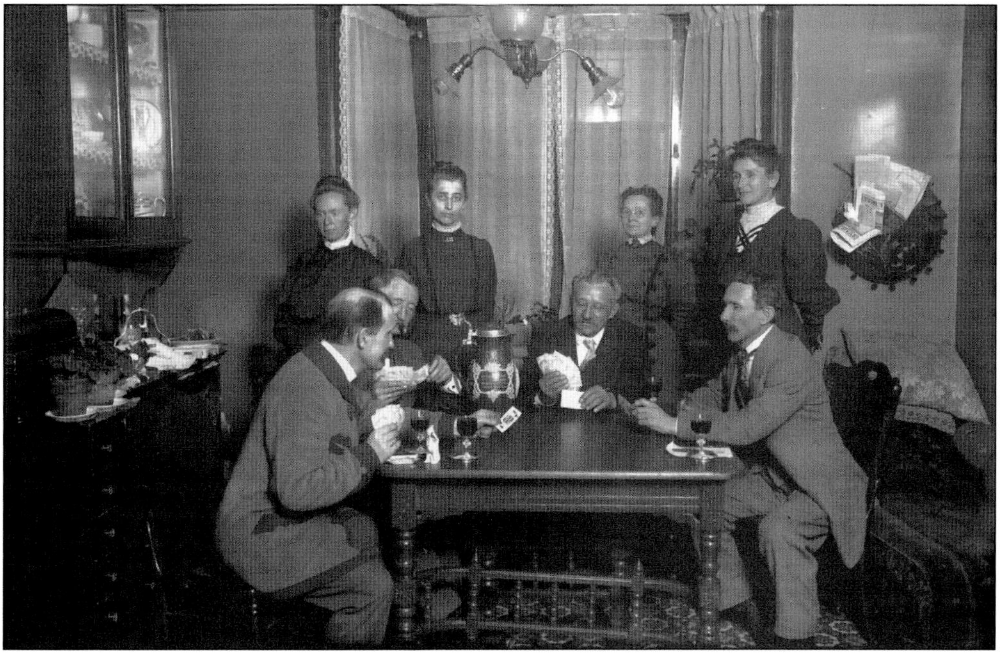

A group of friends gathers in the home of Julius Leschinsky to play cards in about 1910. Leschinsky is seated at the table on the far left. His wife Minnie is the second woman standing from the left. Featured prominently in the center of the table is a ceramic pitcher featuring a grape-and-vine motif, indicating it was designed to serve wine.

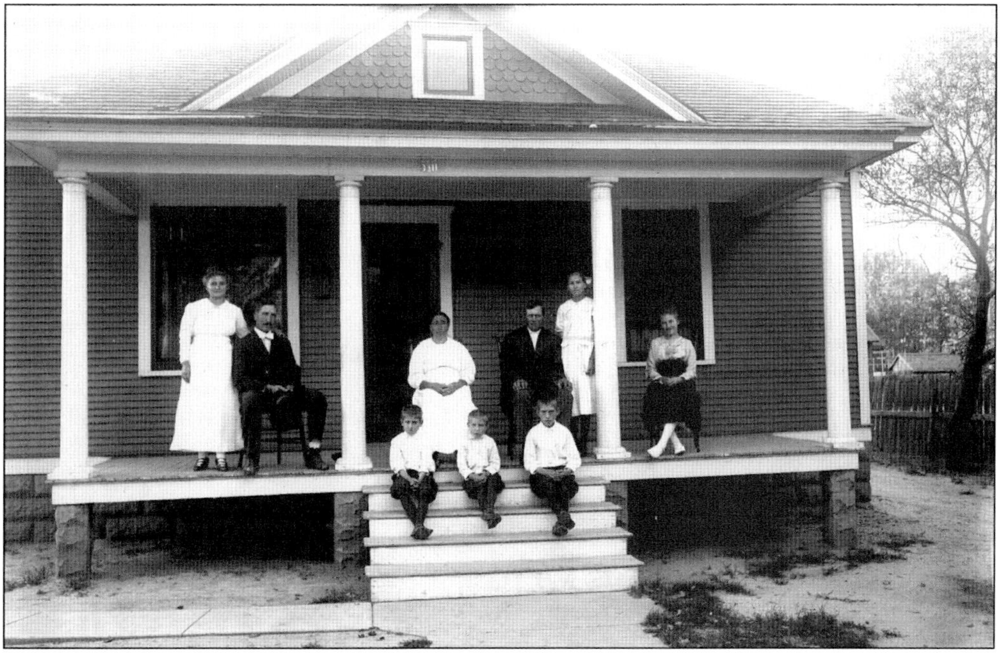

Members of the Henry Wilman family pose on the front porch of their home at 510 East Division Street in September 1917. The three young boys seated on the steps are likely David, Daniel, and John. Other possible identifications are from left to right, Kate (wife of Henry Jr.), Henry Jr., Marie (wife of Henry Sr.), Henry Sr., and Marie and Mollie (daughters of Henry Sr. and Marie).

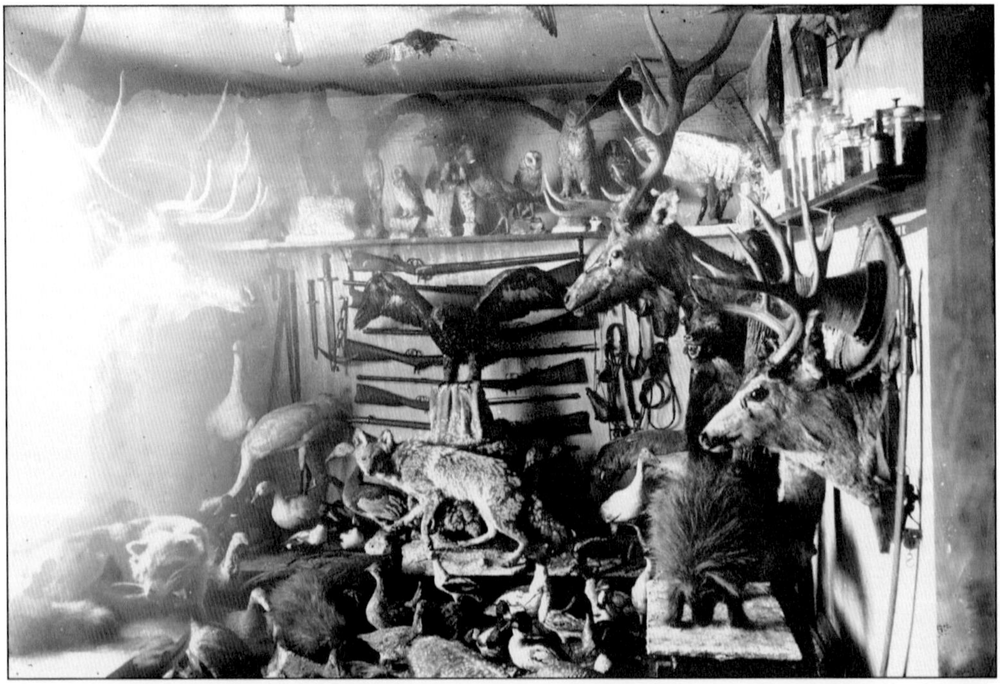

George Guenther operated a sporting-goods store on South Wheeler Street. The photograph at the top of the page shows a room full of various stuffed animals and sporting equipment. Guenther commissioned this photograph in April 1916. He and his wife Lillie lived at 1212 West Second Street. It is unclear if this room of taxidermy artistry was in the Guenther home or at his place of business. Guenther asked Julius Leschinsky to take the photograph below in October 1913. In his business records, Leschinsky describes the celebration as a stag party. Note the bottles of Budweiser beer and empty bowls of chili.

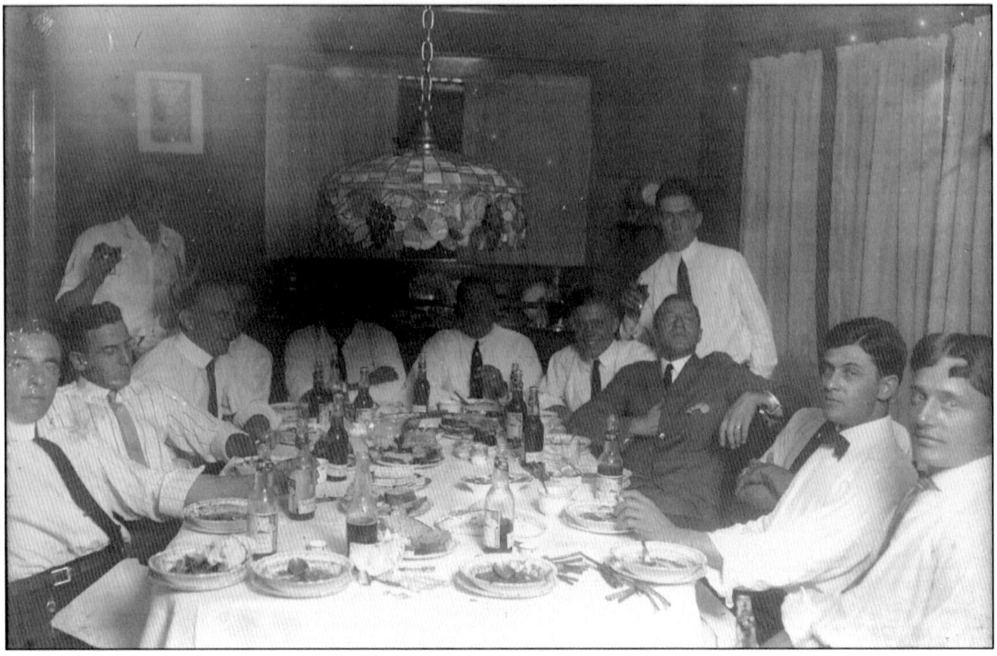

Four

Celebrating Community

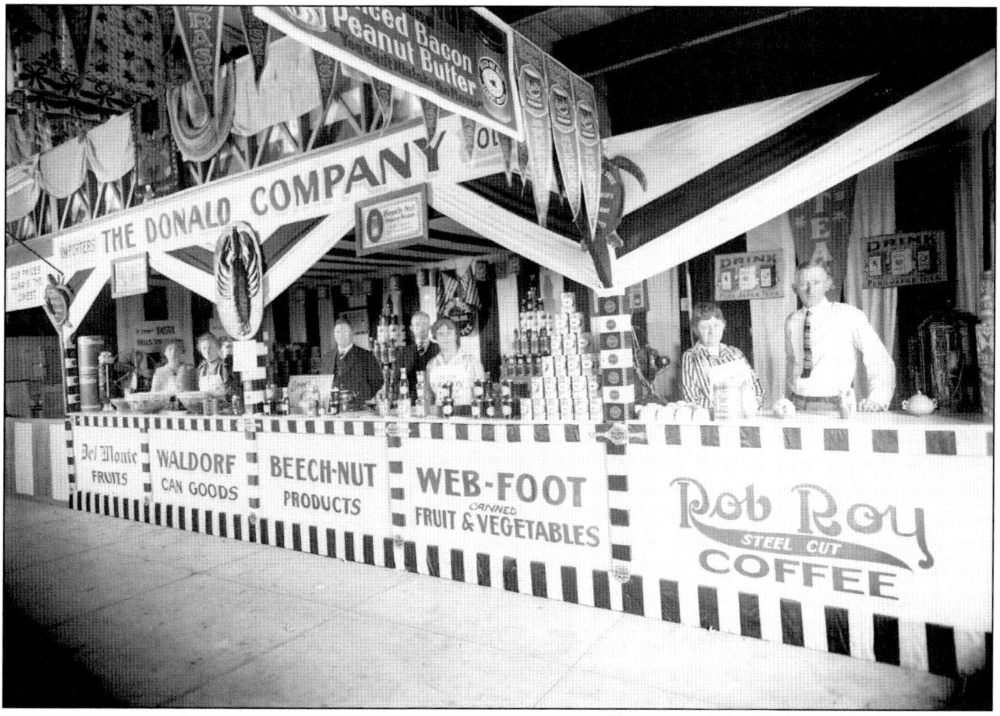

In this photograph, employees of the Donald Company staff their booth at the Central Nebraska Fair in September 1916. Signs advertise the many products sold and distributed by the wholesale fruit and grocery company. While some companies like Del Monte and Beech-Nut are nationally known, Rob Roy coffee and Web-Foot fruit and vegetables were packaged and produced in Grand Island.

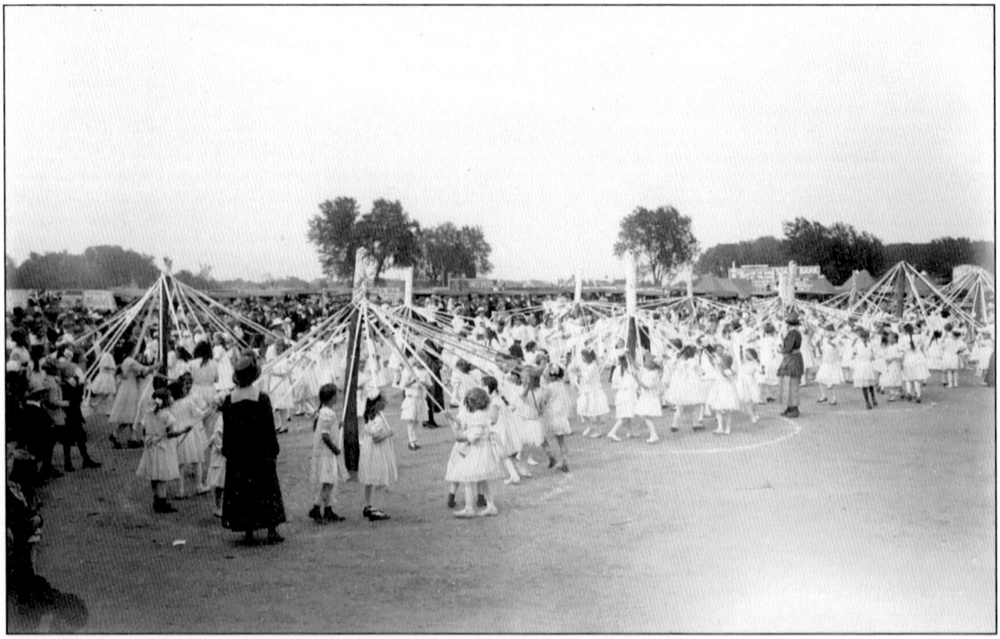

The May festival seen in this photograph was held at Grand Island's old Athletic Park on May 24, 1917. Young girls from Howard, Jefferson, and Dodge schools, wearing white dresses, are seen winding ribbons around maypoles while a large crowd looks on. The Athletic Park was located in the southwest corner of today's Pier Park.

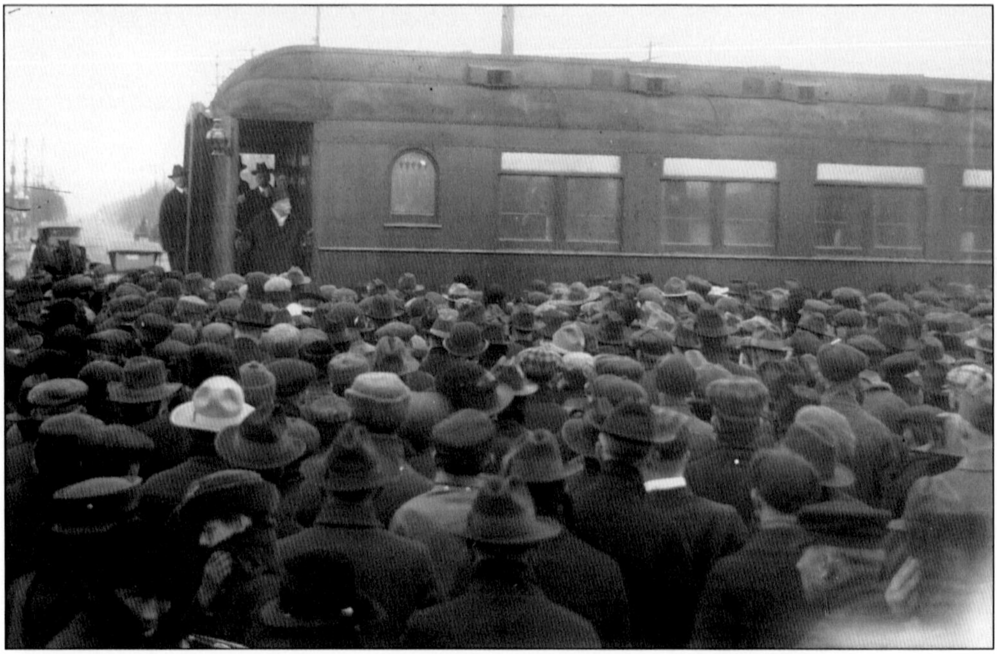

On February 24, 1919, a crowd of nearly 1,500 people gathered at the Wheeler Street crossing of the Union Pacific Railroad to see former president William Howard Taft. Taft arrived in Grand Island at 1:00 p.m. and gave a short speech on a plan outlining the League of Nations as the only method of assuring continued peace. Taft's train left Grand Island at 1:20 p.m. for Omaha.

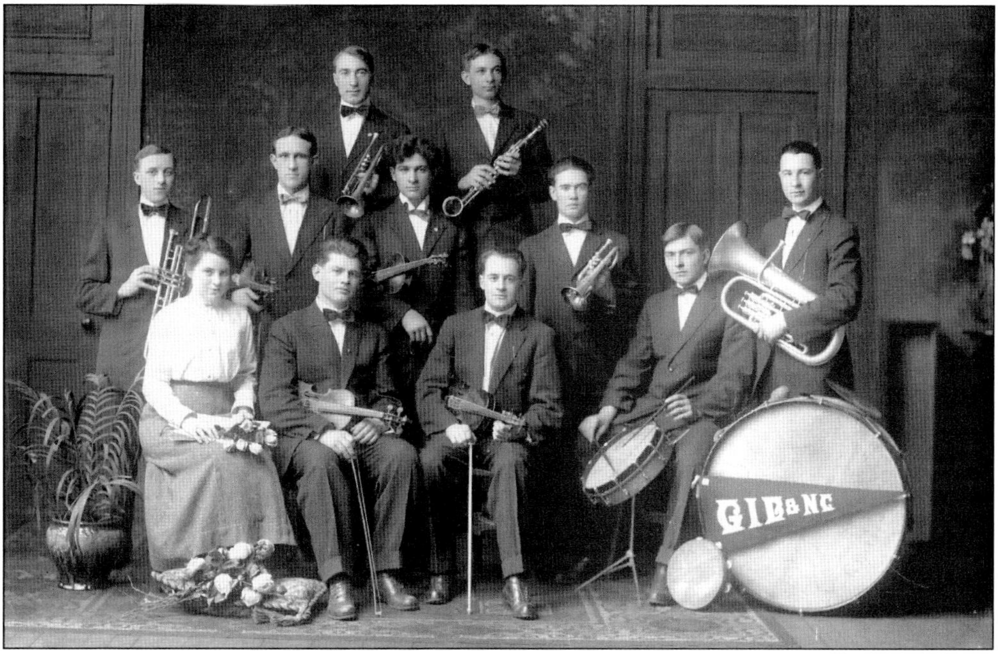

In March 1913, 11 members of the Grand Island Business and Normal College orchestra pose for this photograph. The 10 male members are holding their musical instruments. The only female member is seated at the far left. She is holding music in her lap, and Julius Leschinsky placed flowers at her feet. It could be that she was the vocal soloist.

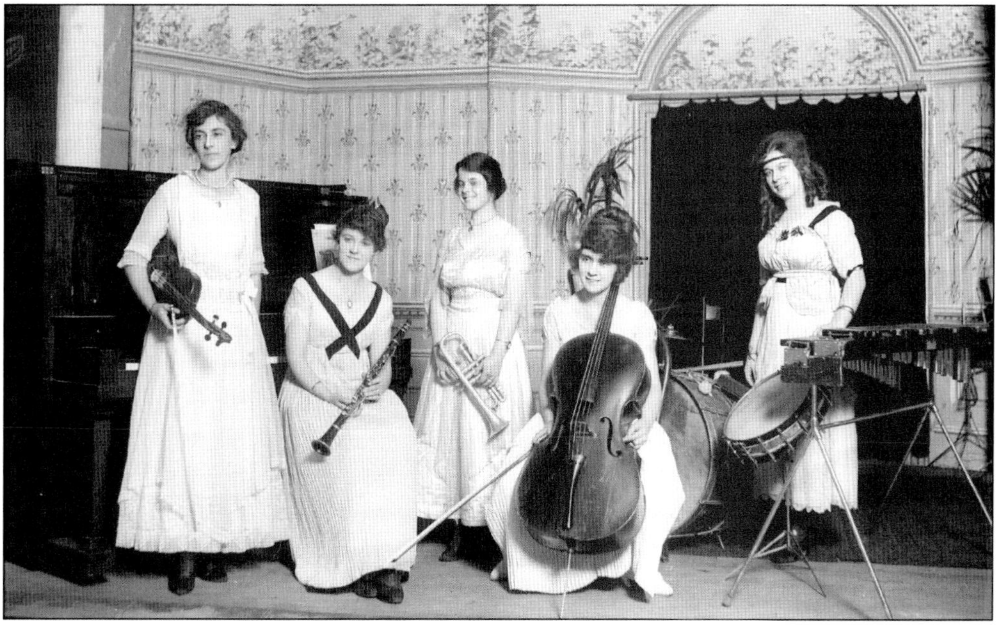

The five young ladies seen in this photograph were part of a traveling musical vaudevillian act that billed themselves as "Miss Gove and her Pilgrim Girls." They performed at the Majestic Theater from October 29 to 31, 1916. According to the newspaper, Miss Gove and her girls promised "good music, well played." Admission was 10¢ for the matinee and 15¢ for the evening performance.

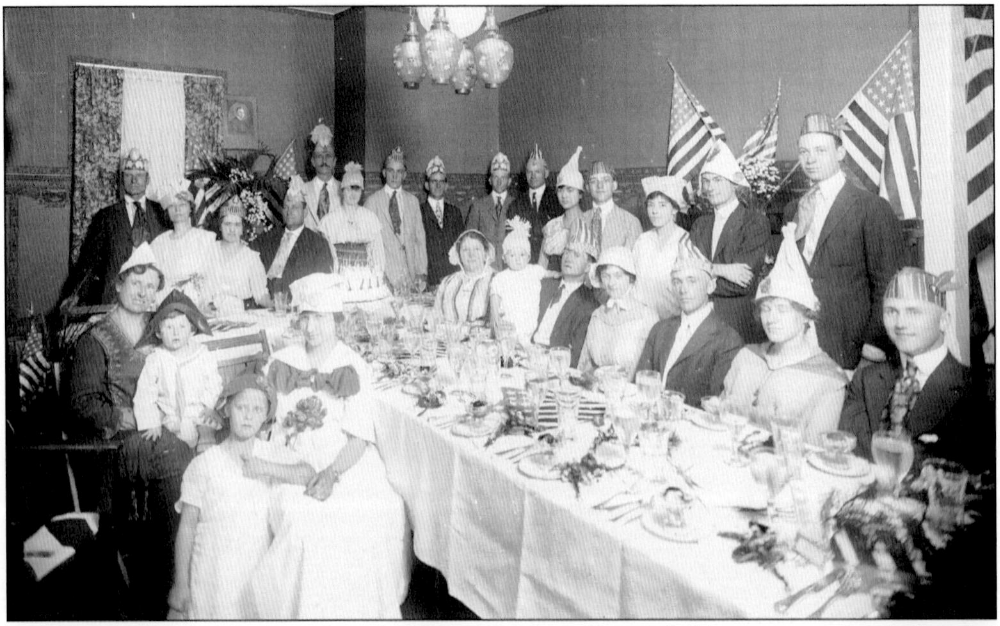

On Sunday, July 1, 1917, the wife and brother of C. M. Robinson held a surprise party for his 43rd birthday. The two brothers were president and vice president of Western Chemical Manufacturing Company. Bertha Robinson hosted a four-course luncheon at their home at 809 West First Street. According to the *Grand Island Independent*, the dining room was decorated with flowers, flags, and candles, all visible in this photograph.

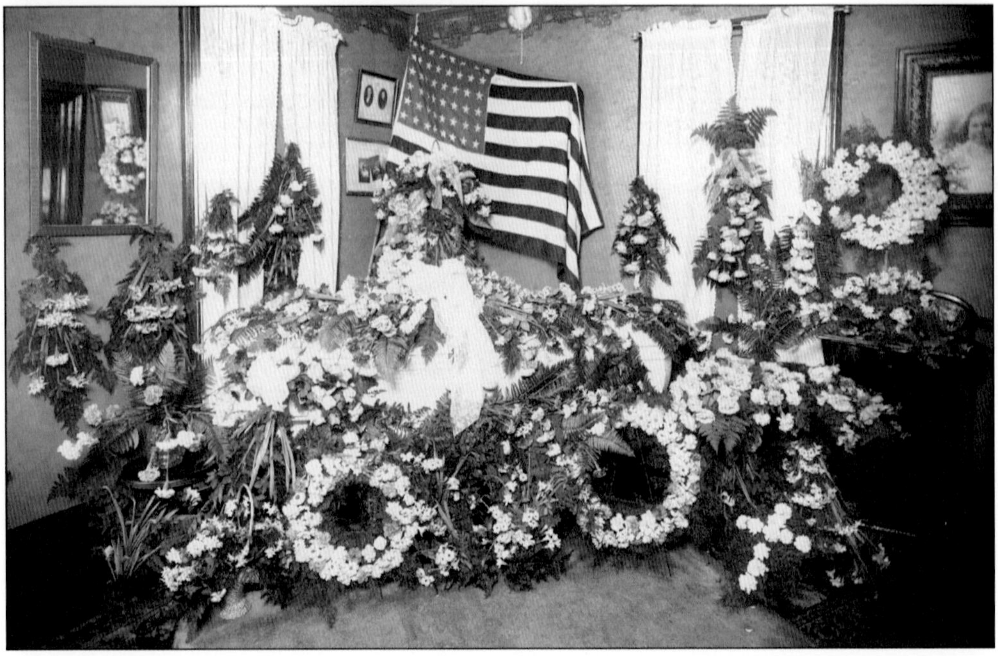

The sad scene captured in this photograph was all too common during the influenza epidemic of 1918–1919. Roe Powell was 27 years old when he succumbed to the deadly infection on February 2, 1919. His funeral was held in the home he shared with his parents and siblings. His casket is barely visible beneath numerous floral tributes received by the Powell family.

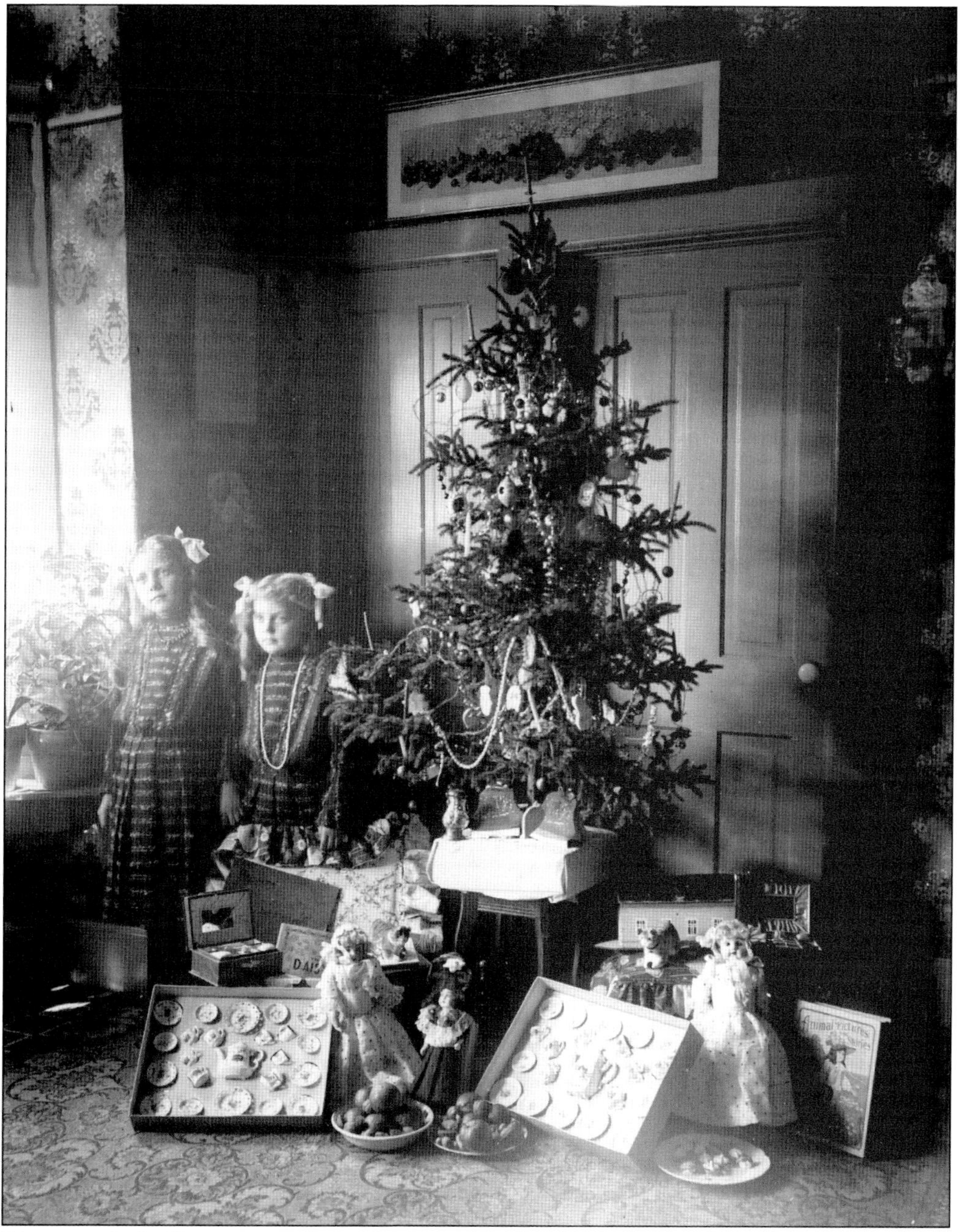

These two little Christmas cuties pose next to their family Christmas tree in about 1914. Judging from the number of gifts under the tree, the girls appear to have been very good that year. The girls are likely sisters and received similar presents. Found under the tree are matching tea sets, dolls, toy cats, books, sewing kits, and pillows. Also under the tree are traditional treats of nuts, fruits, and sweets. The Christmas tree sits on a small wooden table, a common practice during the 19th and early 20th centuries. Decorations include glass and paper ornaments, strings of popcorn, beads, and tinsel. Unlit red and white candles can also be seen. As was tradition, the Christmas tree was set up in what appears to be a parlor. Note the interesting and intricate designs featured in both the carpeting and wallpaper.

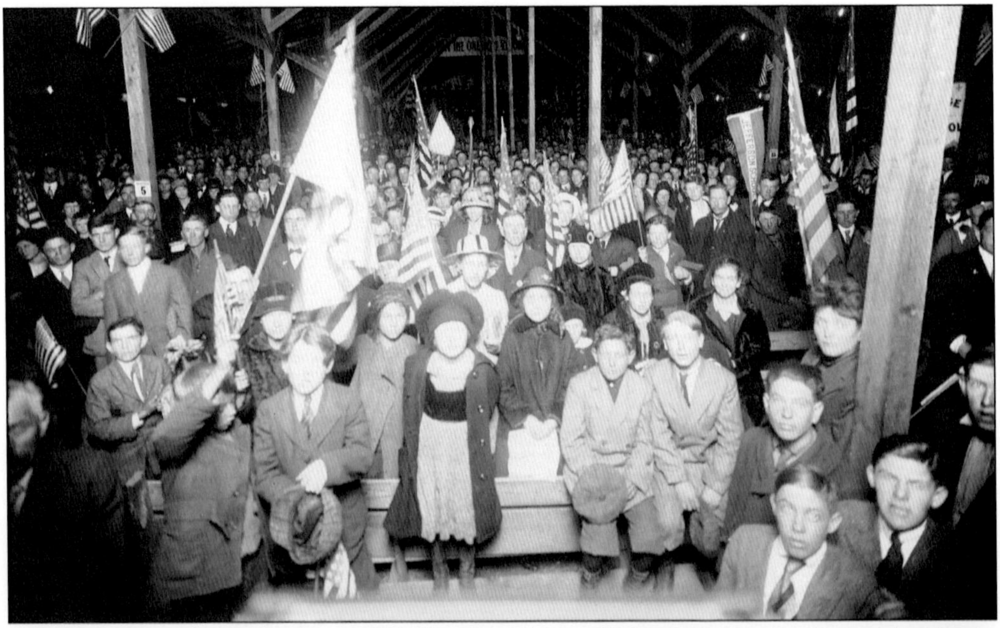

During the spring of 1917, various churches around Grand Island organized a five-week religious campaign. The tabernacle building shown in this photograph was constructed at the corner of Fifth and Cedar Streets specifically for this revival. The J. Q. A. Henry evangelistic party gave many sermons, including "Profanity, the Fool's Prayer," "Is Grand Island a Twentieth Century Sodom?," and "God's Second Best."

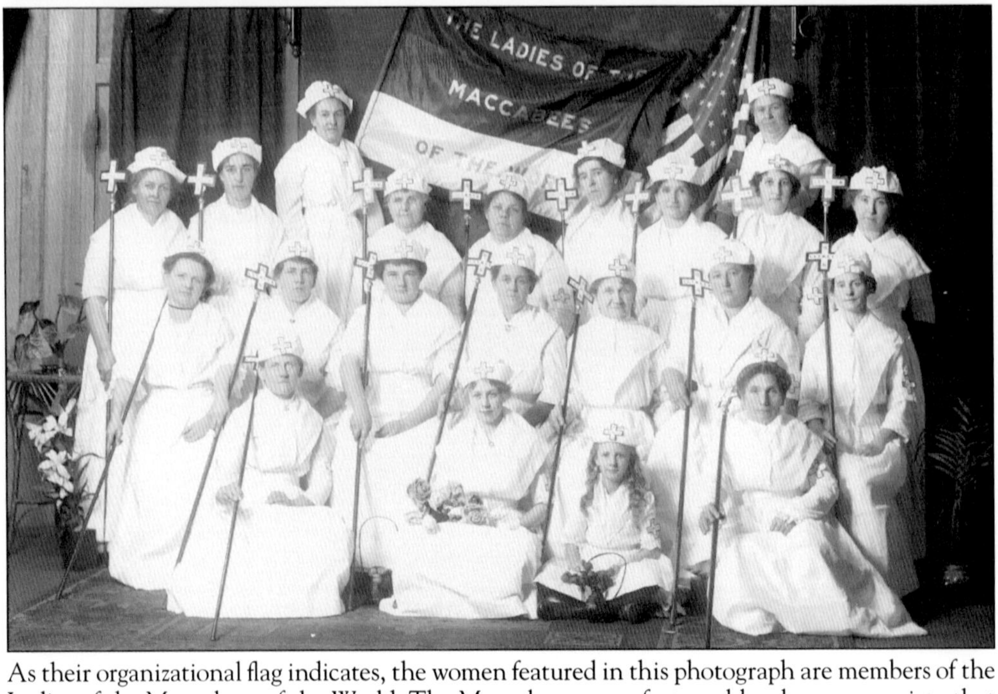

As their organizational flag indicates, the women featured in this photograph are members of the Ladies of the Maccabees of the World. The Maccabees was a fraternal legal reserve society that provided life insurance to its members. Organized in the mid-1880s, the Ladies of the Maccabees of the World was one of the first societies of this type to offer benefits to women.

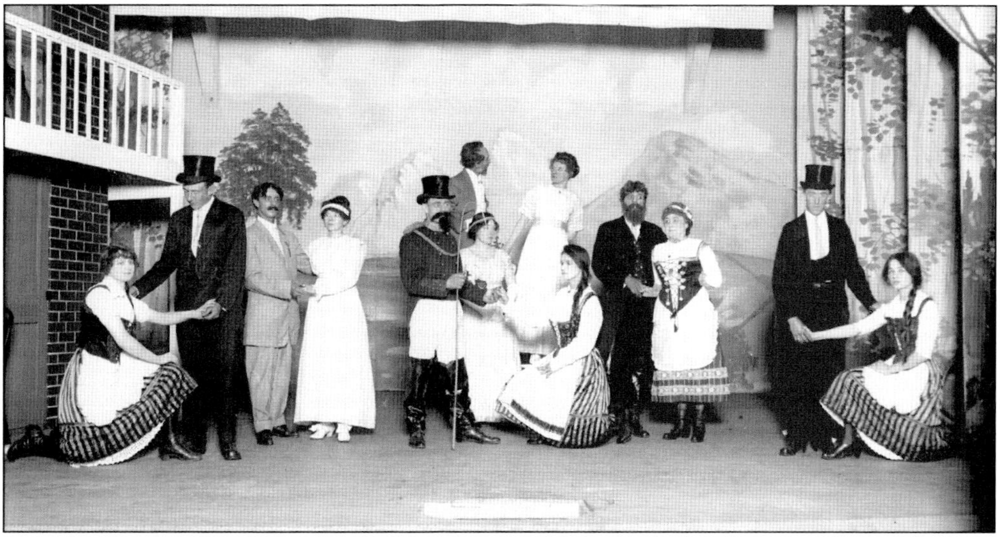

The cast of the German play *Durch das Fenster* poses on the stage of the Plattduetsche Verein in May 1913. The Plattduetsche was founded in 1884 as a social club for German emigrants and their families to socialize and relax with other emigrants. In 1910, it purchased and remodeled a former icehouse located at the corner of Adams and Anna Streets for its clubhouse, the location of this production.

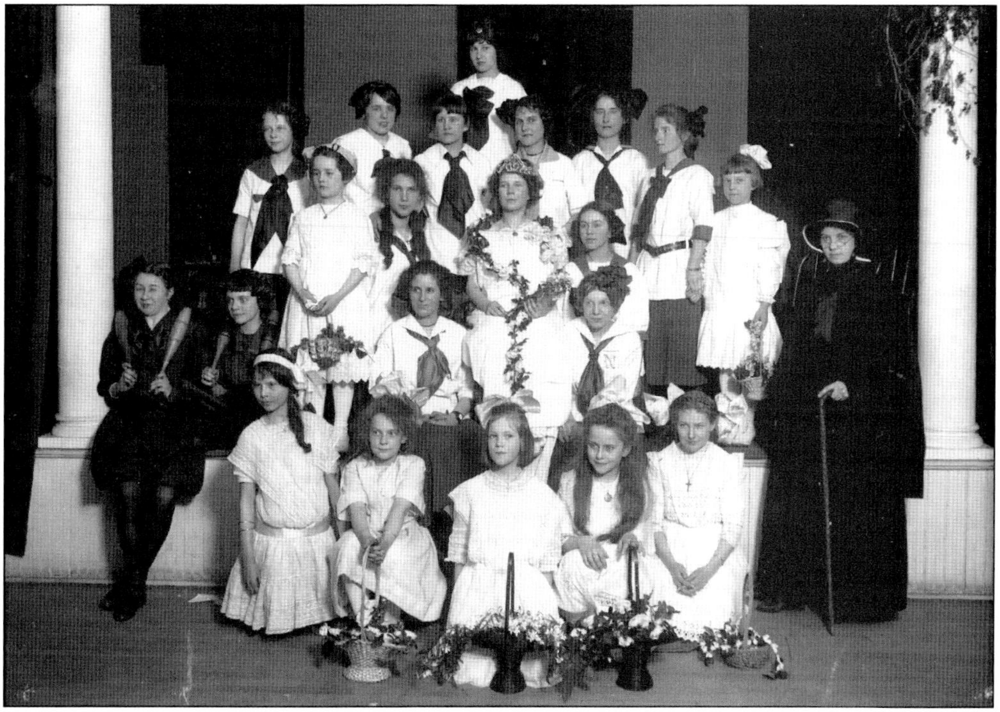

According to Julius Leschinsky's business records, this photograph was taken in March 1913 of "Miss Hill's gymnasium class." Harriette E. Hill listed her occupation in the 1912 to 1913 city directory as the director of expression and physical education at the Grand Island Conservatory of Music. Hill was well known locally for her coaching and directing of plays and productions like the one seen here.

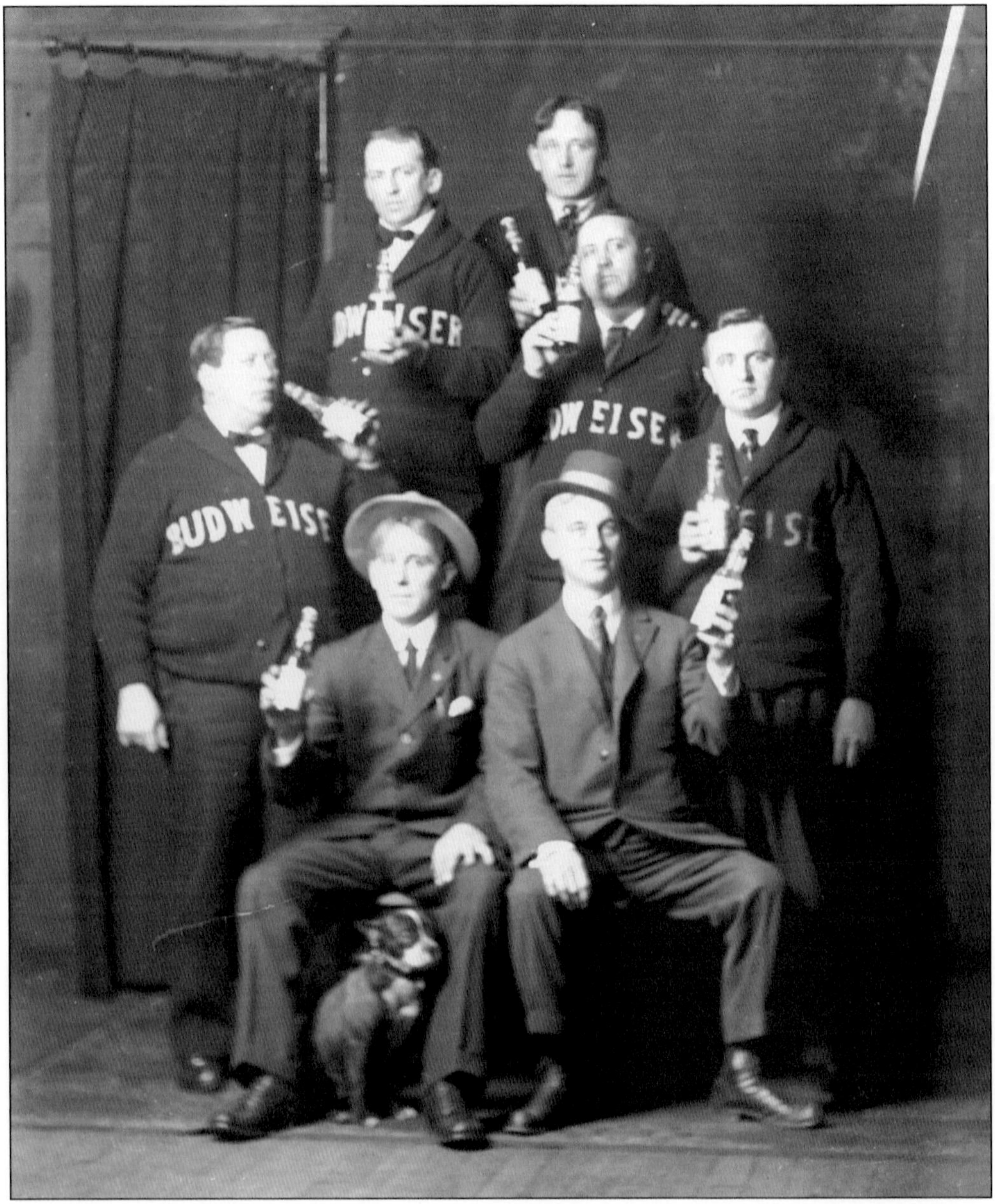

Seen here are seven unidentified members of the Budweiser bowling team in April 1915. Five of the gentlemen are sporting sweaters emblazoned with the team's name across their chests. The team's trusty mascot, a Boston terrier, can be seen posing between the legs of the man seated on the left. The photograph appears to have been taken in celebration, as the teammates toast each other with, what else, a bottle of Budweiser. Bowling was a popular pastime in Grand Island at this time. Numerous tournaments and exhibitions were held throughout the city. One of the most popular bowling alleys was located in the basement of the Liederkranz building. According to the newspaper, the Budweiser team placed fifth out of six teams in the league for the 1915 season. The Budweiser team members included Carl Hehnke, "Lefty" Eggers, Fred Schlotfeldt, Bowen, and Buenger with Straw and George Guenther acting as substitutes. Most of the team members' first names were not reported in the newspaper.

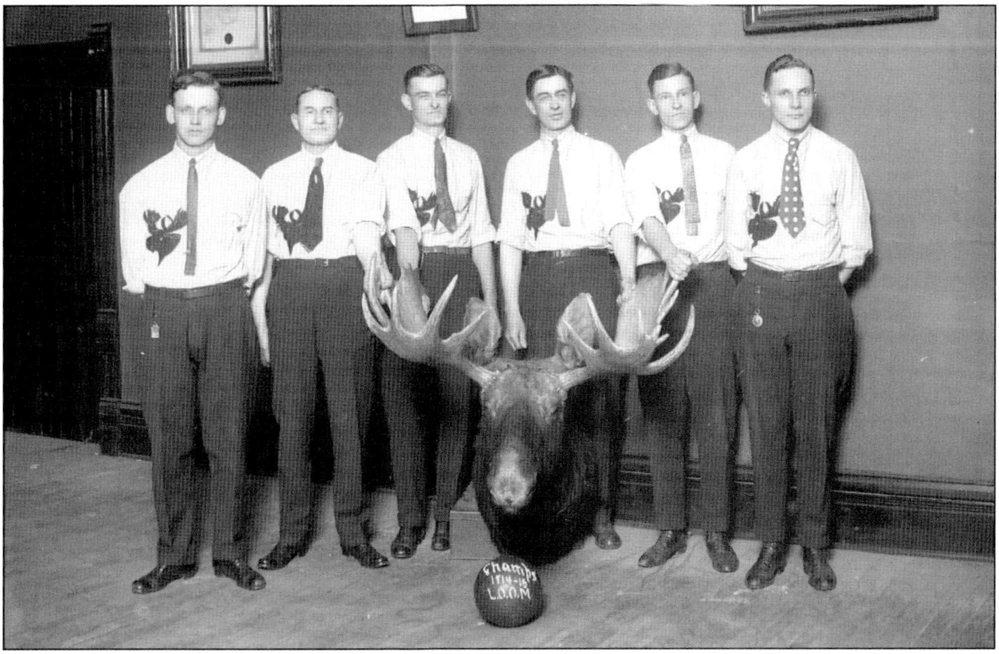

Six members of the Moose Lodge championship bowling team pose with their team's mascot in this photograph. Below the moose head, a bowling ball can be seen with the words "Champs, 1914–1915, L.O.O.M." written on it. L.O.O.M stood for Loyal Order of Moose. The Grand Island Lodge No. 356 was organized on October 4, 1910.

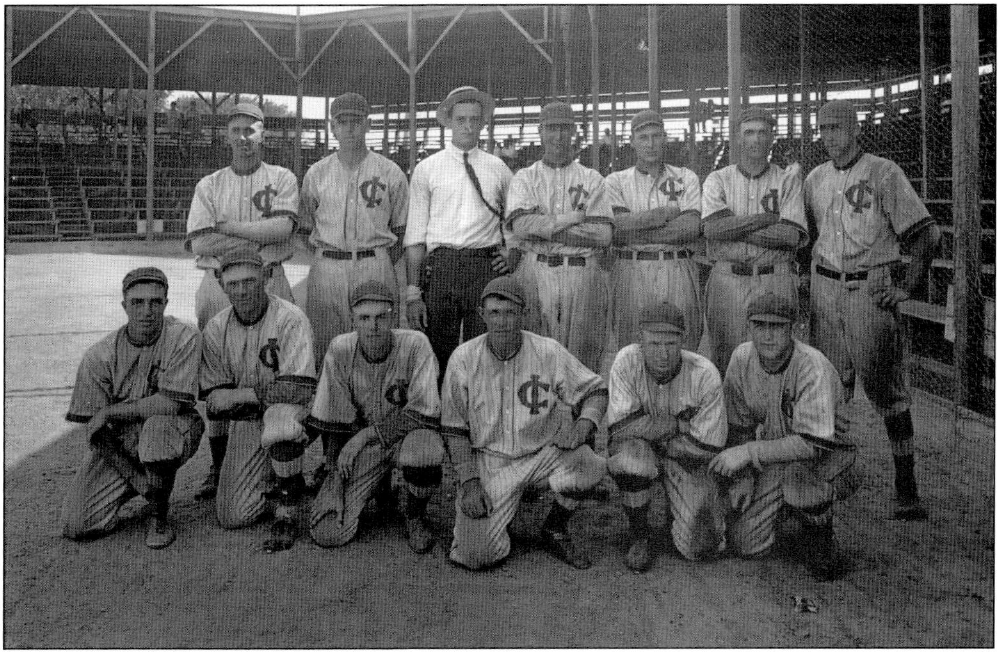

The first baseball game played in Grand Island was in July 1870. Since that time, baseball has been an important part of Grand Island's culture and a favorite pastime. In this photograph, the members of Grand Island's baseball team pose in front of wooden bleachers in August 1914. The team seen here took home the Nebraska state pennant, winning 66 games and losing only 46.

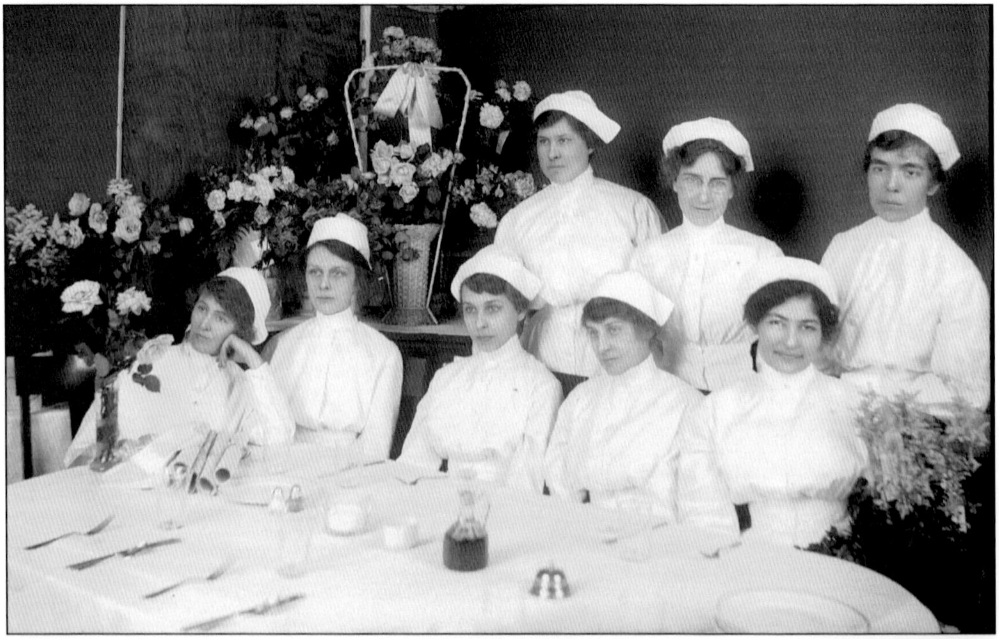

Graduates from the Grand Island General Hospital nursing school pose for this photograph in May 1917. Once located on the northwest corner of First and Locust Streets, the hospital was completed in 1913 under the guidance of Dr. Peter Conway Kelley. In 1937, it was taken over by the Lutheran Hospitals and Homes Society. After the new Lutheran hospital opened in 1958 on Faidley Avenue, the original General Hospital was razed.

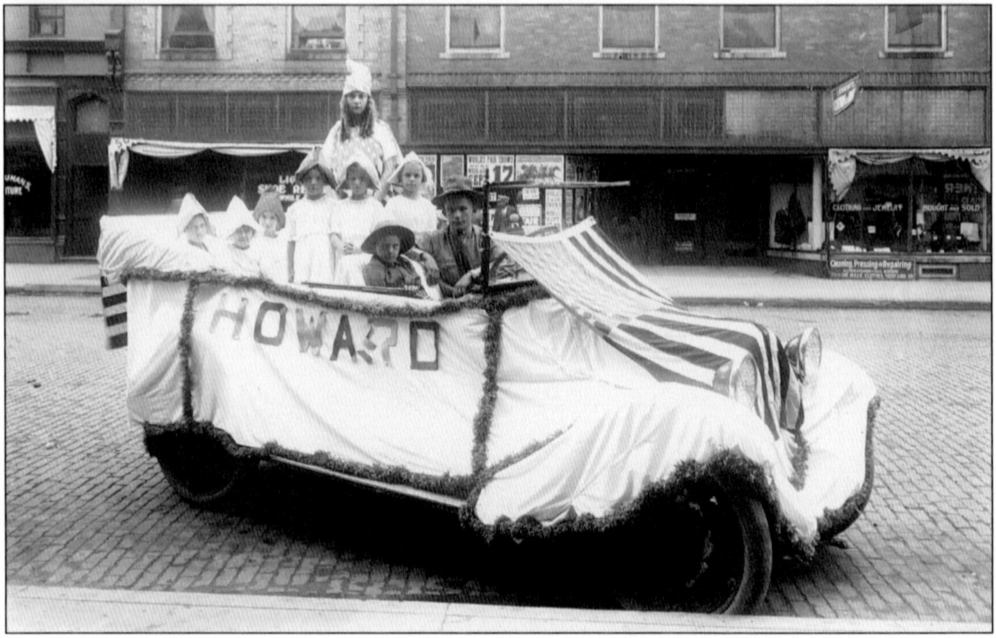

This patriotic float was created by the students of Howard Elementary School. It appeared in the parade held in honor of Children's Day at the Central Nebraska Fair on Friday, September 21, 1917. Schools from all over Hall County participated. Many of the floats featured similar patriotic themes in a time when the country and the city rallied to support the troops during World War I.

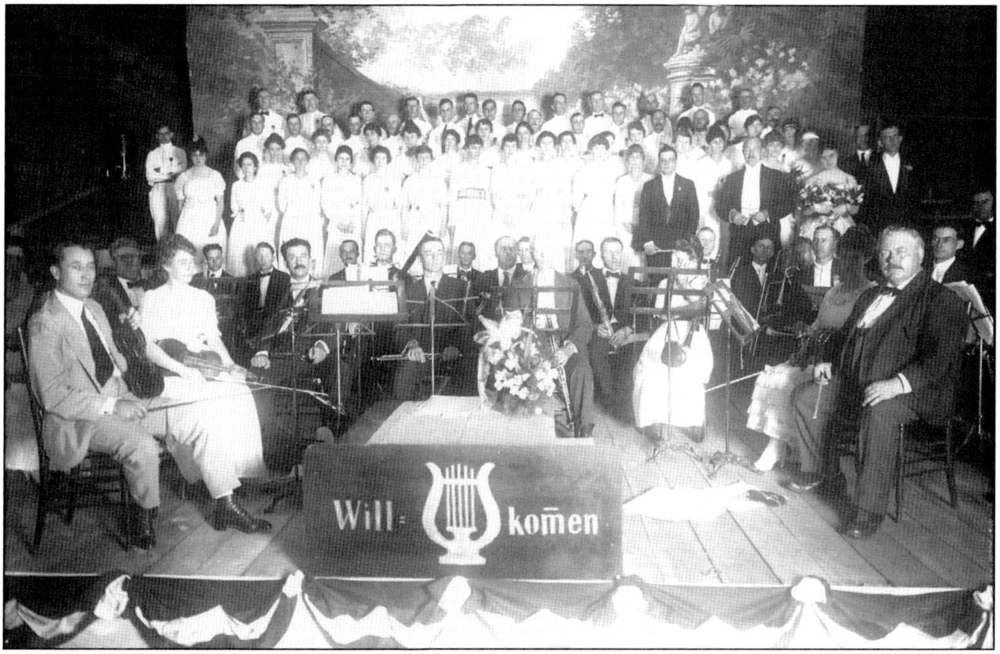

In this photograph, the Liederkranz's orchestra and mixed choir is seated on the organization's stage, located at the corner of First and Walnut Streets. *Liederkranz* means "a wreath of song" in German. The club was organized in 1870 by German settlers who wanted to retain and cultivate German music, literature, and culture.

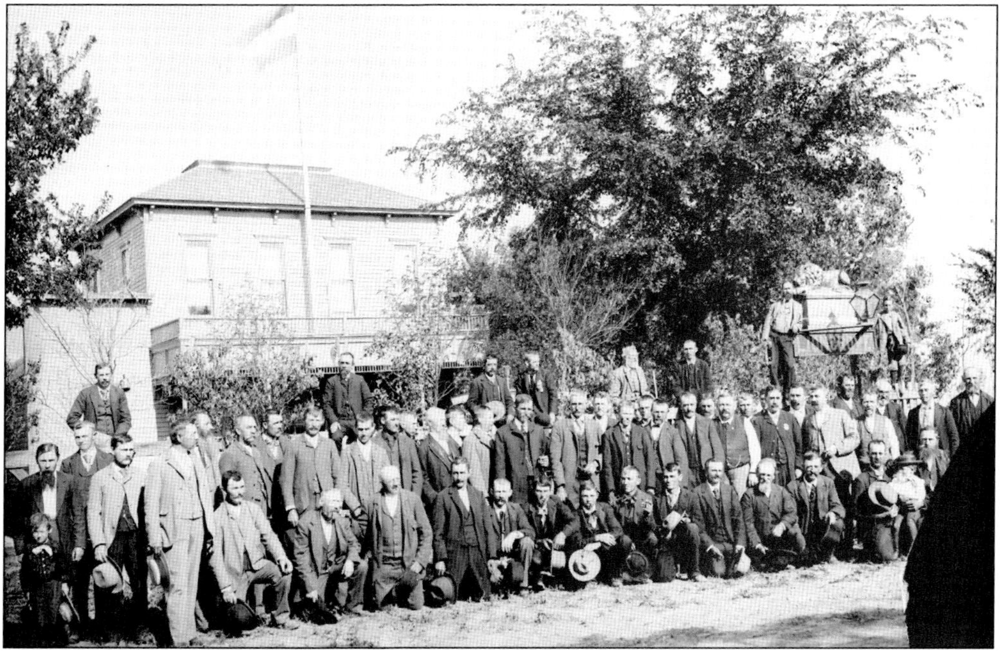

A large group of unidentified men is posing in front of the gates to the Lion Grove. The Lion Grove was a popular gathering place south of Grand Island on the north side of the Wood River's main channel, along today's South Locust Street. Behind the men, a two-story frame building can be seen. It featured a saloon and a large hall for dining and dancing.

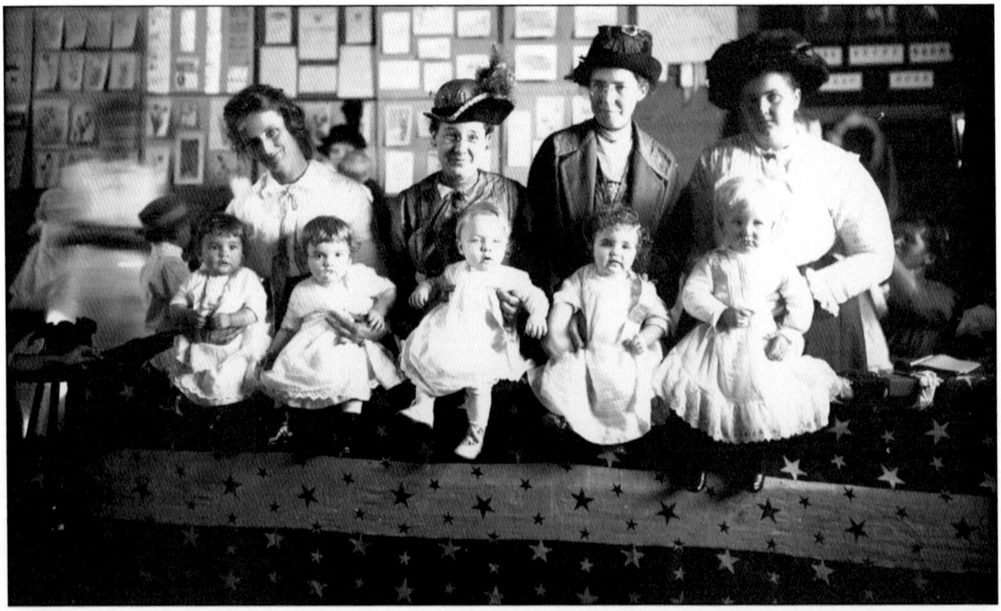

During the 1914 Central Nebraska Fair, a contest was held to find the prettiest baby in the county. The honor went to Florence Mecham, 11-month-old daughter of Earl and Nettie Mecham. Prizes included a silver loving cup from the Carey and Nietfelt Company. Julius Leschinsky, who took the image of the winners seen above, presented gilt framed photographs of the prize-winning babies to their families. Other winners included Helen and Hazel Gideon, likely the two babies at far left, as the prettiest pair of twins and the babies with the most relatives registered. The fair was held from September 29 to October 2, 1914. The photograph below shows prize-winning vegetables on display in one of the exhibit halls. A group of children stands in front of an exhibit of plants sponsored by the Ellsworth Greenhouse of Grand Island.

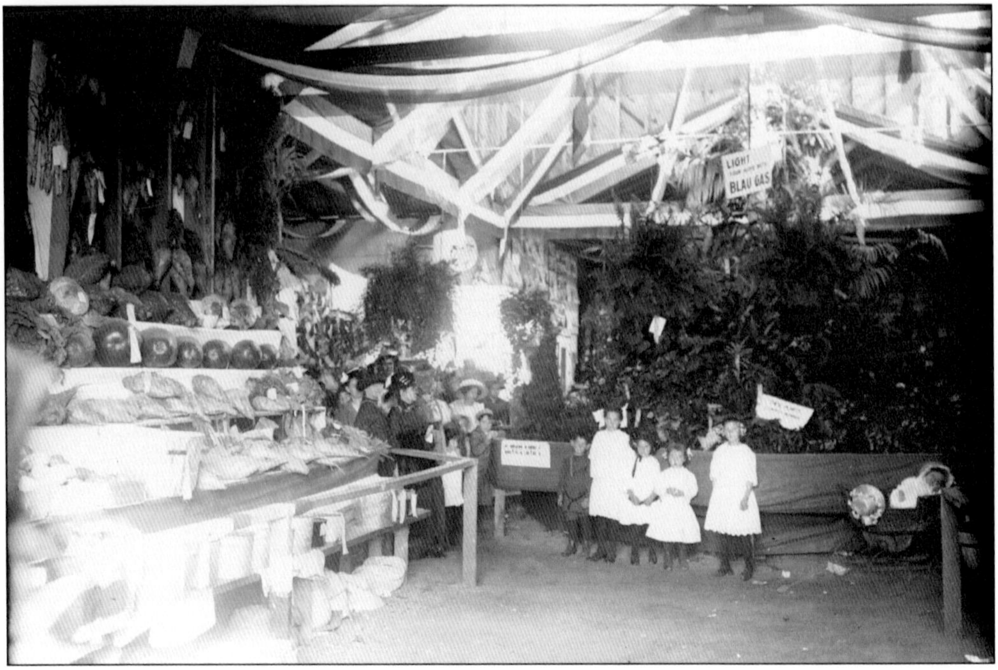

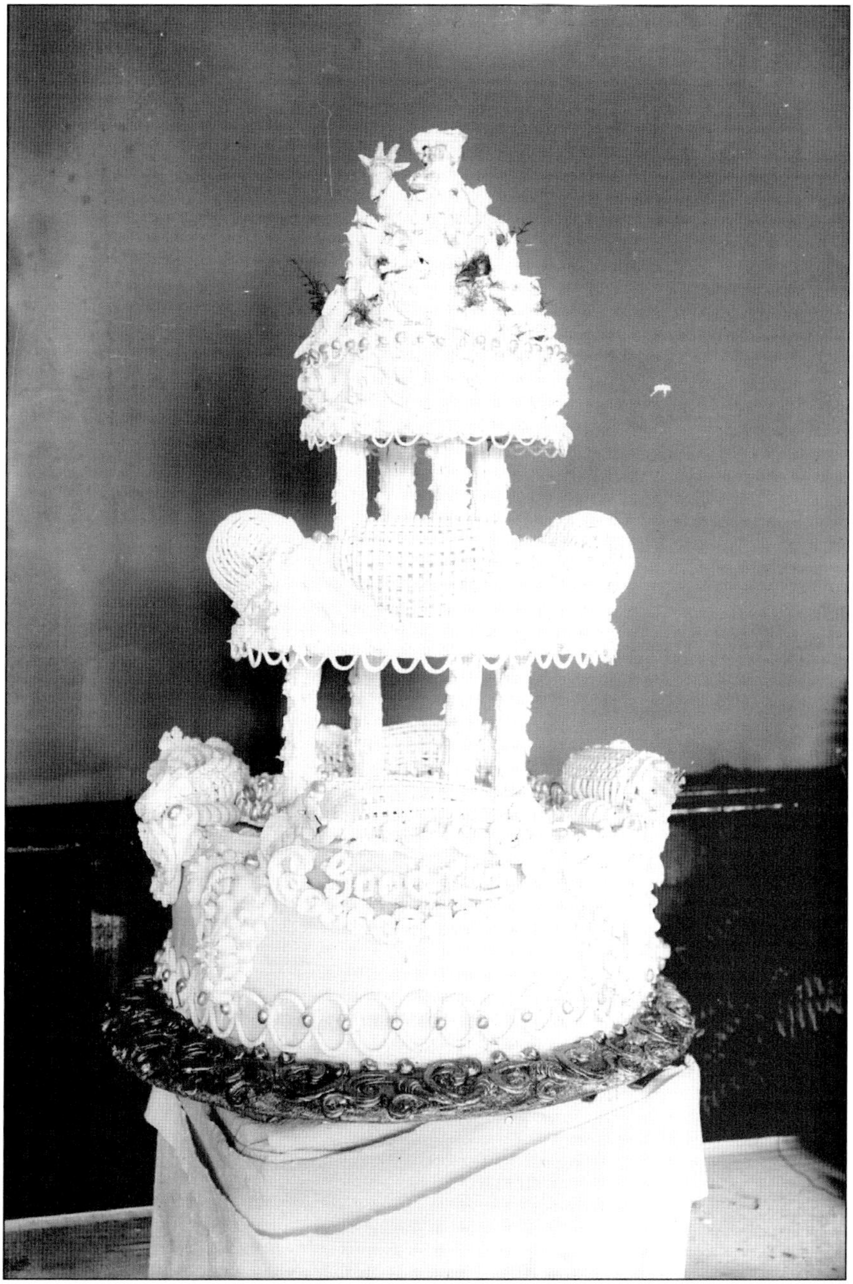

This amazing three-tier cake was created by the Monogram Bakery in November 1912. The occasion for which this masterpiece was created is unknown. On the bottom tier the words "Good Luck" can be seen. Atop the cake is a figure of a girl riding a goat. The Monogram Bakery was started in Grand Island in 1911 by Scottish-born baker Robert Teviotdale, who immigrated to the United States in 1905. At the time this cake was created, the Monogram Bakery was located in the Dolan Building at the corner of Wheeler and Fourth Streets. In 1917, Teviotdale built a two-story brick building at 376 North Walnut Street. By 1919, the modern facility was turning out 7,000 loaves of its Butter Nut bread daily and claimed that Teviotdale was the first baker in Nebraska to introduce the wrapping of bread loaves in waxed paper.

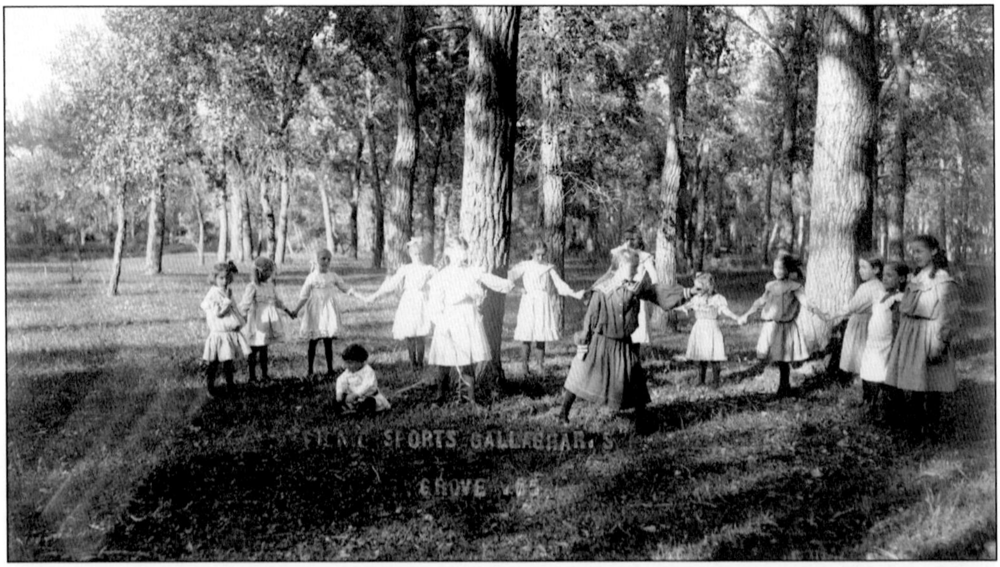

Gallacher's Grove was a popular gathering spot south of Grand Island near Doniphan on Nine Bridges Road. The grove was often the site of the Burns Club annual picnic. The Burns Club was a local social organization that celebrated Scottish heritage and the writings of Robert Burns. The grove was owned by John Gallacher, who emigrated from Scotland in 1872. According to accounts in the newspaper, many games and sports were played at the Burns Club picnic. Participants enjoyed traditional Scottish games like rounders, quoits, and the throwing of the hammer, as well as lawn tennis, races, and shooting competitions. In the top photograph, children play a game of blindman's bluff. In the bottom photograph, a crowd gathers to watch two young men box. Unfortunately, Julius Leschinsky incorrectly spelled Gallacher's name when he created these photographs in 1905.

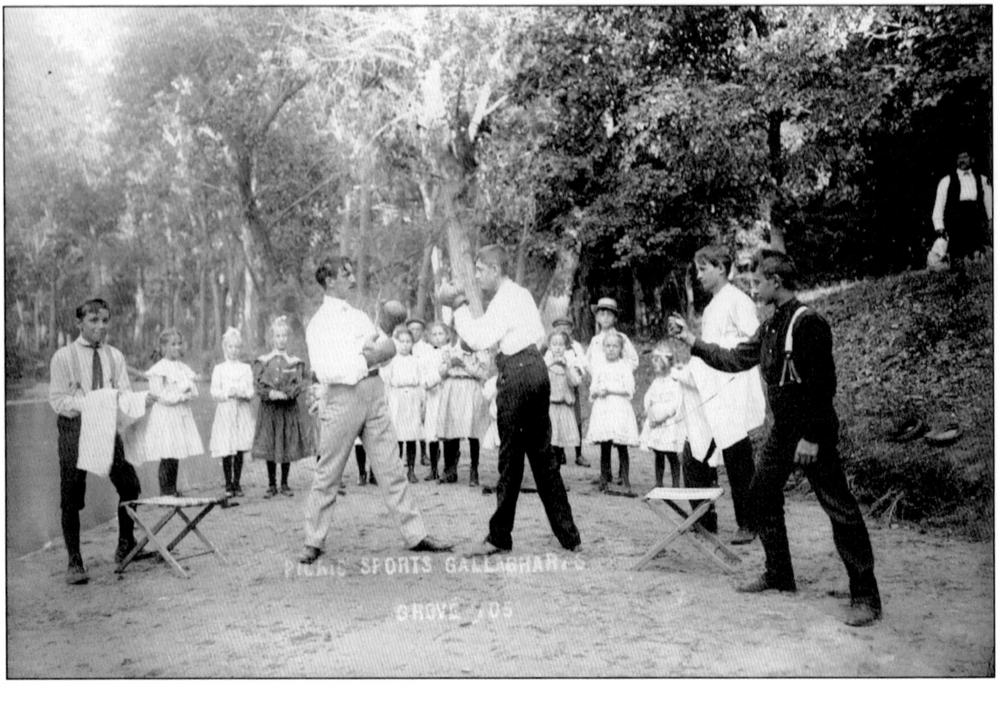

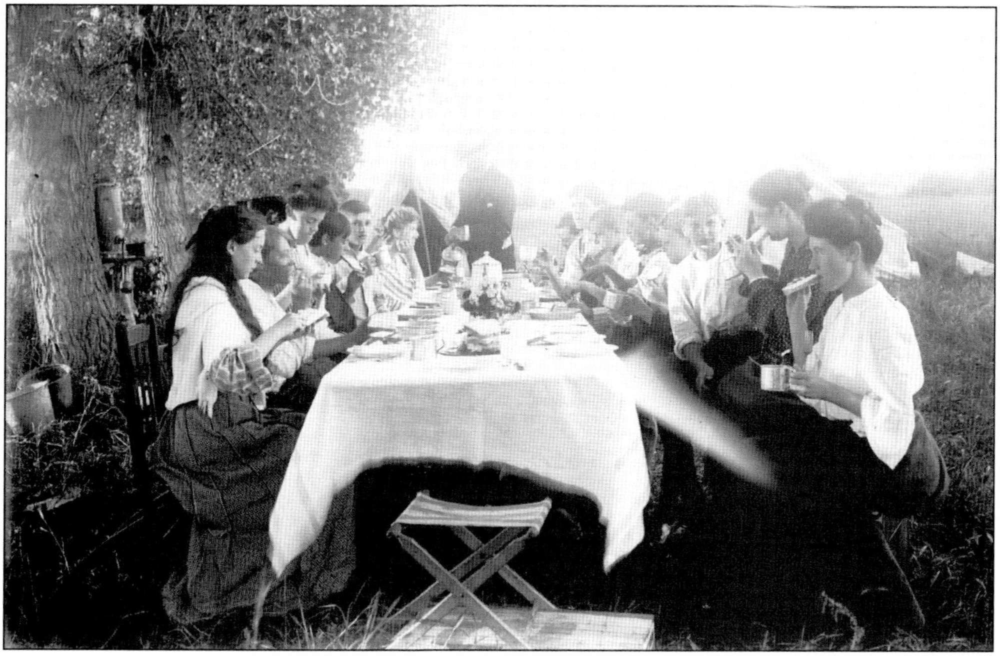

Taken in about 1910, this group of teenagers is enjoying a picnic outing. Note that the man at the end of the table pouring from a tin coffee pot is wearing a minister's collar. The young lady at the far right holds a tin cup while nibbling on a slice of bread. A small bouquet of wild flowers adds a certain charm to the linen-covered picnic table.

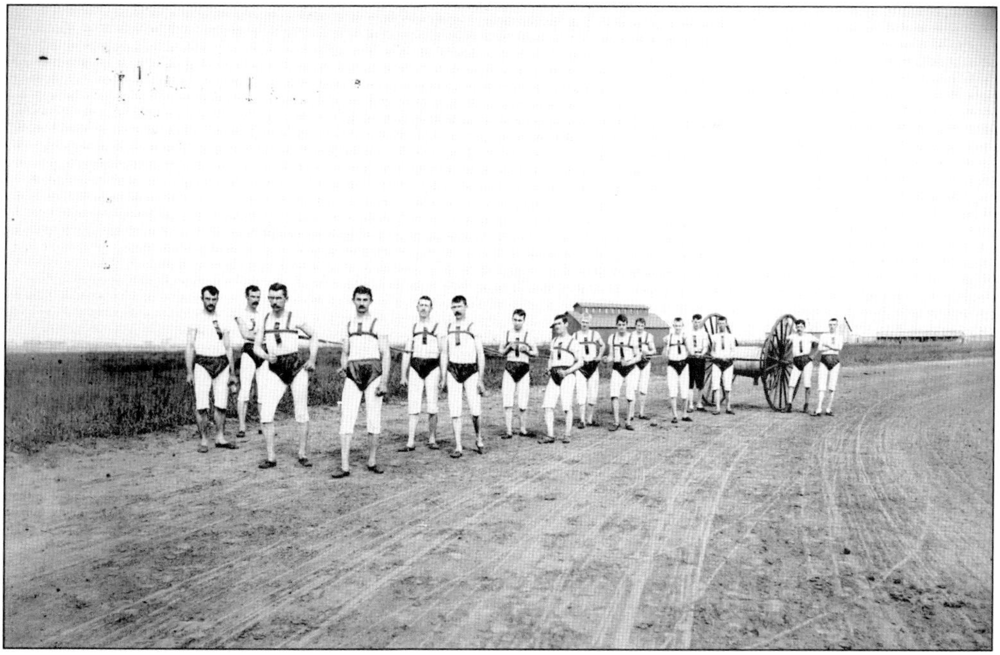

Members of the Grand Island Fire Department are shown harnessed to a hose cart in the early 1900s. In 1906, the volunteer firemen won the hook-and-ladder competition at the Nebraska State Fireman's Association tournament held in Fremont on August 16–18. They set a state record by pulling a cart 250 yards and sending a man up a 24-foot ladder in just over 38 seconds.

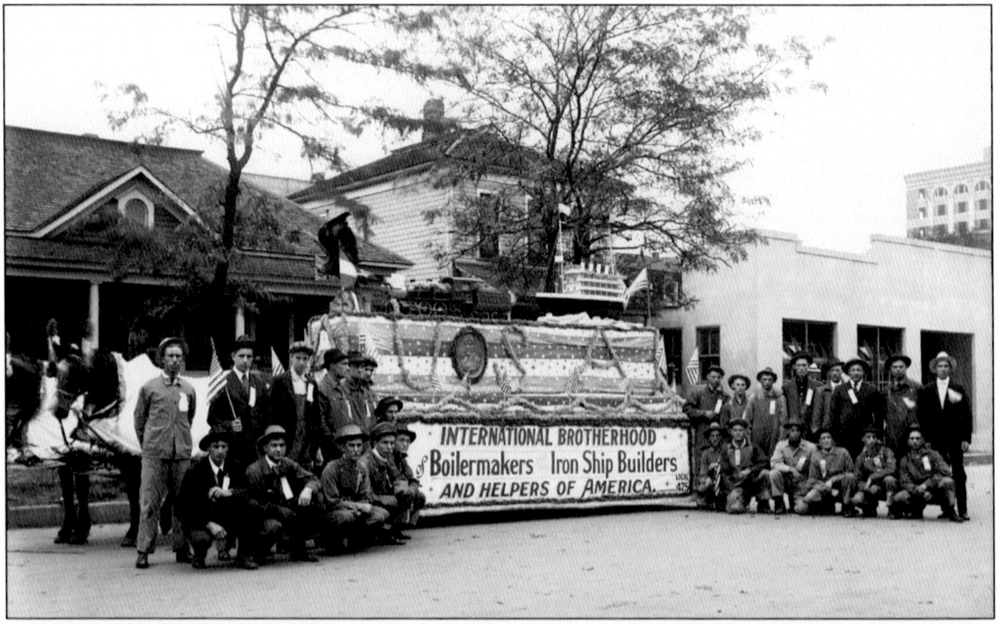

Members of International Brotherhood of Boilermakers, Iron Ship Builders, and Helpers of America, Local Union 475 gather around their 1918 Labor Day float. The horse-drawn float features a model of a railroad engine as well as a ship. "USA" is spelled out in garland on a background of patriotic bunting. A portrait of Pres. Woodrow Wilson can also be seen attached to the side of the float.

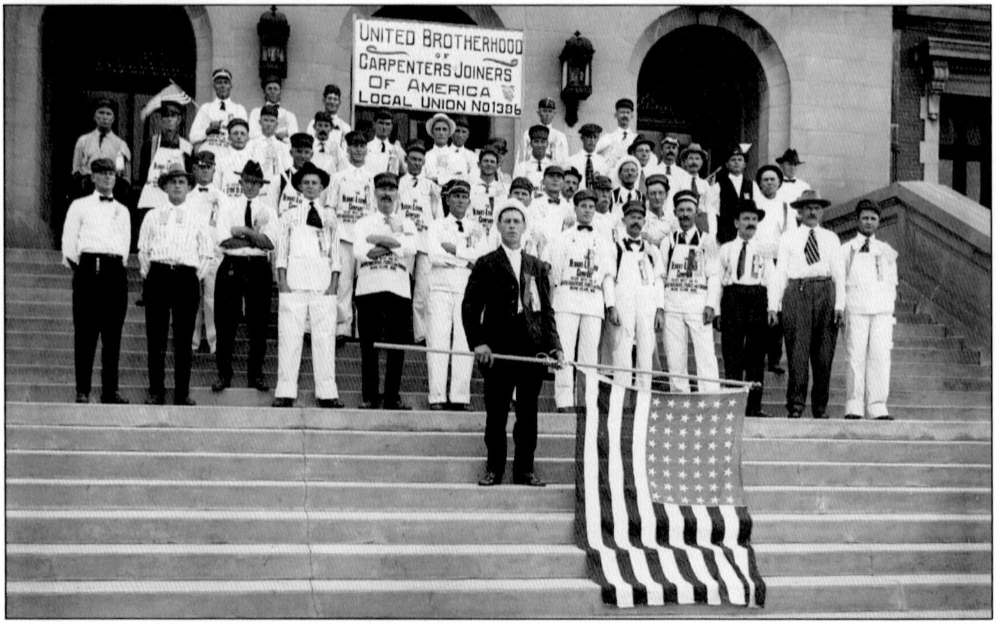

Members of the United Brotherhood of Carpenters and Joiners of America, Local Union 1306 pose on the steps of the Hall County Courthouse in September 1917. They have likely gathered to celebrate the Labor Day holiday. The courthouse was complete in 1904 at the intersection of South Locust and First Streets. Several of the men are wearing aprons from Hehnke-Lohman Hardware Company of Grand Island.

Five

All Dressed Up

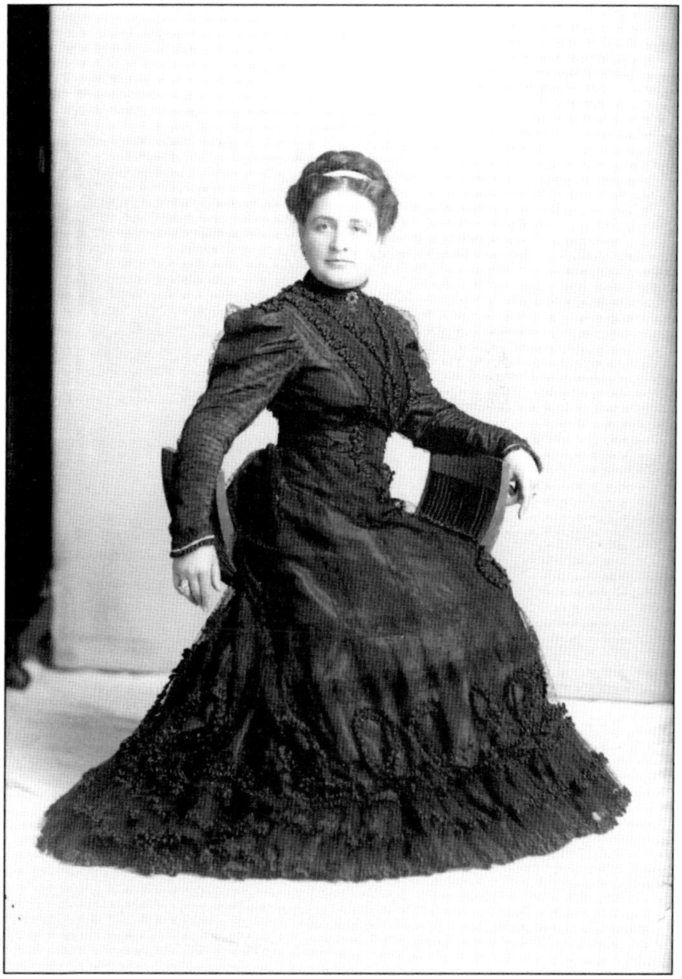

Josephine White of North Platte poses for this photograph in April 1910. Josephine's husband Wood White was an engineer for the railroad. She is wearing a stunning dress with a net overlay featuring flocked dots. The bodice neckline, front, and sleeve edges all have ribbon ruching. Julius Leschinsky's reputation and award-winning talents brought in customers from all over the region, including western Nebraska.

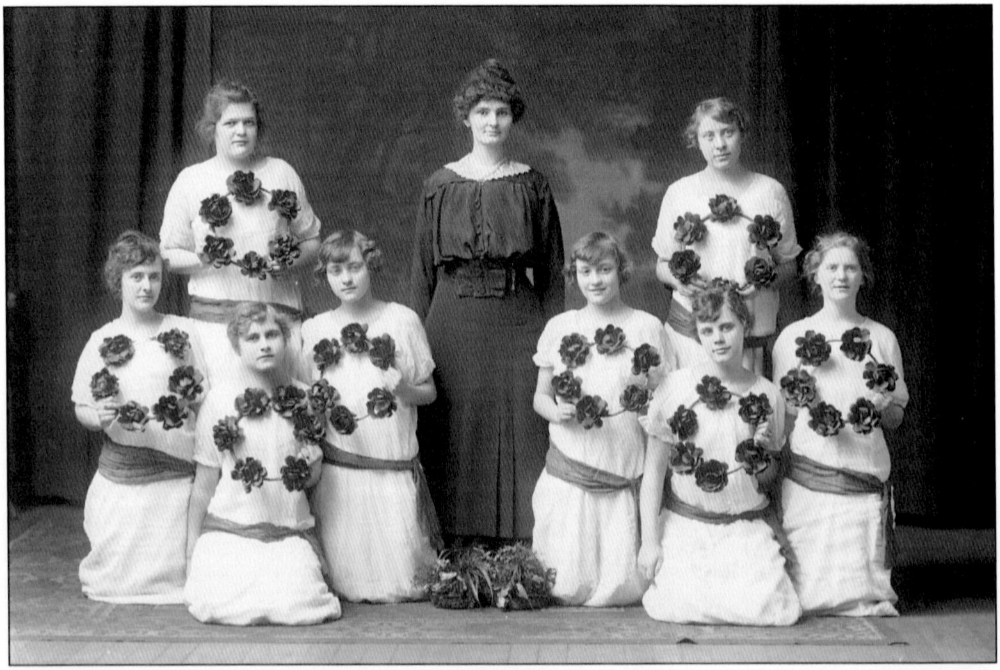

According to Julius Leschinsky's business records, the young ladies featured in this photograph were members of the Grand Island Business and Normal College Rose Drill Team. The photograph was taken in March 1915. The woman in the center appears to be the team instructor. The eight young women are wearing matching white dresses with colored sashes. They are holding rings with six paper roses, likely used to perform a synchronized dance.

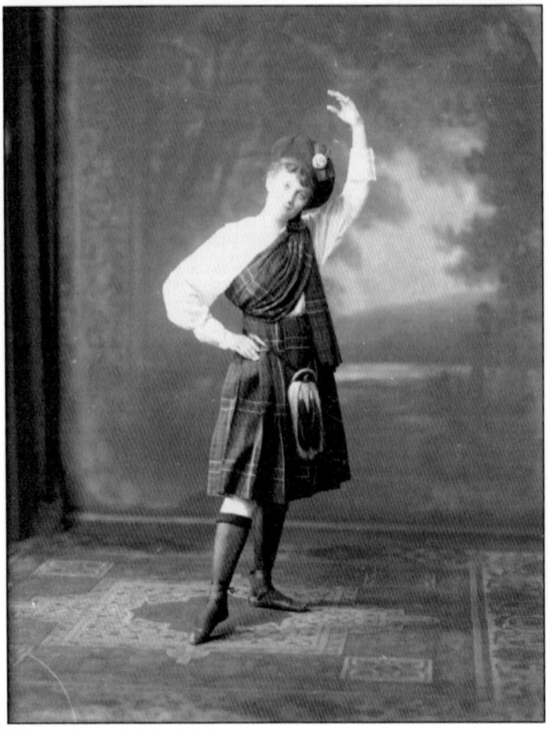

In 1885, local Scottish residents formed the Central Nebraska and Republican Valley chapter of the St. Andrew's Society to "keep alive the memory of Scotland, her manners and customs, literature and games." The St. Andrew's Society, and later the Burns Club, sponsored programs of traditional Scottish readings, music, and dancing. This lovely young lass poses for Leschinsky in May 1915.

The young lady in this photograph shows off the volumes of material used to make her dress. She was likely a performer or dancer of some kind. Note that her skirt reached to just below her knees and she wears patent leather Mary Jane–type shoes similar to modern tap shoes. The dress is likely a silk crepe, which would have flowed beautifully as she danced and twirled.

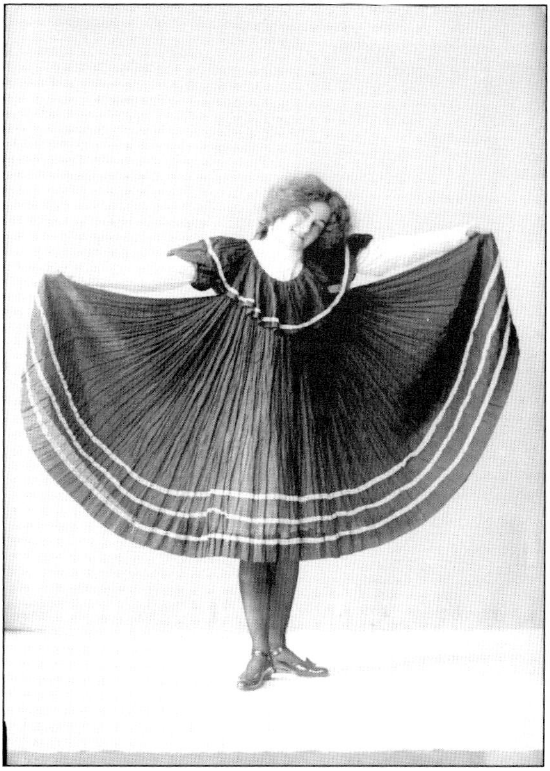

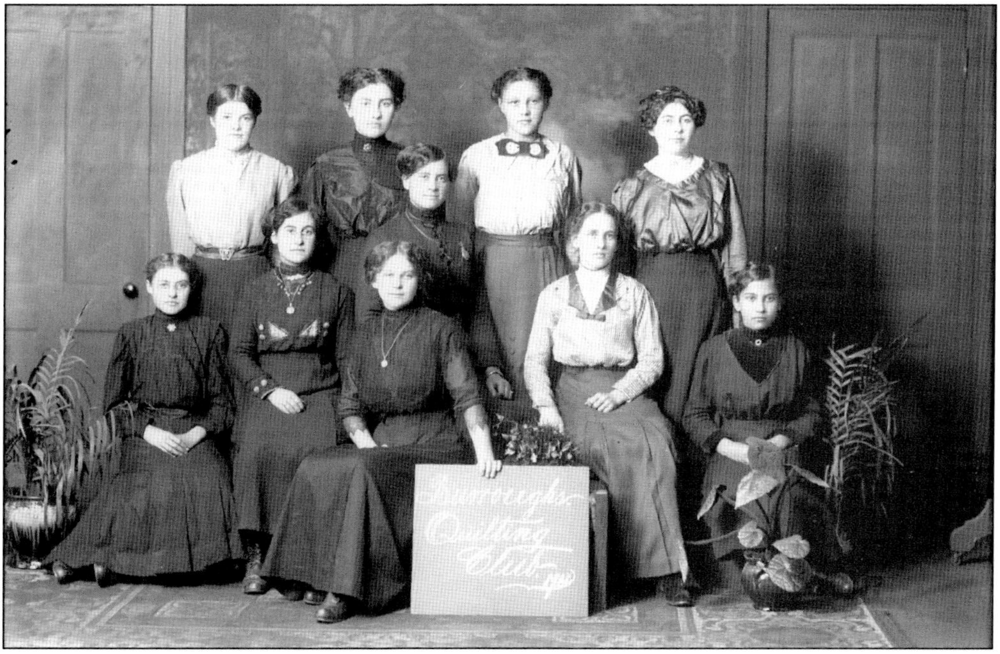

Members of the Burroughs Quilting Club pose for this photograph in December 1913. Grand Island was home to many quilting and sewing clubs during this time. They were one of the few opportunities for women to gather and network socially. The quilts they created were often given as special gifts to friends or important people or donated to less fortunate families.

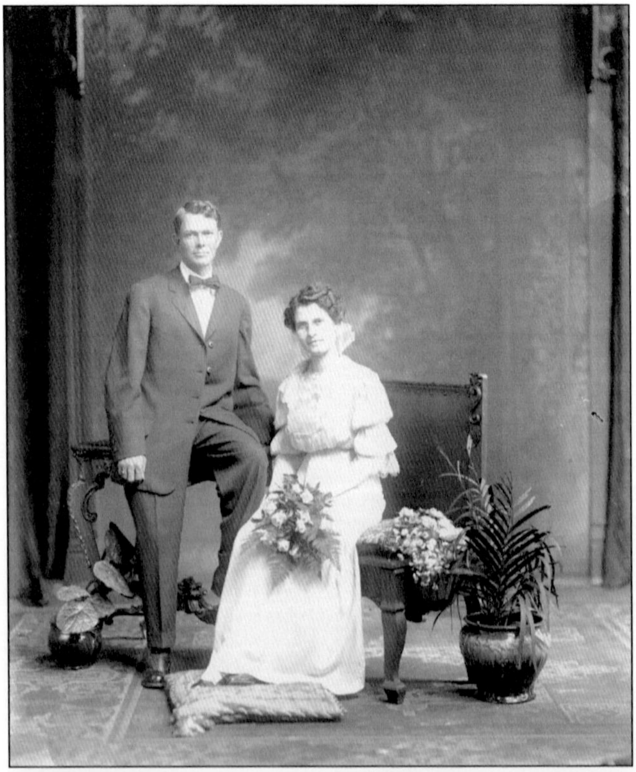

On June 25, 1915, James Hanna married Alta Story in Grand Island, and together they pose for this wedding portrait. According to the couple's marriage license, they were from Brownlee in Cherry County, which is about 180 miles northwest of Grand Island. James lists his occupation as a ranch hand on the marriage record, and Alta was a schoolteacher.

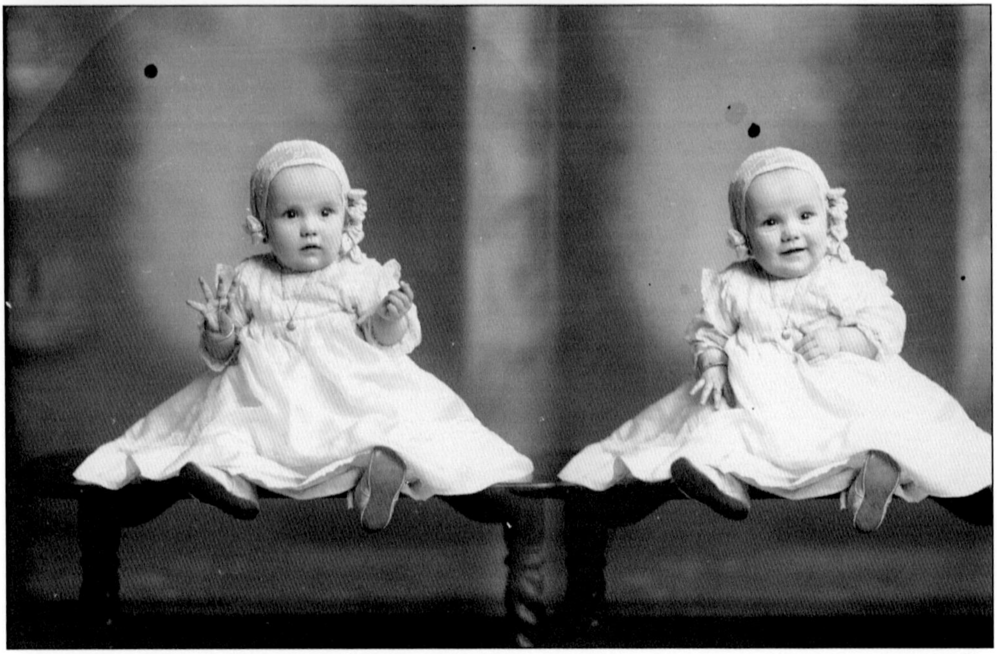

This little cutie is likely Harriett Hansen. Her mother Lena Hansen commissioned this photograph in May 1912. Around her neck Harriett is wearing a gold locket with the initials H. B. inscribed on it. The necklace likely belonged to Lena, whose maiden name was Helena Brooks. Harriett is also wearing a gold ring and bracelet.

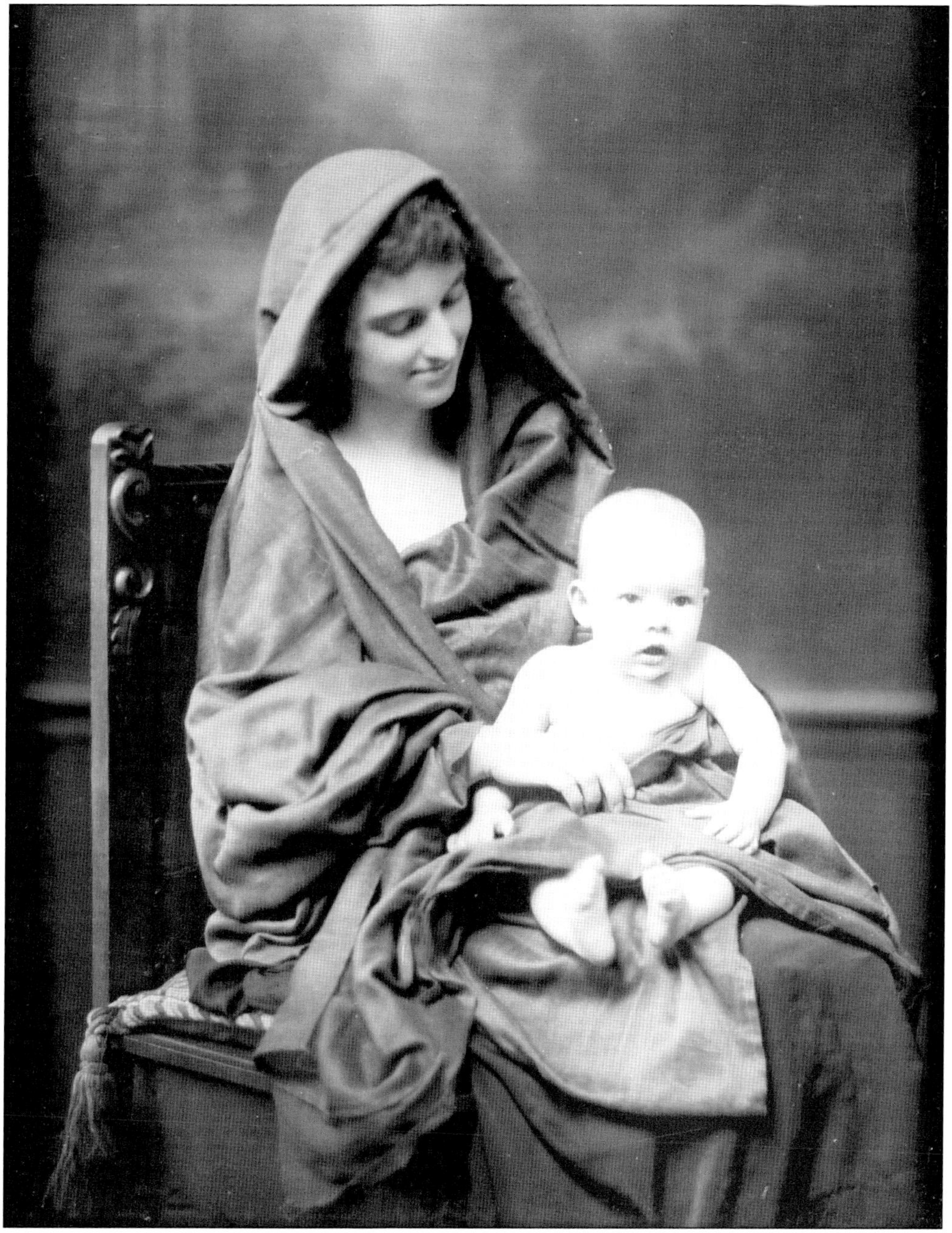

Alma Warren poses with her son Virgil E. Warren Jr. in September 1918. Julius Leschinsky modeled this mother and child in a way that evokes paintings of a European Renaissance master. This was a favorite pose of Leschinsky, and numerous examples can be found in his collection. Leschinsky won multiple awards for his photography, including the Nebraska State Photography Association's highest award, the Silver Loving Cup, three times. Alma was the wife of Virgil E. Warren. Virgil Sr. was a cashier for the Commercial State Bank. According to the 1920 census, Alma would have been about 25 at the time of this photograph and Virgil Jr. about six months old.

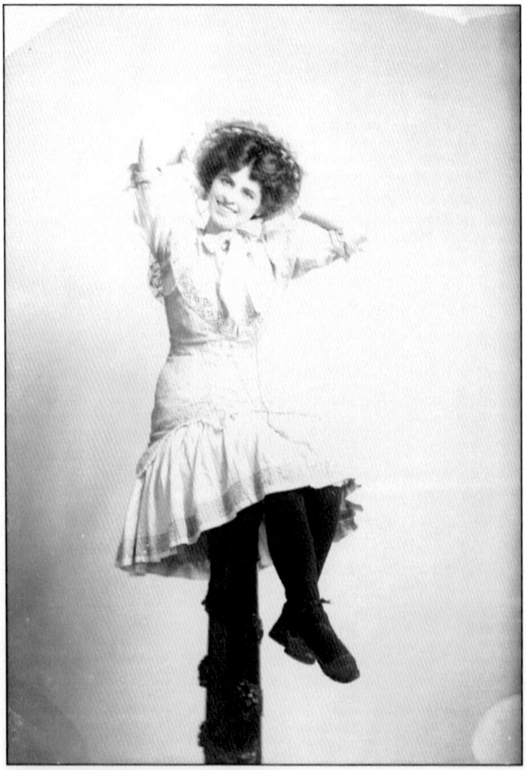

Little is known about this photograph. According to Julius Leschinsky's business records it was commissioned in November 1910 by Mrs. R. F. Daugherty. A search of city directories and census records reveal no Daughertys living in the area. By the look of her costume she may have been a traveling performer. Her skirt is far shorter than would have been fashionable and would have been considered scandalous anywhere outside the theater.

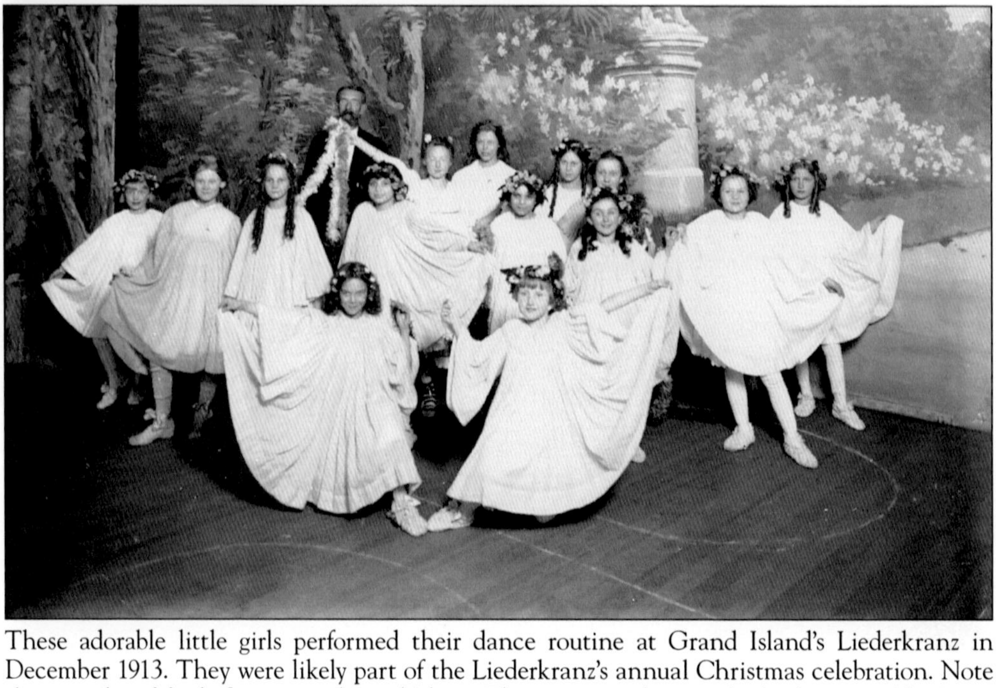

These adorable little girls performed their dance routine at Grand Island's Liederkranz in December 1913. They were likely part of the Liederkranz's annual Christmas celebration. Note the wreaths of fresh flowers in the girls' hair. The man standing at the back is possibly Oscar Niemann, a German immigrant who traveled the United States as an actor before settling in Grand Island with his wife Margot, also an actor.

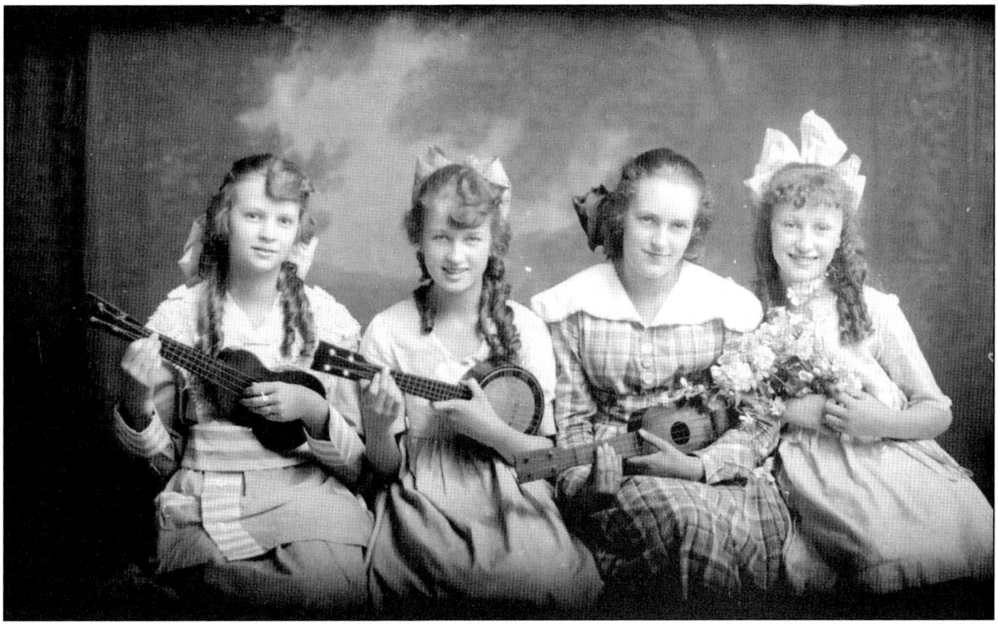

These four lovely young ladies pose for Julius Leschinsky in July 1918. Two of the girls hold ukuleles. The girl sitting second from the left holds a banjo ukulele, sometimes called a banjolele. A close examination of the banjo ukulele in this photograph reveals the four strings typical of this type of instrument. The small head is made of wood that appears to be painted in contrasting colors.

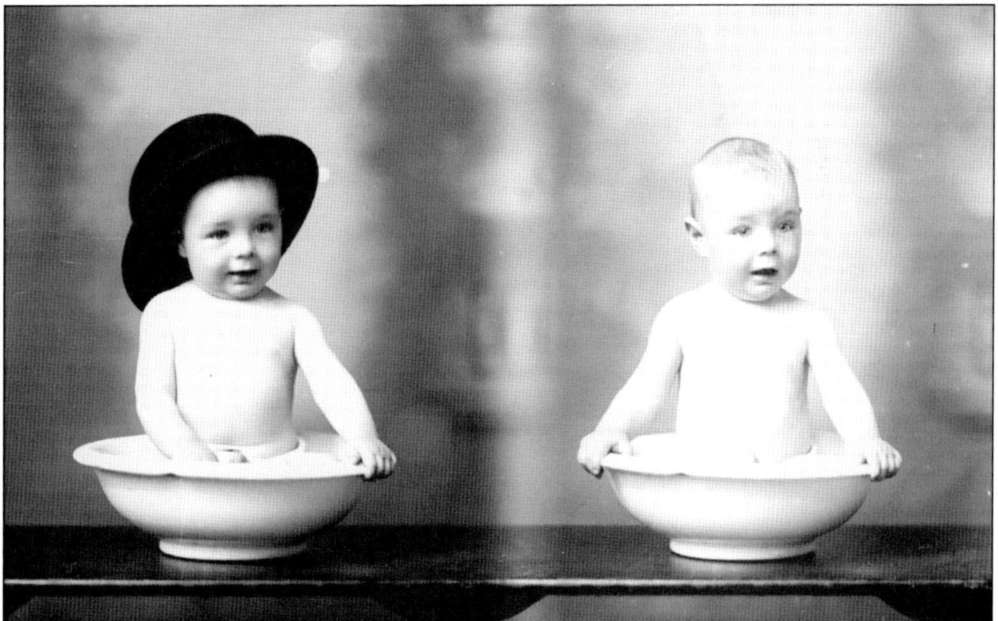

Leschinsky shows off his sense of humor in this photograph taken in July 1911. The images were commissioned by Mrs. T. M. Lyttaker. Leschinsky used a single glass plate to capture two images of the same subject, a common photographer's technique that saved time and money. In the image on the left, the child is wearing a felt bowler hat, a popular fashion for men at the time.

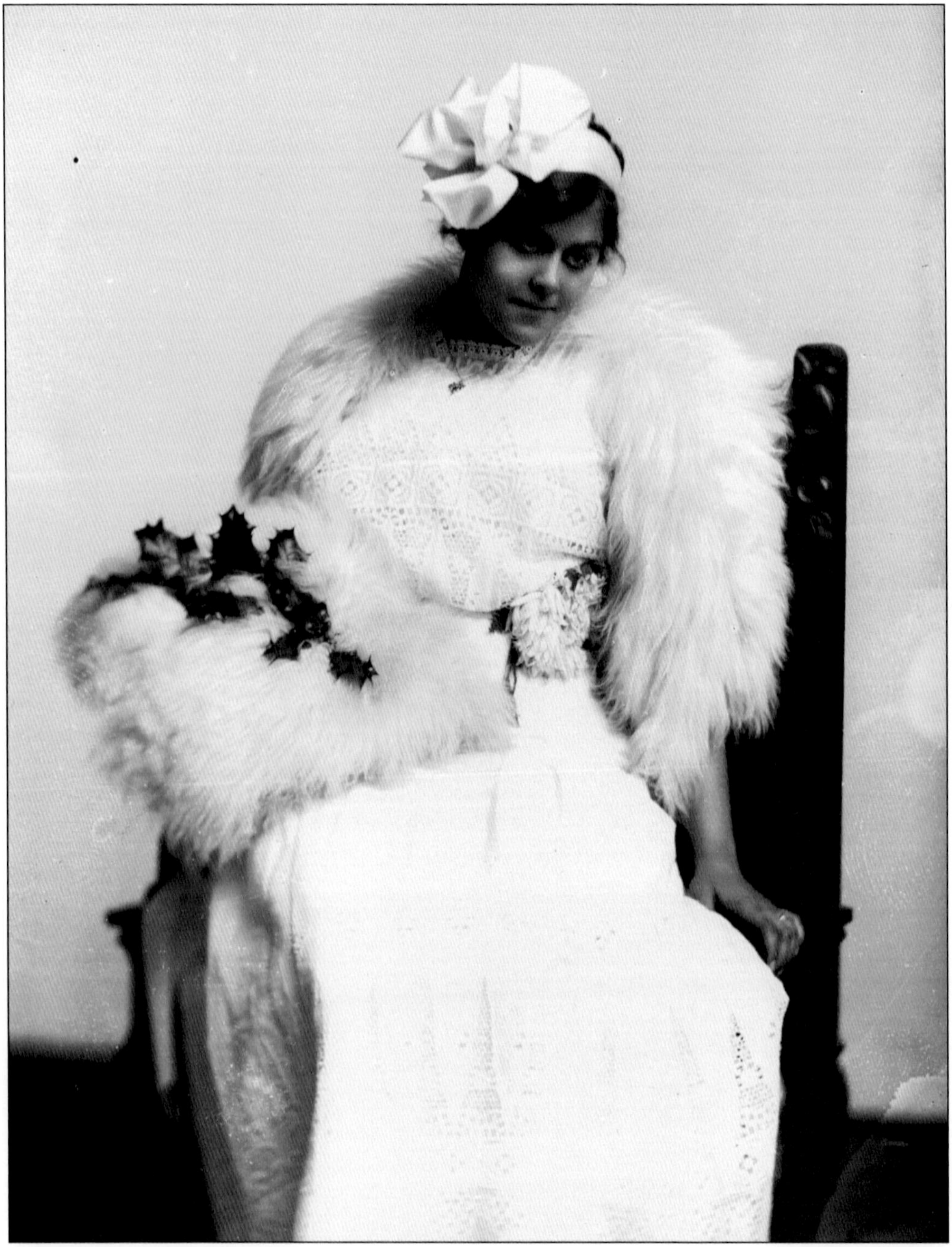

Syble Flippin poses for this photograph in December 1912. Note the sprig of holly on her fur muff. Syble was the daughter of Dr. Charles Flippin and his third wife, Dr. Mary Belle Reed. Dr. Flippin was born into slavery in Tennessee in 1848. During the Civil War, Charles ran away from his owner to enlist in the Union army. He graduated from the Bennett Eclectic Medical College of Chicago in 1881. Charles met Mary Belle, who was described as a white lady of much beauty, while they were both practicing medicine in Marion County, Kansas. They came to Nebraska in about 1888. Syble was born in 1894. Charles married his fourth wife, Nettie Lohmann, in 1909, and they moved to Grand Island with Syble in about 1910.

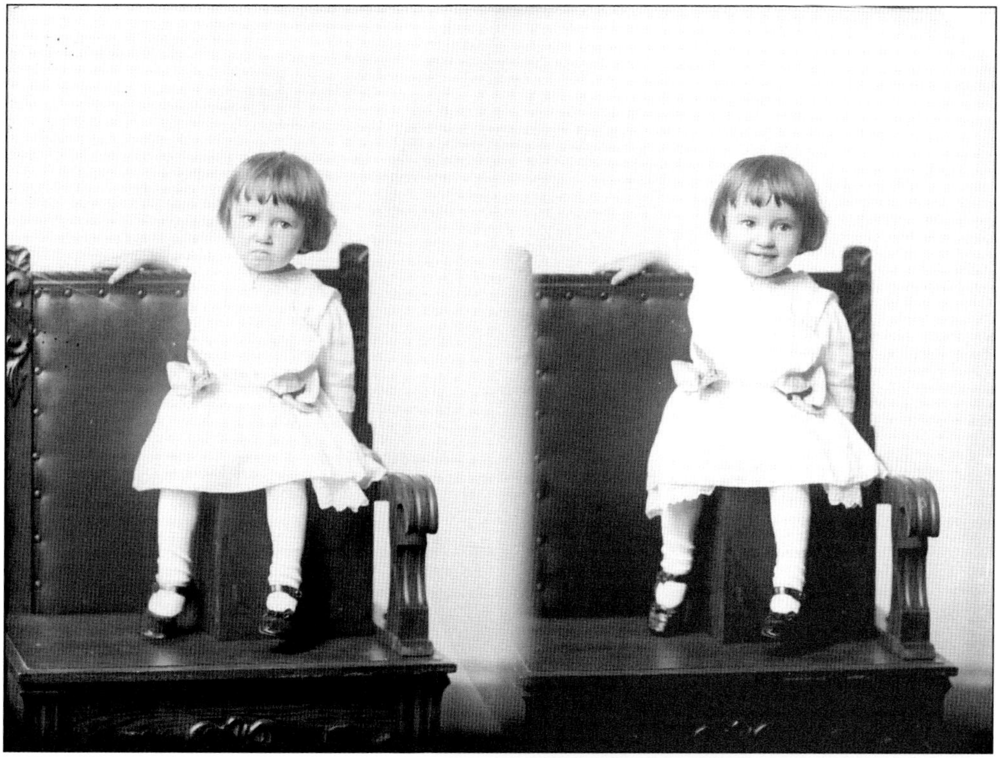

Families are often loyal to one photographer, as seen in these portraits of the children of Charles and Johanna Bosselman. The top images, taken in July 1913, feature Lillie Hattie Rose Bosselman. Lillie was born on the family farm near Worms on December 21, 1911. In the left image, Lillie gives the perfect pout and then turns on a brilliant smile in the second image. In the bottom photograph, Charles Orval Bosselman reaches out to the camera in October 1914. Charles was born on March 28, 1914. As an adult, Charles started a manufacturing business in 1946 with his own inventions and patents. In 1948, he moved his business to Grand Island. It was here that he, his brother Fred, and brother-in-law Al Eaton started the Bosselman-Eaton Oil Station. The company grew into the Bosselman Family of Companies.

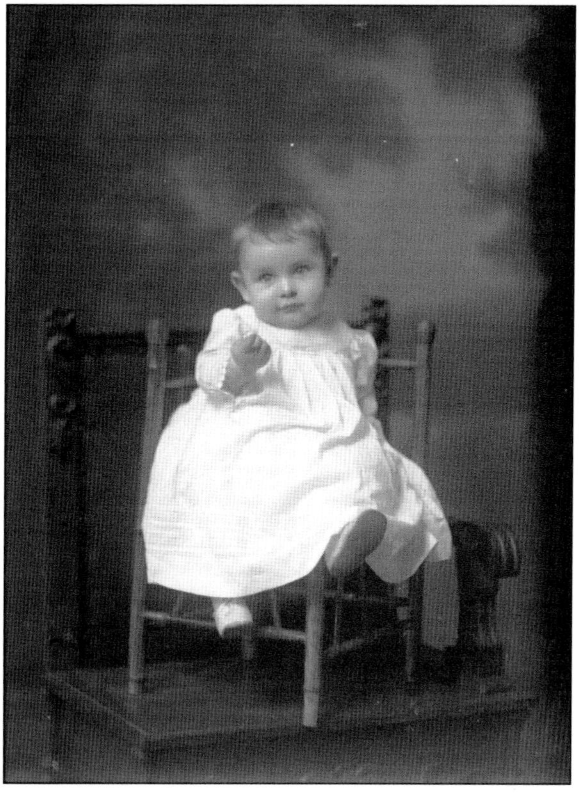

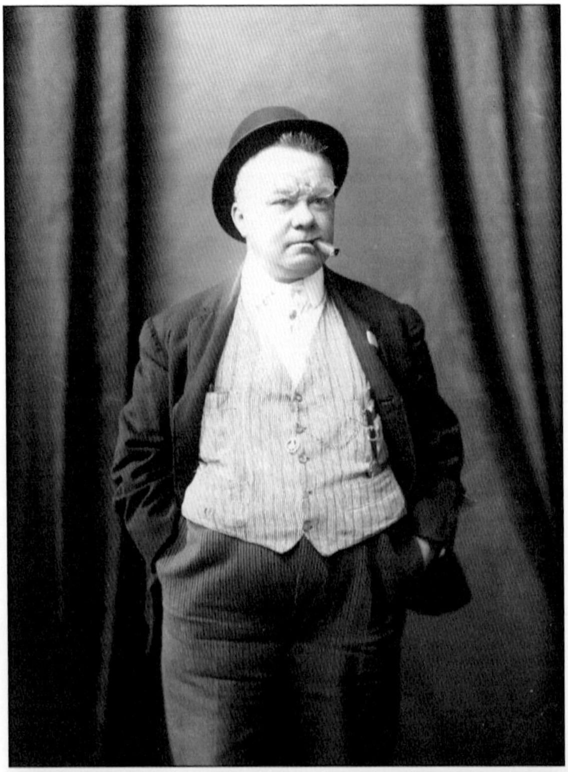

Julius Leschinsky had a knack for capturing the personality of his subject. In this photograph, Daniel C. Brown poses with his glasses perched on his forehead while chomping on a cigar in November 1913. Born in Philadelphia, Brown came to Grand Island in 1903. He established the Phelps Cigar Company, Pool and Billiards at 113 South Locust Street in 1910.

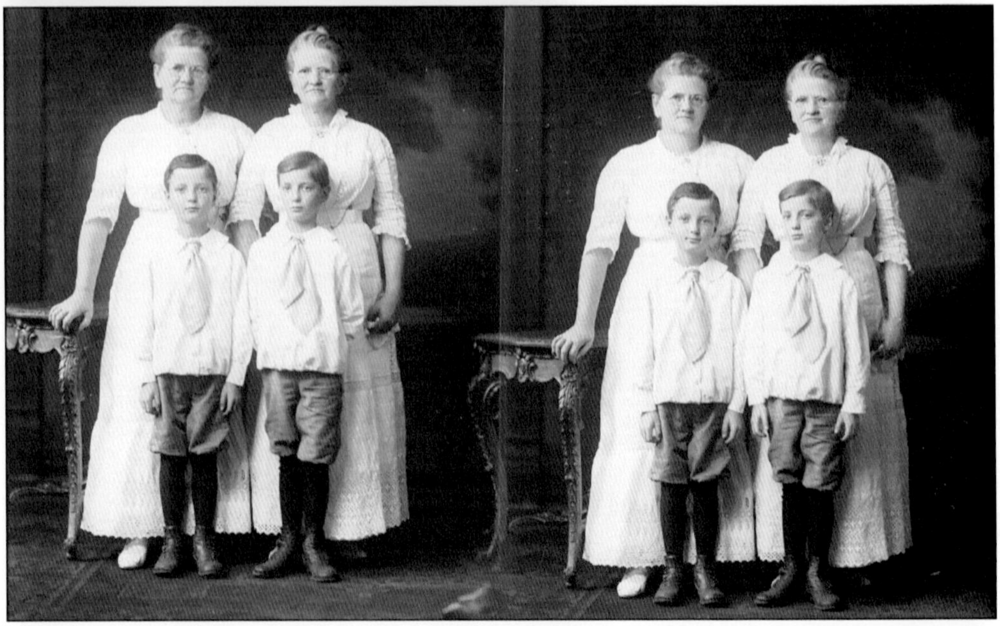

In this photograph, Emily Travis poses with her twin sister Emma Stinchcomb and her twin grandsons Elmer and Earl Engleman in October 1917. Emily and Emma were born in October 1862 to Stephen and Elizabeth Buzza. Emily's daughter Elizabeth Minerva Travis married William T. Engleman in 1909 and gave birth to Elmer and Earl in 1911. Note that both sets of twins wear matching outfits.

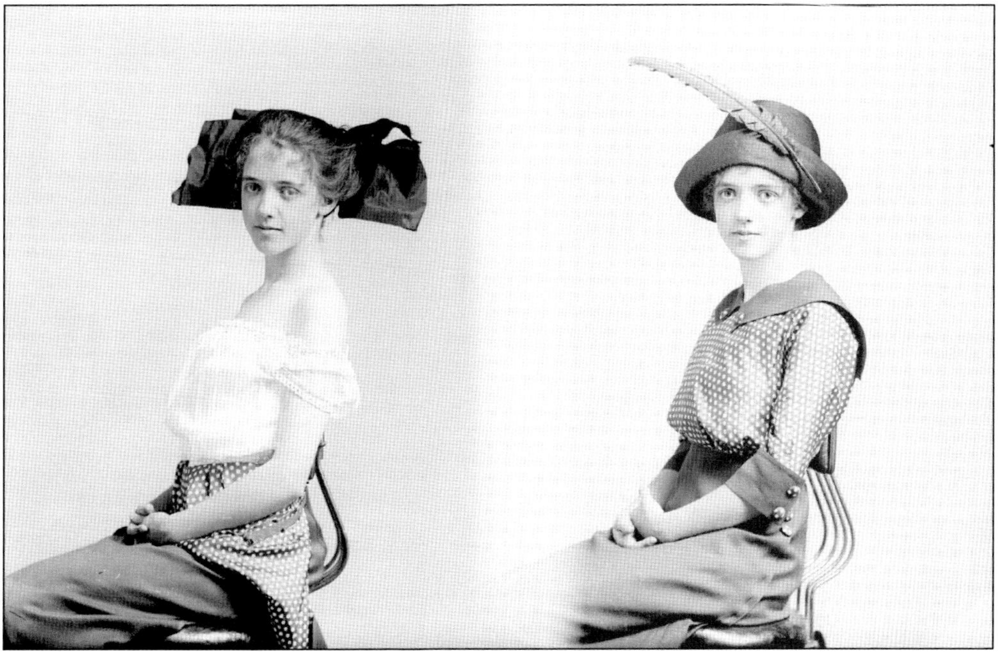

At first look, this series of photographs taken in May 1911 appears to be quite scandalous. In the image at right Helen Dill poses wearing a hat with a large feather. In the left image, her blouse has been removed and the straps of her chemise are pulled down, but it is likely that the finished product was very innocent with only Helen's head and bare shoulders visible.

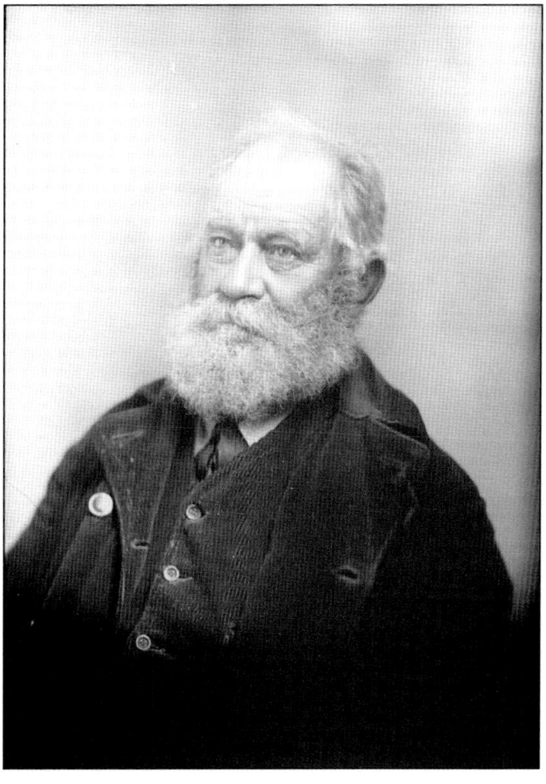

In November 1911, August Wendt poses for this photograph. Wendt was born in Germany in 1843 and immigrated to the United States in 1870. He took a homestead in Lake Township, Hall County, in 1872, and he farmed it for over 46 years. He died in 1920 at the age of 76 years, 6 months, and 13 days.

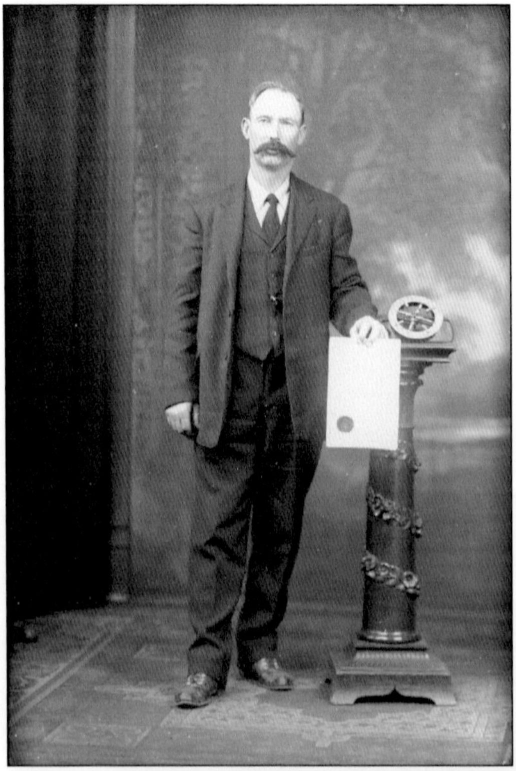

On December 7, 1915, Hugo Grotzky of Chapman received patent number 71915 for a specialized wheel attachment. In this photograph, Grotzky is holding the official patent and his invention can be seen atop the wooden pedestal. According to his patent, Grotzky's invention related to attachments for wheels to prevent lateral movements or skidding.

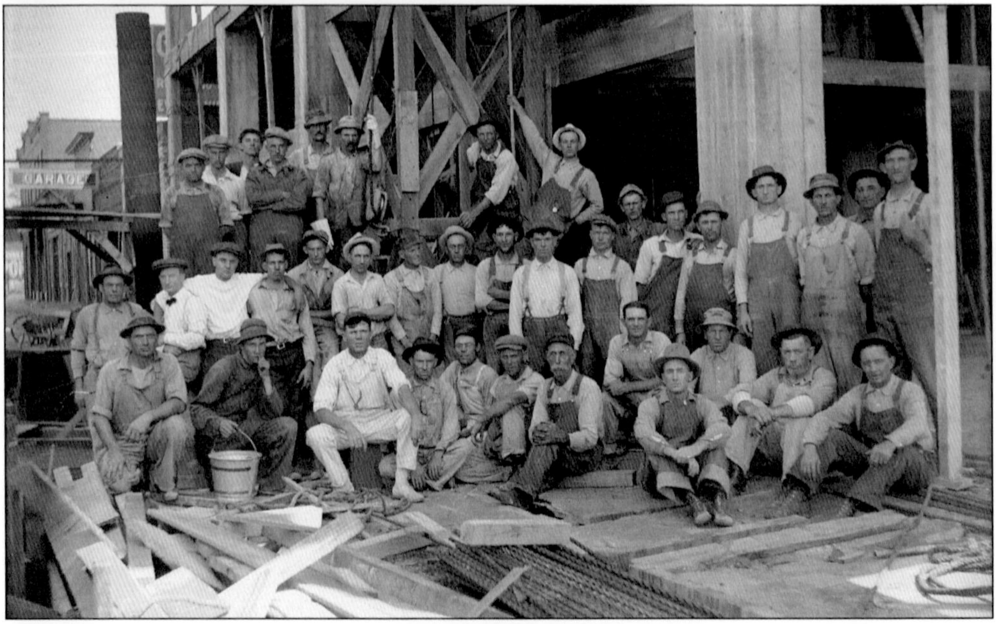

This photograph, taken in September 1917, features the hardworking men who built the Yancey Hotel. At 10 stories, the Yancey was the tallest building in town for nearly 90 years. In 1918, financial difficulties caused construction to stop, and the hotel sat unfinished until 1923. Once completed, the Yancey had over 150 rooms, a diner, a news and cigar stand, and an elegant ballroom known as the Gold Room.

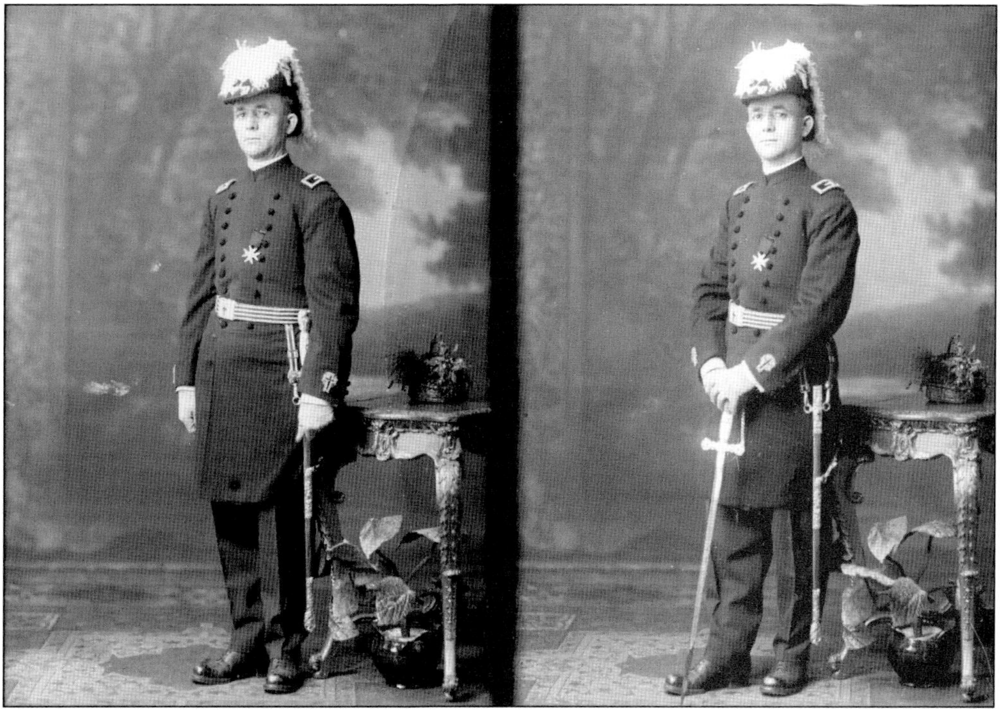

In December 1915, Charles T. McElroy poses for Julius Leschinsky wearing the uniform of the Knights Templar, a degree of the Freemasons. As a member of the Masons, McElroy advanced to a high position, becoming a Knight Templar and a Shriner. He also served as a high priest and eminent commander. He was also an active member of the Episcopal Church and the fraternal order of Elks.

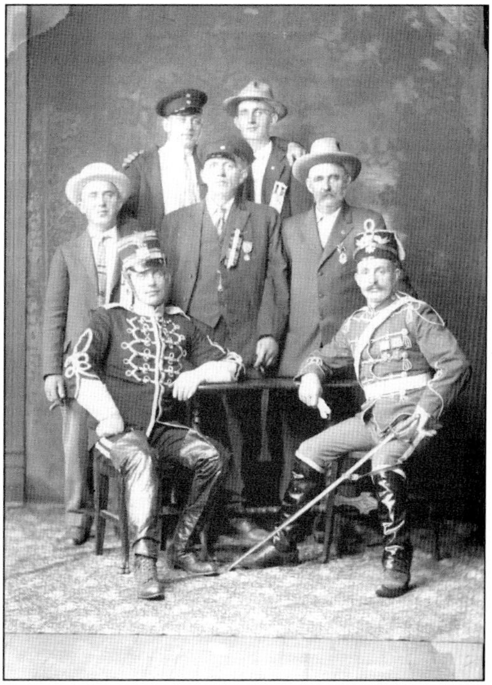

This photograph was commissioned by Jacob Pahl in October 1913. Two of the seven men are wearing German-style military uniform costumes. The other men wear ribbons or medals associated with Grand Island's German heritage societies such as the Liederkranz, Plattduetsche Verein, and the Sons of Herman. It is unfortunately unclear with which organization these men are associated.

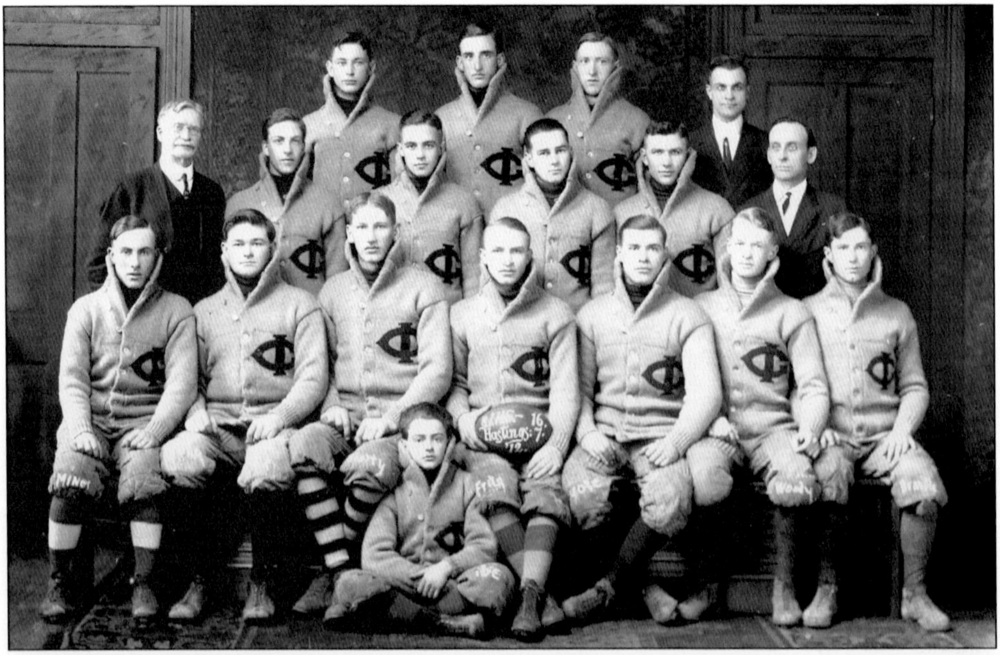

In this photograph, members of the Grand Island High School football team pose in their letterman sweaters. A player in the center of the first row holds a football. Written on the football is "G.I.H.S. – 16, Hastings – 7, '12." Grand Island High School beat rival Hastings High School 16 to 7 on November 26, 1912. Note the nicknames written on the knees of the players seated in the first row.

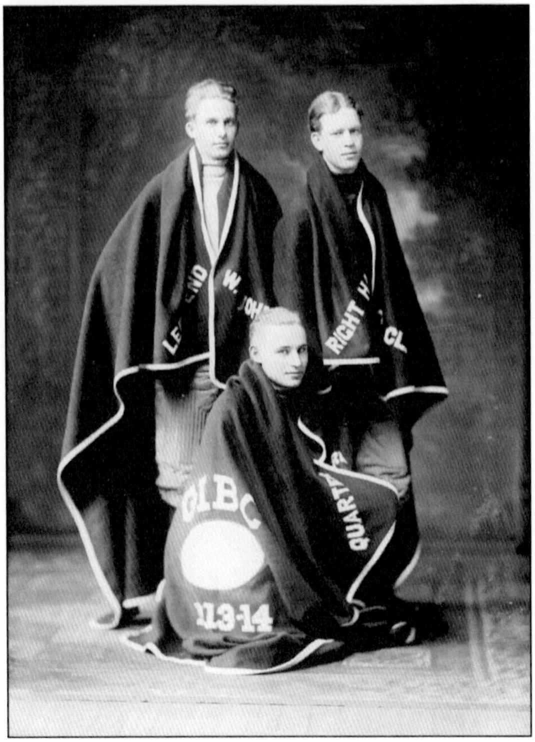

Three of the members of the Grand Island Business College football team are dressed in their padded football pants and sweaters in 1915. The three men have award blankets draped over their shoulders, likely given to honor them for their athletic accomplishments. The blankets are stitched with lettering including their name and position. The two men standing played left end and right halfback, and the man sitting was the quarterback.

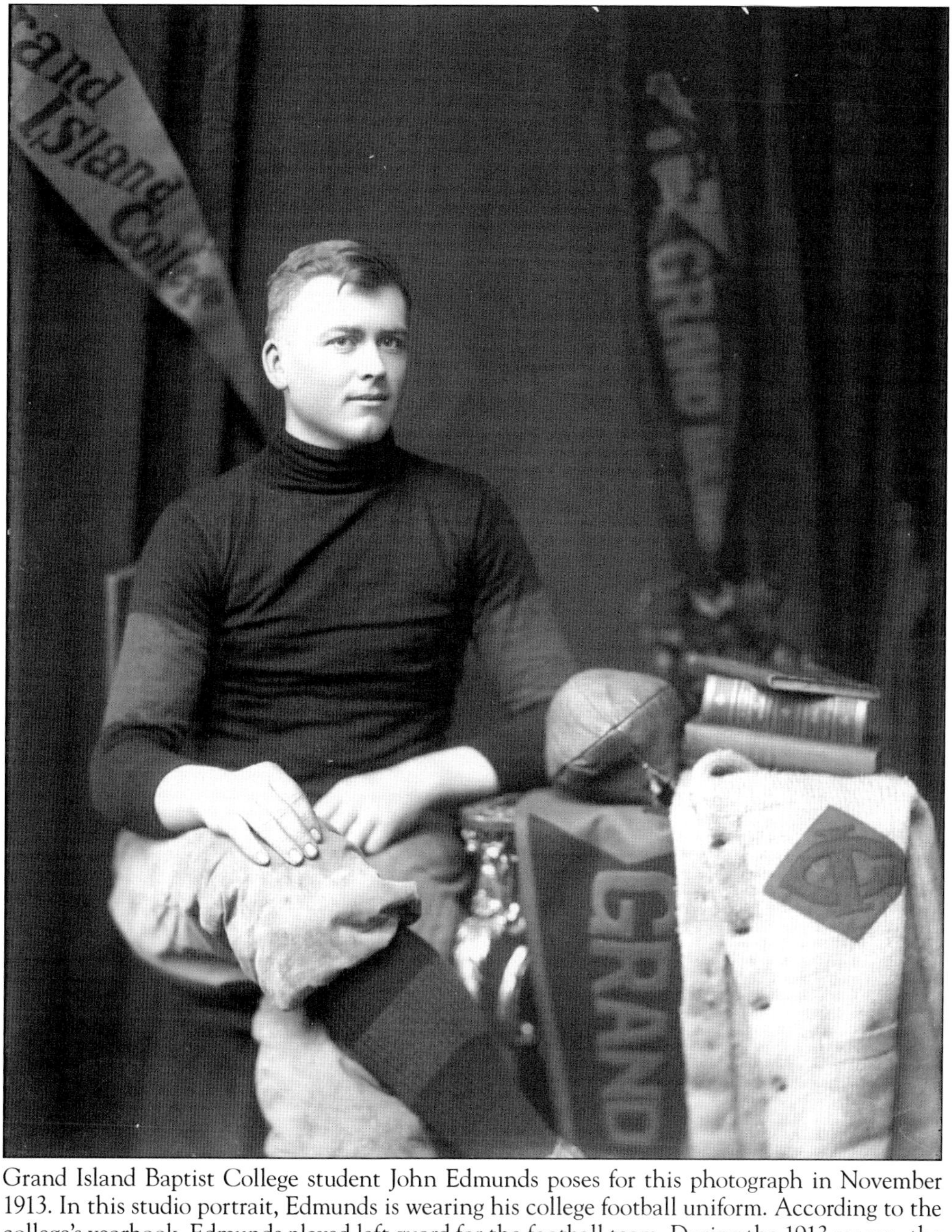

Grand Island Baptist College student John Edmunds poses for this photograph in November 1913. In this studio portrait, Edmunds is wearing his college football uniform. According to the college's yearbook, Edmunds played left guard for the football team. During the 1913 season, the Grand Island Baptist College boasted an undefeated season. Behind Edmunds, several Grand Island college pennants have been pinned to the photographer's backdrop. To his right, another pennant, football, stack of books, and Edmunds's letter sweater sit on the table.

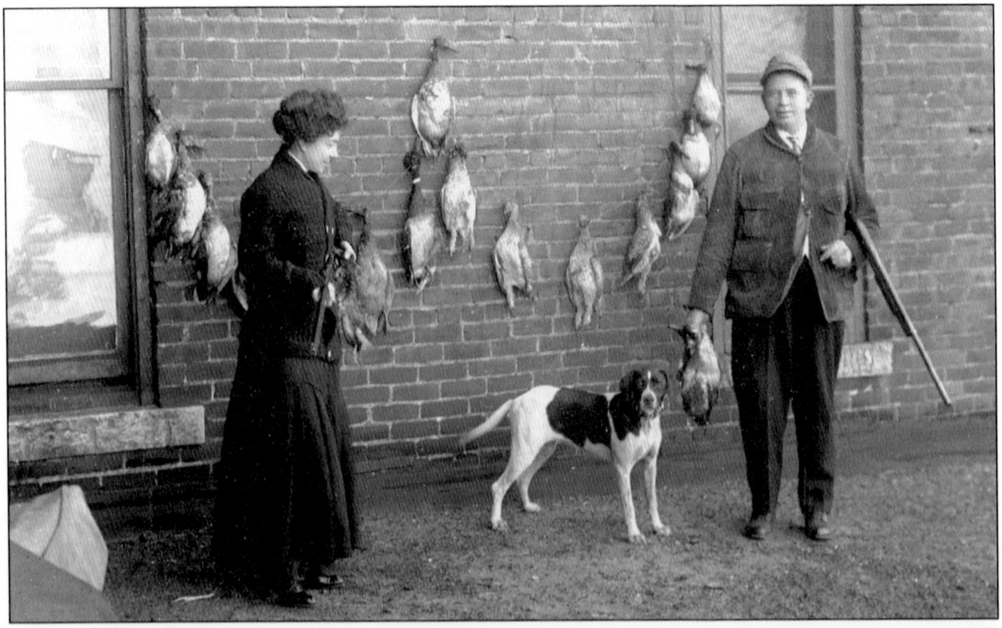

Posed with the trophies of a successful hunt, this couple seems to have enjoyed a crisp fall day in 1910. This photograph was commissioned by J. M. Totten, the manager of the Palmer House hotel at the time. Numerous ducks and grouse have been strung up behind the couple and their hunting dog. At the time of this photograph, grouse season was from October 1 to November 1.

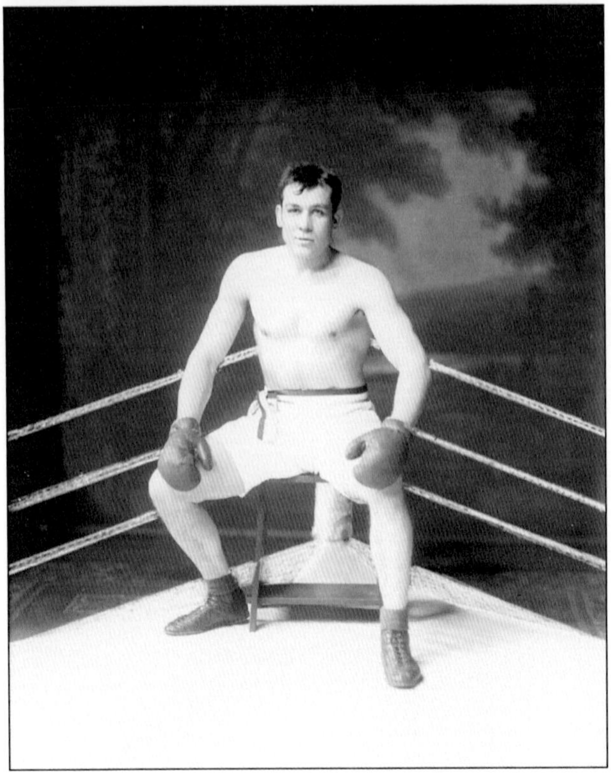

Local amateur boxer Jack Price poses for this photograph in March 1915. The photograph was taken prior to Price fighting against Tommy Smith of Omaha. The fight was held on March 29, 1915, and was well attended. The Grand Island Athletic Association was careful to call the match an "Athletic Carnival," since prizefights were prohibited by law. According to the newspaper, Price and Smith were closely matched and no clear winner was determined.

This lovely young woman shows her team spirit while sitting for Julius Leschinsky in November 1911. She is wearing what appears to be a hand-knit sweater and matching hat. Draped across her shoulder is a pennant on which "Grand Island" has been stitched. It is unclear if she is rooting for the high school, Baptist college, or business college team.

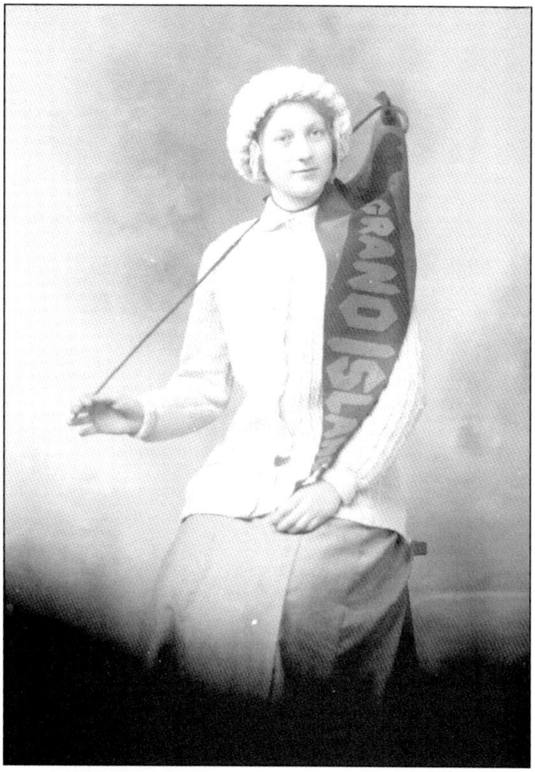

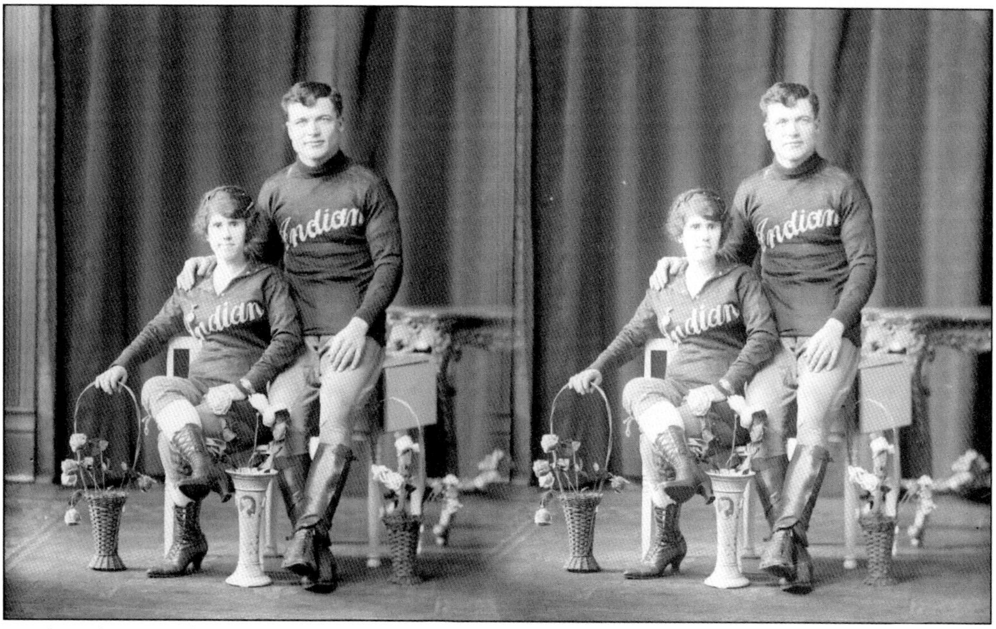

In this photograph, John and Georgina Kallos pose sporting their motorcycle-riding gear in January 1918. Born in Greece, the couple immigrated to the United States in 1910, where they shortened their last name from Kalleoropoulos to Kallos. The couple is wearing matching outfits emblazoned with the Indian Motorcycle logo. Georgina is wearing knicker-style riding pants, which would have been unusual for women to wear in 1918.

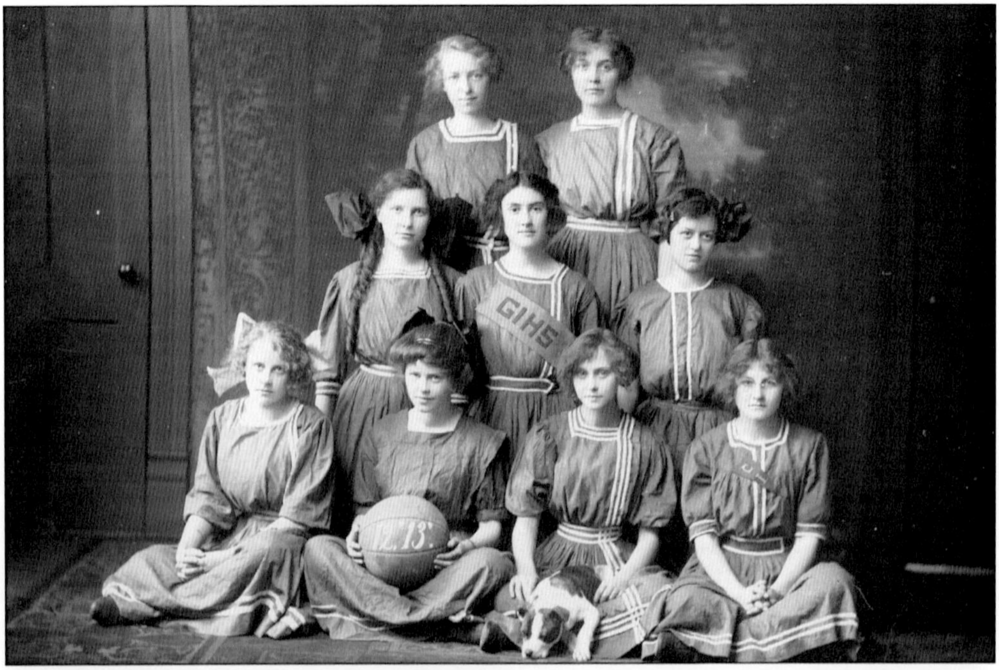

The first exhibition basketball game in Grand Island was played on April 19, 1902, between the Grand Island and St. Paul high school girls' teams. Unfortunately, the Grand Island girls lost 5 to 7. From that time on, basketball became a popular high school sport for both girls and boys. In this photograph, nine members of the 1912–1913 Grand Island High School girls' basketball team pose with their mascot.

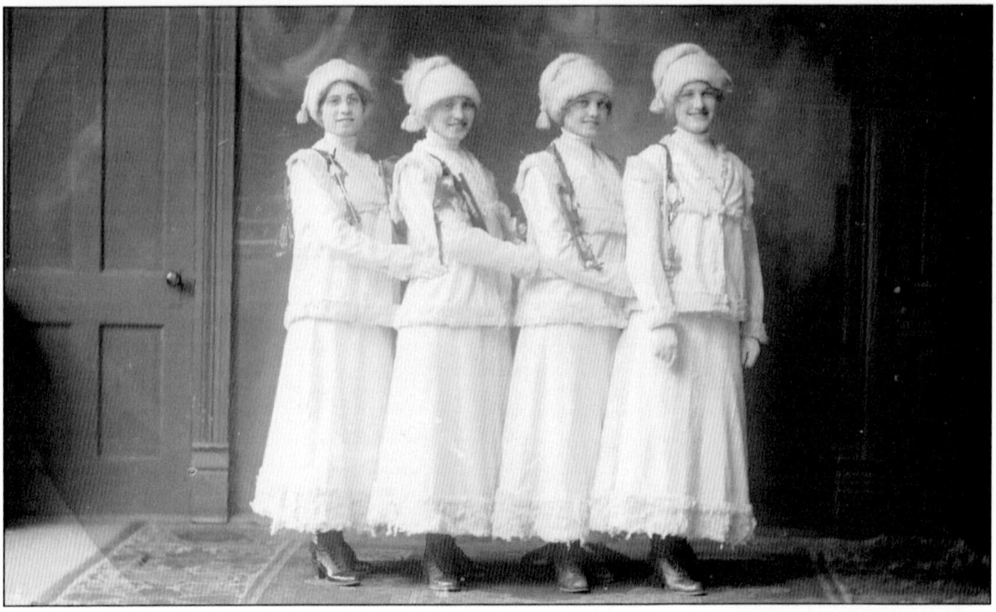

Sporting matching outfits, these four charming young women are likely the Pepper sisters Elizabeth, Minnie, Meta, and Frieda. The sisters pose for this photograph in February 1912 with their ice skates flung over their shoulders. They were the daughters of William and Mary Pepper. The Peppers had 10 children, 8 girls and 2 boys.

Six

GETTING AROUND

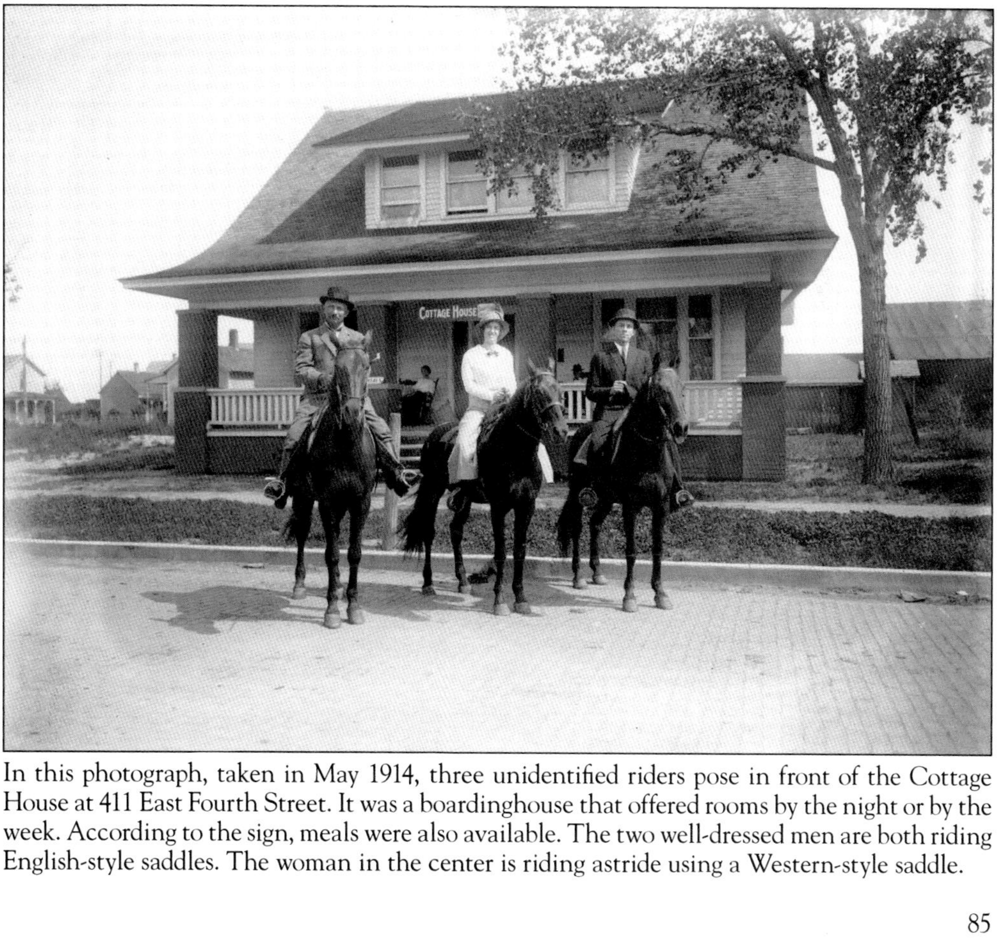

In this photograph, taken in May 1914, three unidentified riders pose in front of the Cottage House at 411 East Fourth Street. It was a boardinghouse that offered rooms by the night or by the week. According to the sign, meals were also available. The two well-dressed men are both riding English-style saddles. The woman in the center is riding astride using a Western-style saddle.

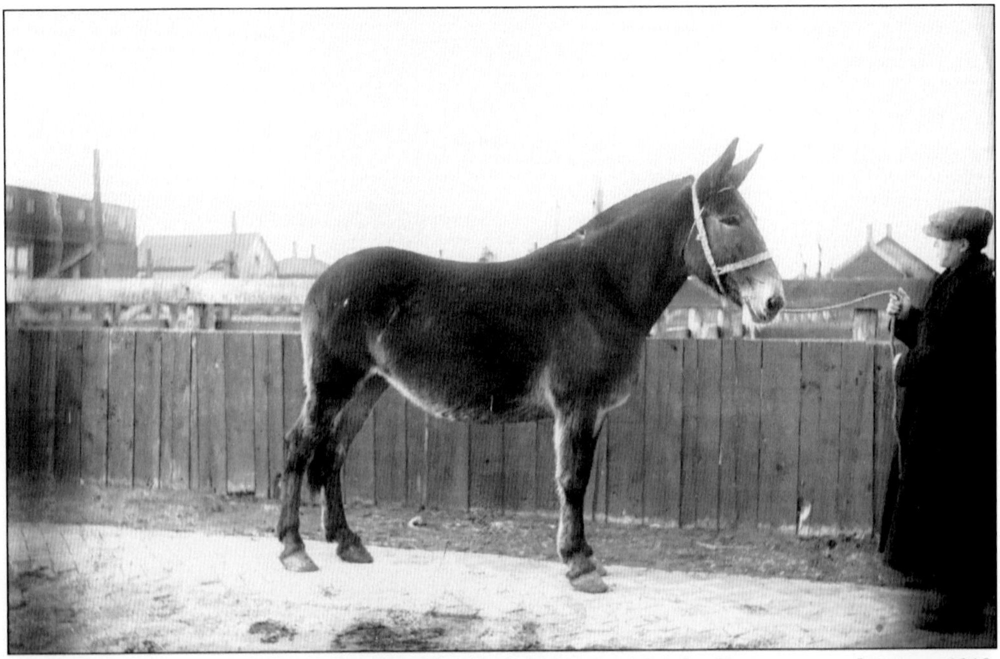

This big boy is on display at the Grand Island Horse and Mule Company in January 1919. Located on East Fourth Street, the sale pen can be seen behind the mule. When the horse market began in Grand Island in 1903, a modest 4,000 animals were sold. From there, it grew to be the second-largest horse and mule market in the world, reaching its peak during World War I.

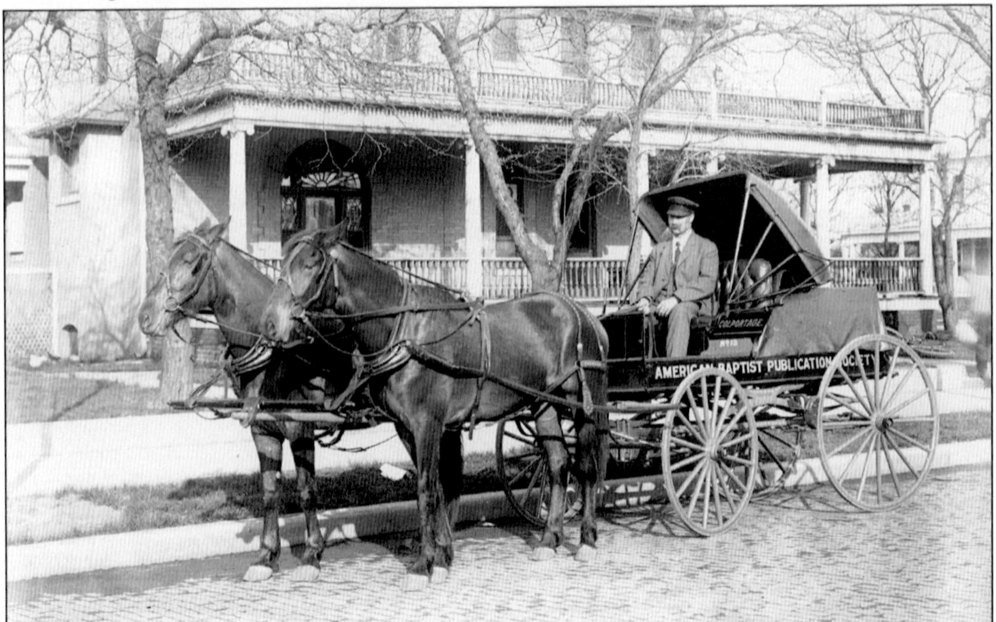

Taken in April 1911, this photograph shows Rev. James E. Judkins holding the reins to the buggy he used as a colporteur for the American Baptist Publication Society. A colporteur refers to a person who travels, selling books and tracks that are usually religious in nature. Judkins also worked as a missionary minister in Grand Island before moving to Omaha.

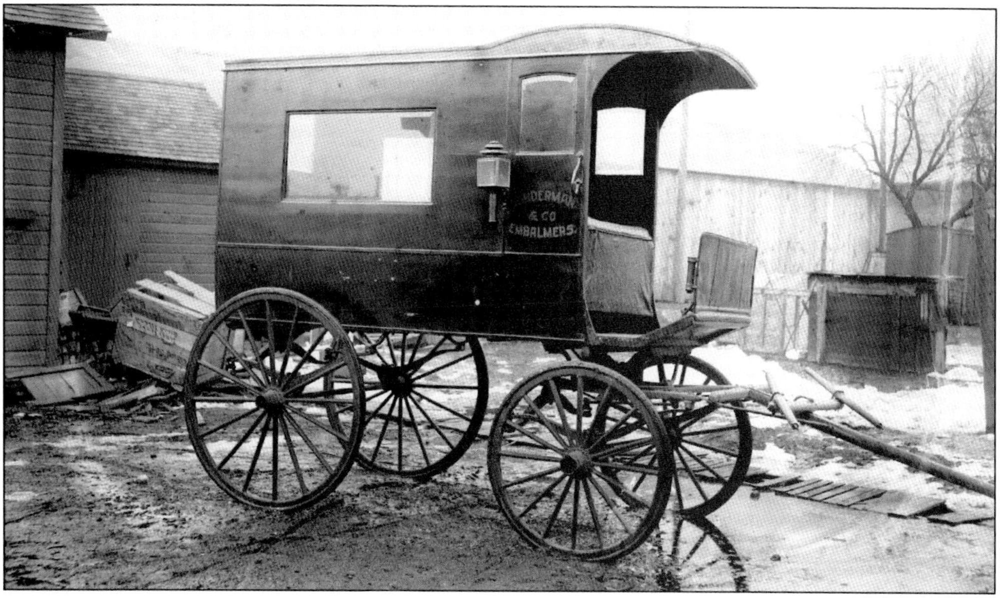

Seen here in February 1912 is the horse-drawn hearse used by Sonderman Furniture and Undertaking. Joseph Sonderman started his family's business in 1891 at 116 West Third Street. The business remained at that location until 1936. Over the years, the business has changed location and owners, but it remains in operation today. Sonderman was a charter member of the Nebraska State Funeral Director's Association and president of the first state board of embalmers' examiners.

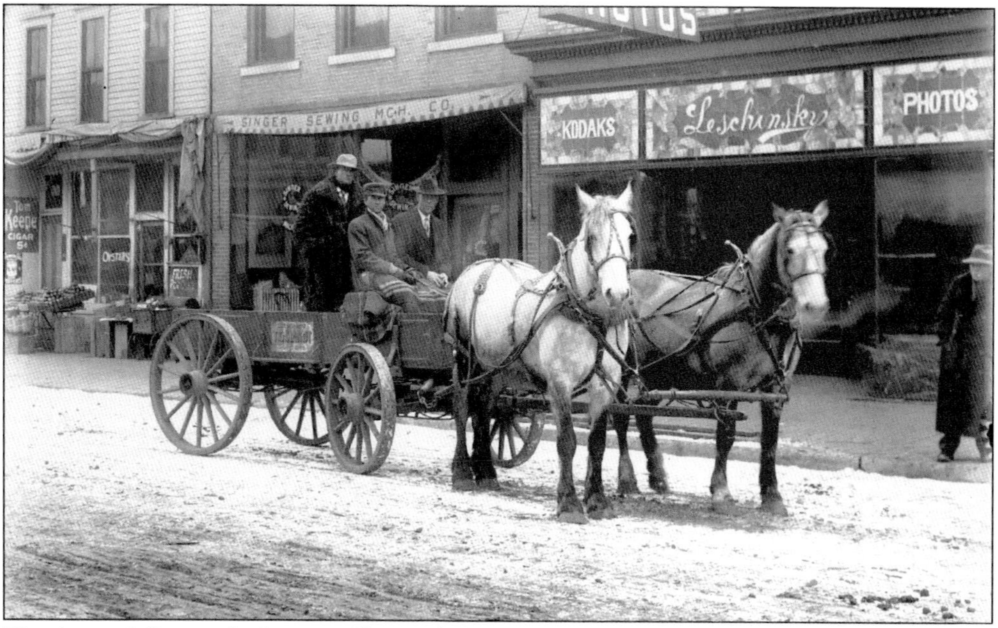

This beautifully matched team of horses belonged to the Tilley family. The Tilleys operated a plant and tree nursery on their farm north of Grand Island where the Grand Island Airport is now located. The Tilleys were responsible for planting and nurturing many of the trees throughout Grand Island. Taken in November 1911, the Tilleys' wagon is parked on the 100 block of East Third Street.

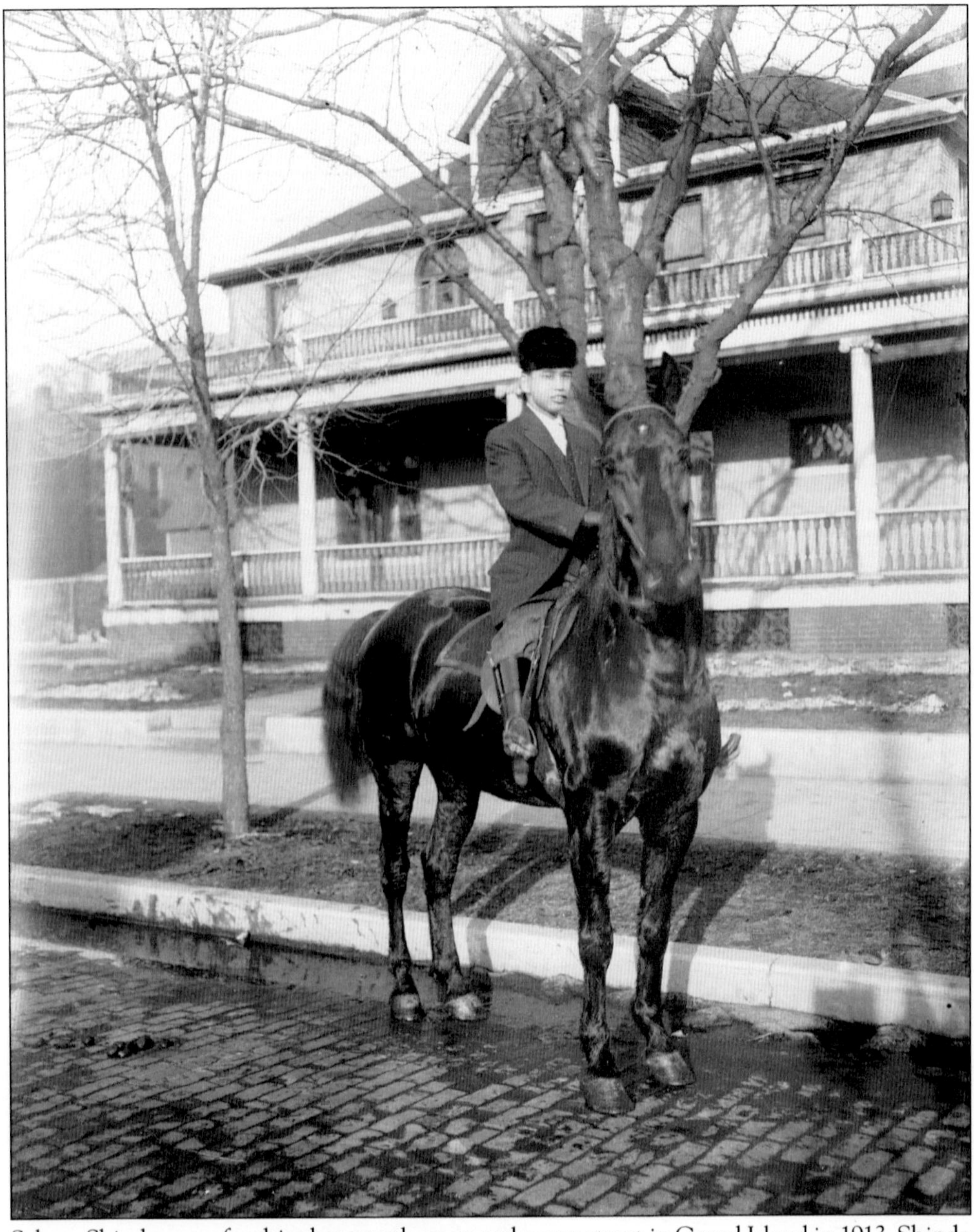

Saburo Shindo poses for this photograph on an unknown street in Grand Island in 1913. Shindo owned and operated the Palace Café, once located at 120 South Locust Street. Born in Aki, Hiroshima, Japan, on May 5, 1879, he came to the United States in 1903, locating first in Evanston, Wyoming. Later that same year, he purchased a restaurant in Lexington, Nebraska. In 1907, Shindo opened a new restaurant in Elm Creek. He came to Grand Island in 1908 and started the Palace Café. He married Evadna Mitchell in 1915, and they had three children, Kenneth, Yalanda, and Rodney. Shindo died on December 26, 1928, from complications due to a ruptured appendix. According to his obituary, Shindo was held in high esteem in local business circles. Note the fine leather riding boots Shindo is wearing. He is also using an English-style saddle.

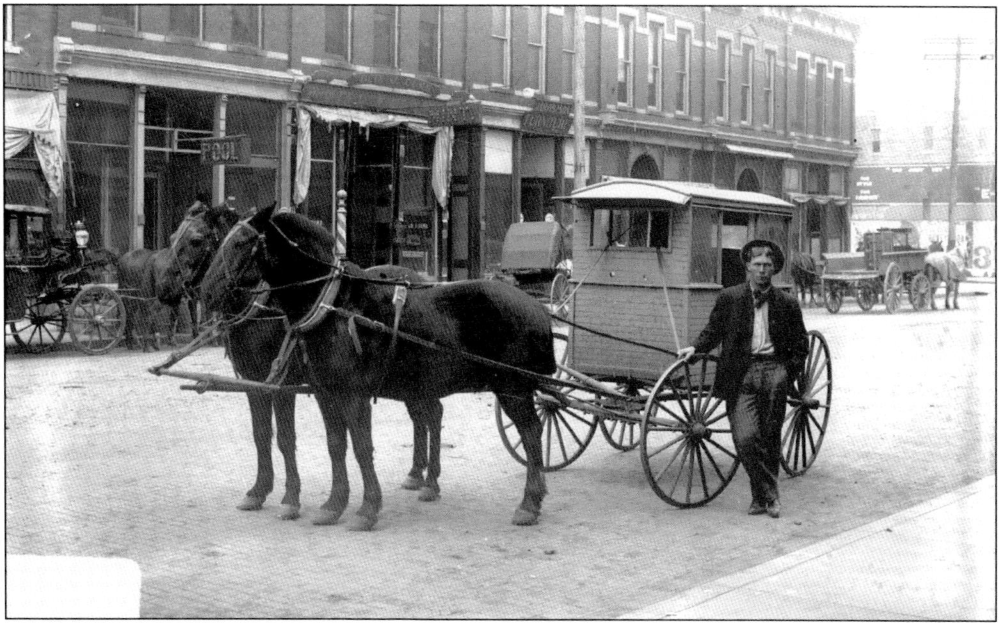

Hired man Sam Madsen is standing outside Julius Leschinsky's studio on East Third Street with a horse-drawn dairy wagon in November 1910. Sam worked for William M. Minor, a Hall County dairy farmer. Minor's farm was located west of Grand Island near the area commonly referred to as Westlawn. According to the 1910 census, Madsen was born in Denmark in about 1886 and immigrated to the United States in 1902.

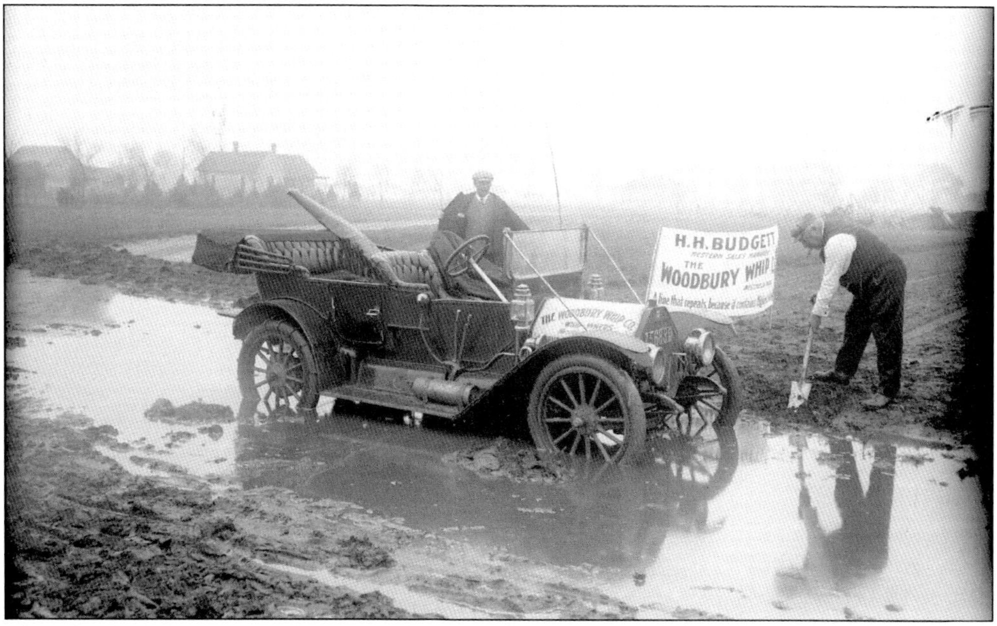

This photograph was commissioned in May 1913 by H. H. Budgett, the western sales manager of the Woodbury Whip Company of Massachusetts. It is one of a series of four photographs showing two unidentified men getting their automobile stuck in and then pulled out of the mud. In the last photograph, a team of horses was hitched to the automobile with a man holding a long whip, presumably as an advertisement for the company.

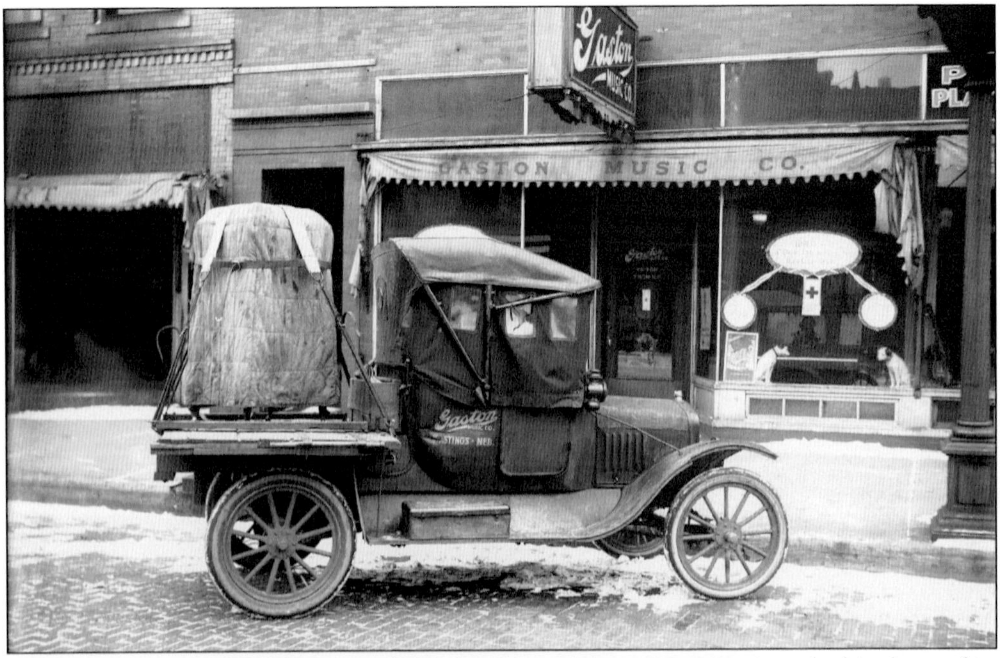

In this photograph, the delivery truck for the Gaston Music Company is parked in front of its store located at 103 East Third Street in February 1919. At this time, Edwin A. Jones was the manager of Gaston's. Loaded on the back of the pickup truck's flatbed is likely a Victor Victrola phonograph player. Advertisements for Victrolas can be seen in the window of the music store.

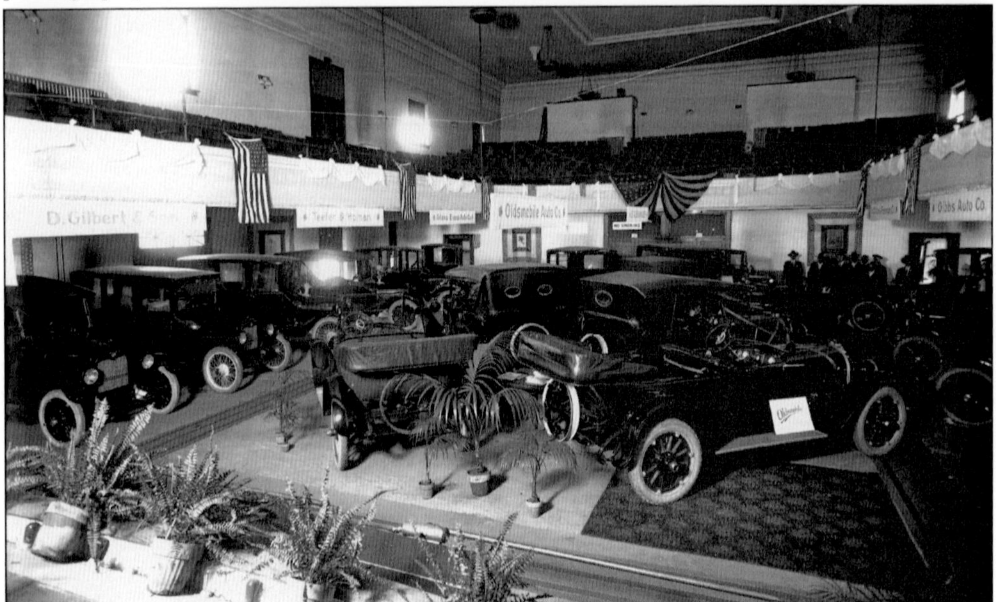

Local dealers held an automobile show (seen here) at the Liederkranz from April 9 to 12, 1919. The auditorium's seats were removed and the latest models of automobiles were moved into the Liederkranz. At left is the display for Gibbs and Sons, which sold Studebakers. In the center, several Oldsmobiles can be seen. According to the newspaper, other automobiles exhibited included an Auburn, a Raulang electric car, and a Chandler Chummy.

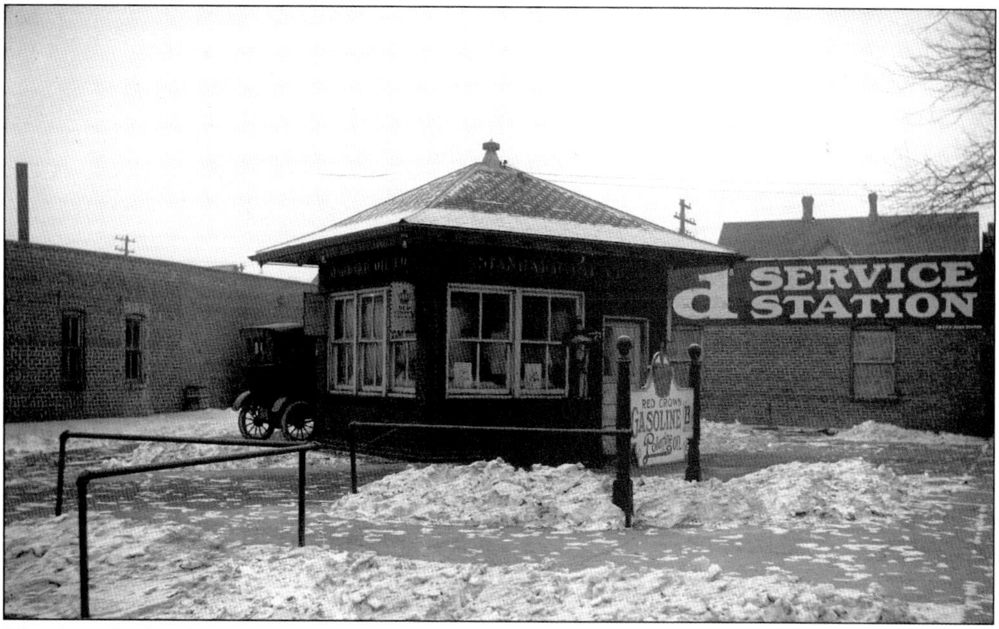

The Standard Oil station seen here was located at the southeast corner of Pine and Second Streets. This address was along the Lincoln Highway, a road that stretched from New York City to San Francisco. Taken in about 1915, the station seen in this photograph was built in the bungalow style designed by Omaha architect Everett S. Dodds for Standard Oil. Standard Oil used this design in numerous cities, including Grand Island.

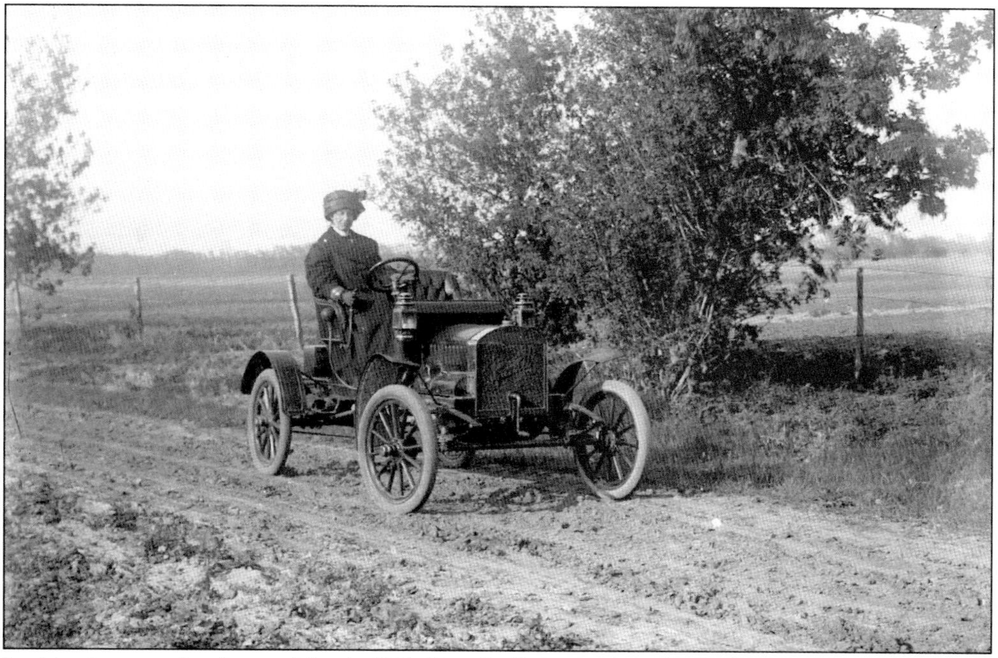

In this photograph taken in March 1910, Dora Kolls sits at the wheel of her automobile. A native of Grand Island, Kolls devoted her life to education, first as a teacher, then as principal of Wasmer School, and later as Hall County superintendent of schools. She served as superintendent from 1910 until her death in 1918 at the age of 44.

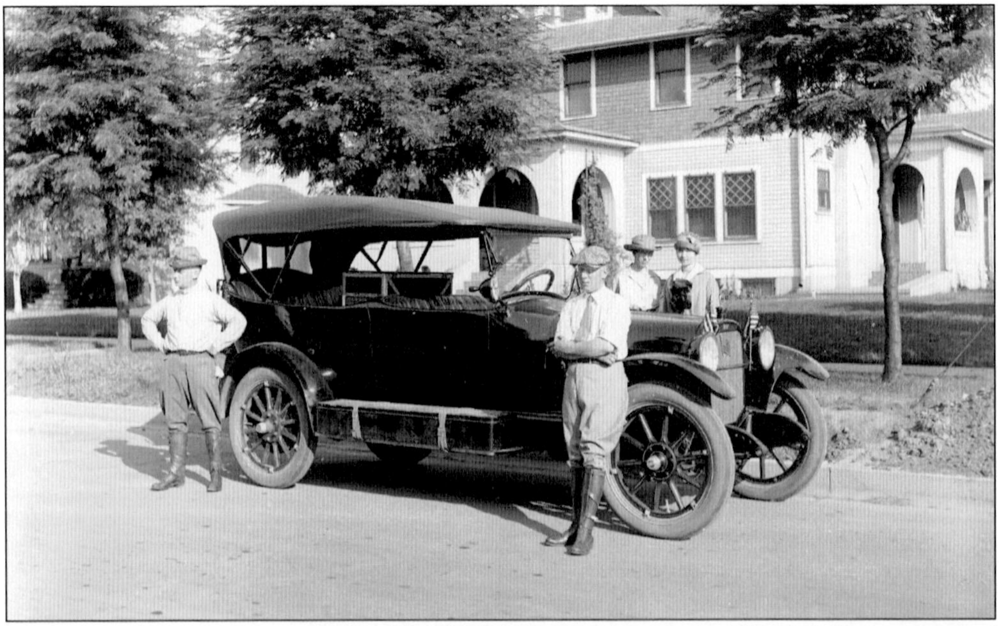

On July 26, 1917, Dr. H. R. and Ethel Hatfield, Minnie Neubert, and S. W. Brock departed Grand Island for a two-week vacation to Denver. According to the newspaper, the photograph seen here was taken as they departed Grand Island and a second photograph was to be taken when they arrived in Denver. The group was traveling in Dr. Hatfield's automobile and was attempting to make a nonstop, record-breaking run.

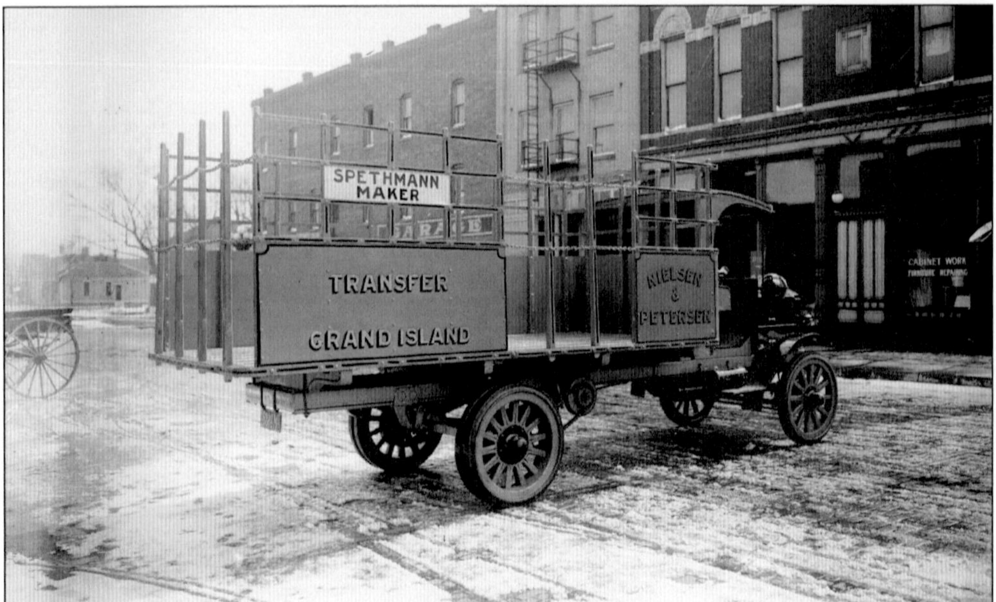

The delivery truck seen in this photograph, taken in March 1918, was fabricated by Spethmann Blacksmith and Auto Works located at 214 East Third Street. It was created for Nielsen and Petersen Dray and Transfer Company. According to its advertisement in the Grand Island City Directory, Nielsen and Petersen specialized in moving pianos. During this time period, many blacksmiths diversified their shops to accommodate the growing popularity of automobiles.

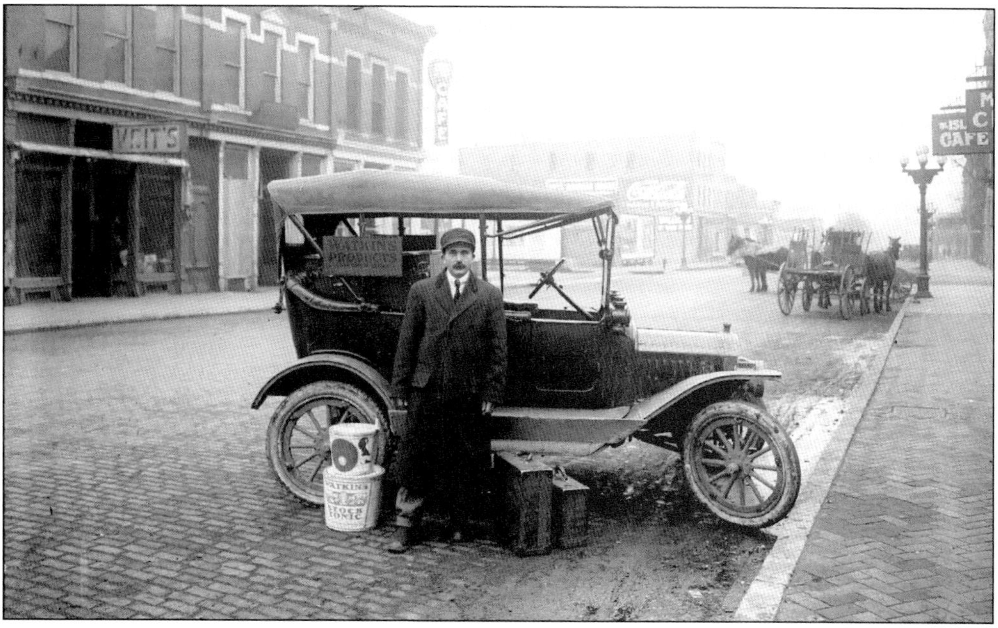

Julius Leschinsky stepped out of his studio at 109 East Third Street to capture this image of a traveling salesman. Taken in February 1918, the unidentified man is selling Watkins Products from his early automobile. The sign attached to the automobile proclaims, "Watkins Products for Sale Here." The buckets to his left are for Watkins Stock Tonic. His sample cases are to his right.

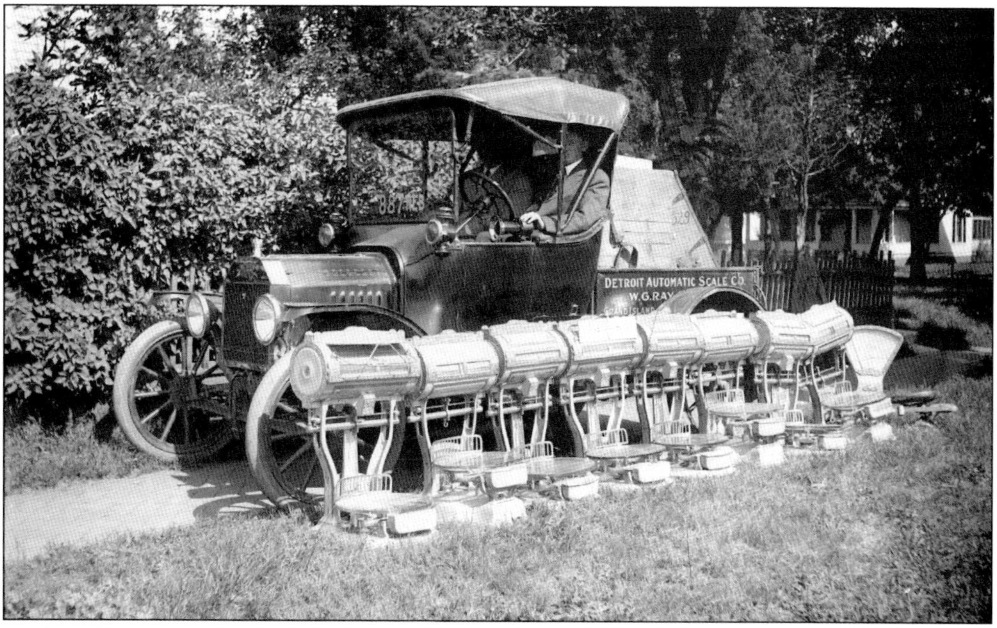

In this photograph, two men are seated inside a Ford pickup truck in August 1913. According to the lettering along the truck bed, it was used by W. G. Ray of the Detroit Automatic Scale Company. Several models of automatic scales have been lined up in front of the truck. Scales such as these were used commercially to measure grains, produce, and candy. Ray likely sold and calibrated the scales.

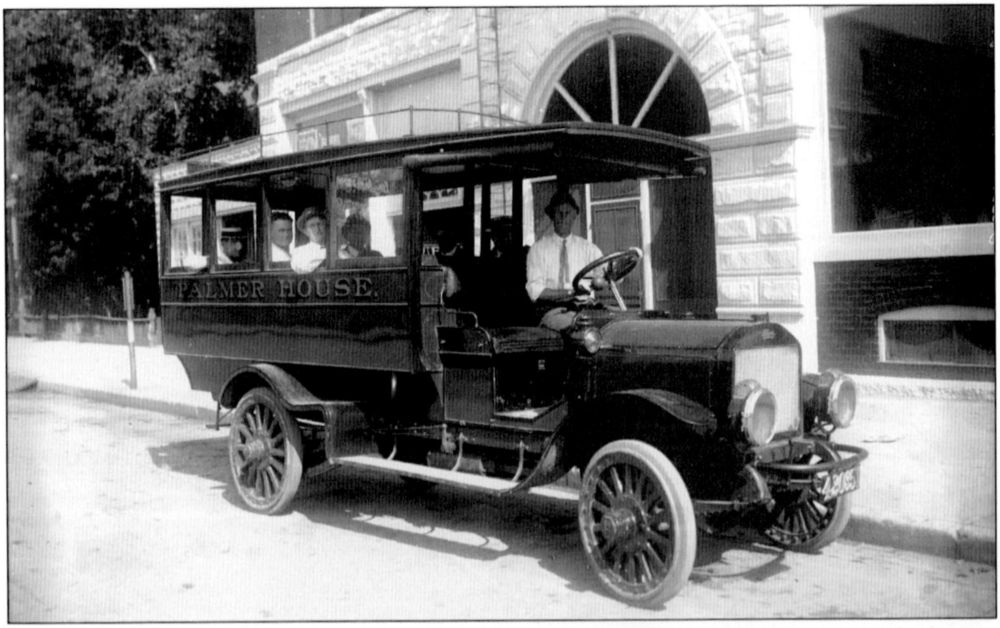

This photograph shows the driver for the Palmer House Hotel omnibus ready to take his six passengers on a trip around town in July 1912. The Palmer House was located at the southeast corner of Third and Sycamore Streets. The distinctive arched doors of the Palmer House are visible behind the bus. According to the emblem visible below the radiator cap, the bus was a Dart.

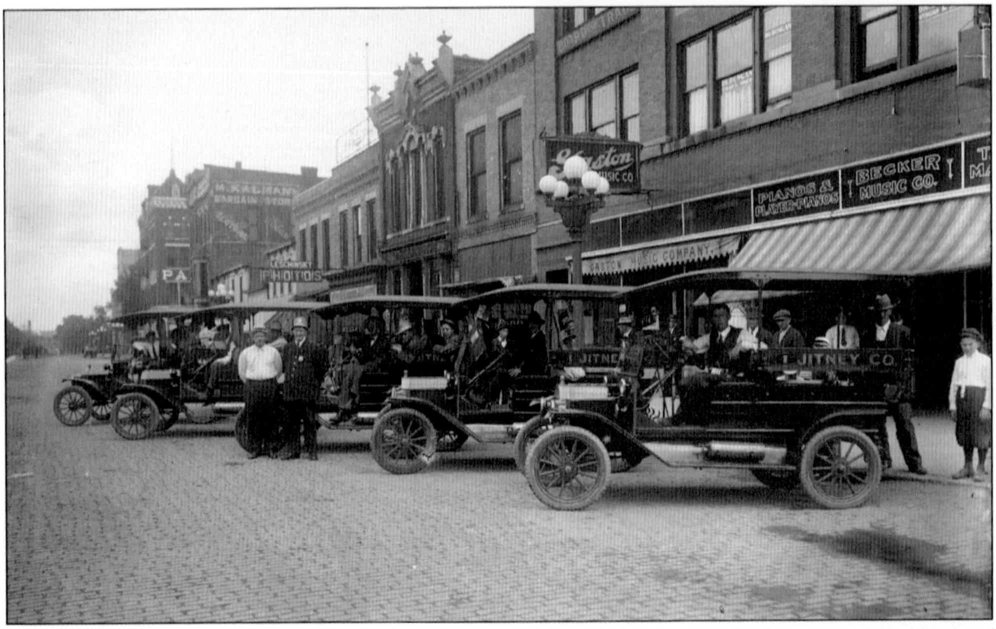

Five buses belonging to the Grand Island Jitney Company are parked along the 200 block of East Third Street in July 1915. The Jitney Company opened on June 4, 1915. The next year in October 1916, high gas prices and poor road conditions forced the company out of business. According to the newspaper, the buses were chrome yellow, the same color as the coaches on the North Western Railway.

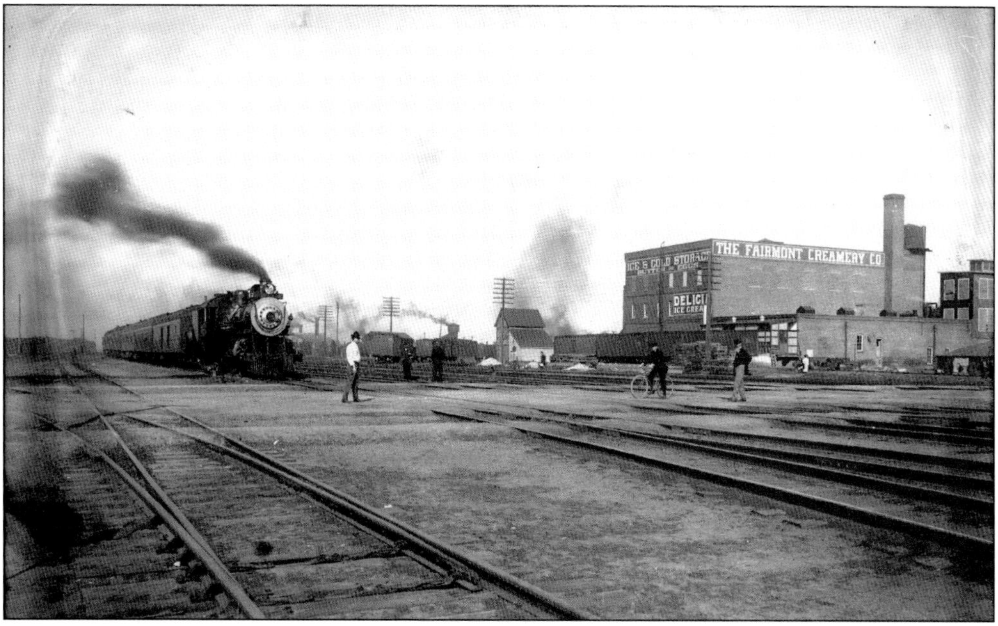

The Fairmont Creamery once stood at 324 North Vine Street, along the main line of the Union Pacific Railroad. The plant seen in this photograph, taken in May 1912, was built in 1909. The four-story building began as a butter manufacturing and cold-storage operation. It quickly expanded to include ice cream, cottage cheese, eggs, and dressed poultry. In 1913, the Fairmont reportedly produced over 63,000 pounds of butter a week.

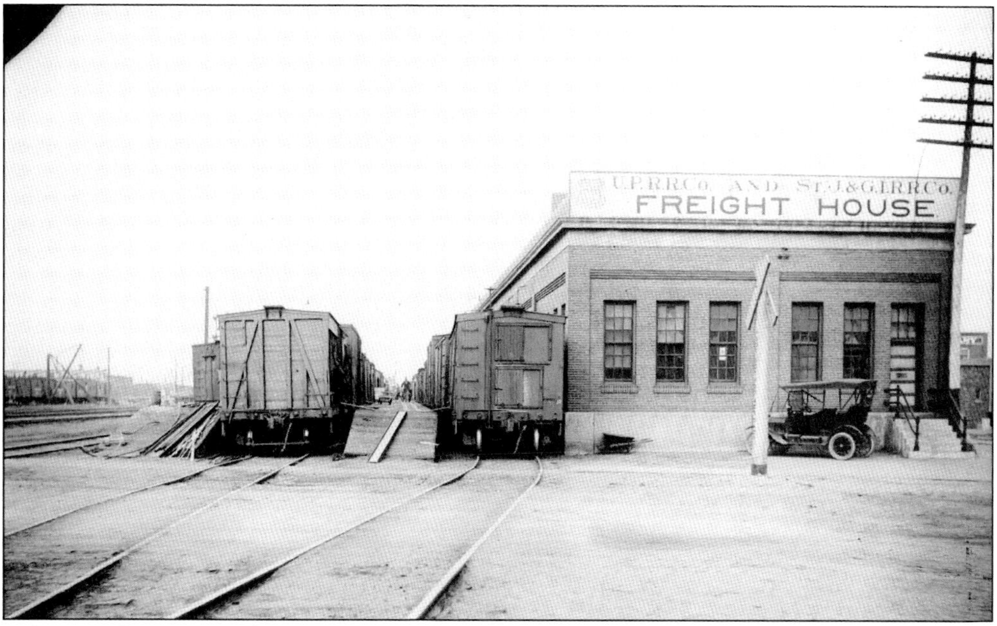

Taken in about 1918, this photograph shows the freight depot in Grand Island used by the Union Pacific Railroad Company and the St. Joseph and Grand Island Railroad Company. It was located at the corner of Front and Sycamore Streets. On the dock, workers can be seen loading and unloading the boxcars. The pole of the railroad crossing sign reads, "Look out for the cars."

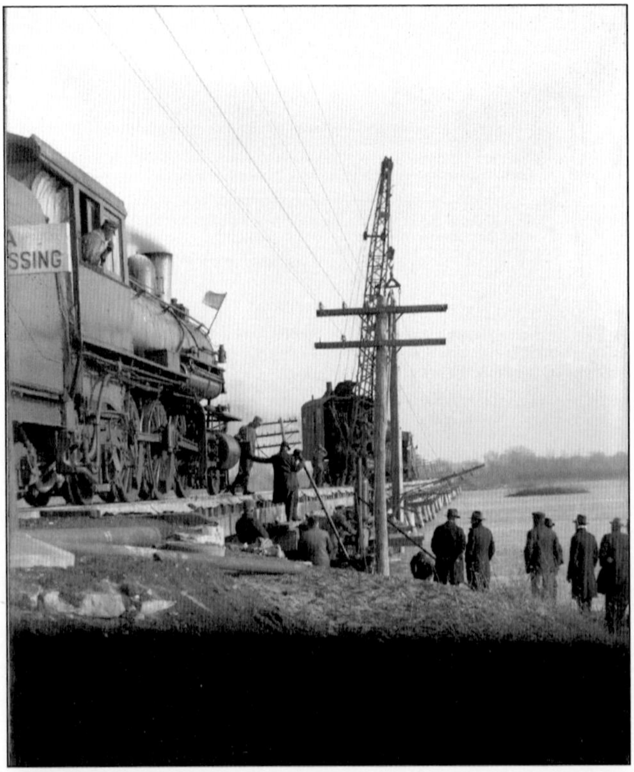

The two photographs seen here are of the construction of the new Burlington Railroad passenger bridge across the Platte River between Phillips and Grand Island. The photograph at left shows the Concrete Piling Company in December 1916 working on the utility lines in preparation for the new bridge. Actual construction of the bridge began in March 1917 and was completed about 18 months later in October 1918. It took the contractors another three months to finish the approaches. The photograph below shows the bridge opening for service in January 1919. The new bridge was 1,000 feet long, 120 feet shorter than the old wooden bridge, which can be seen in both photographs.

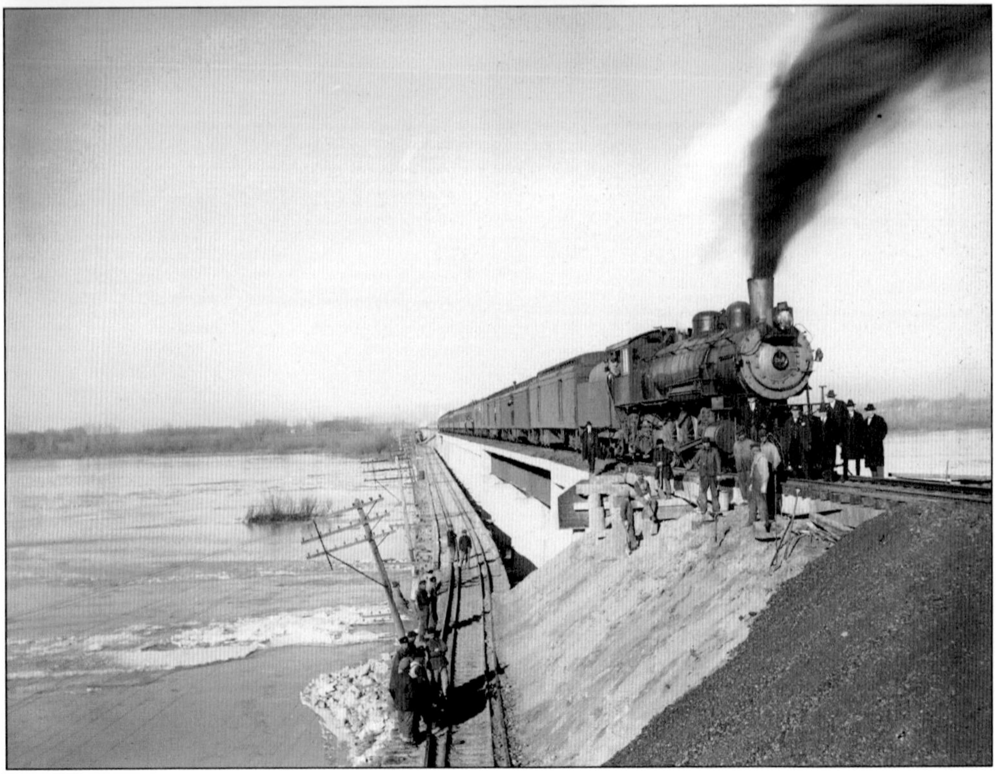

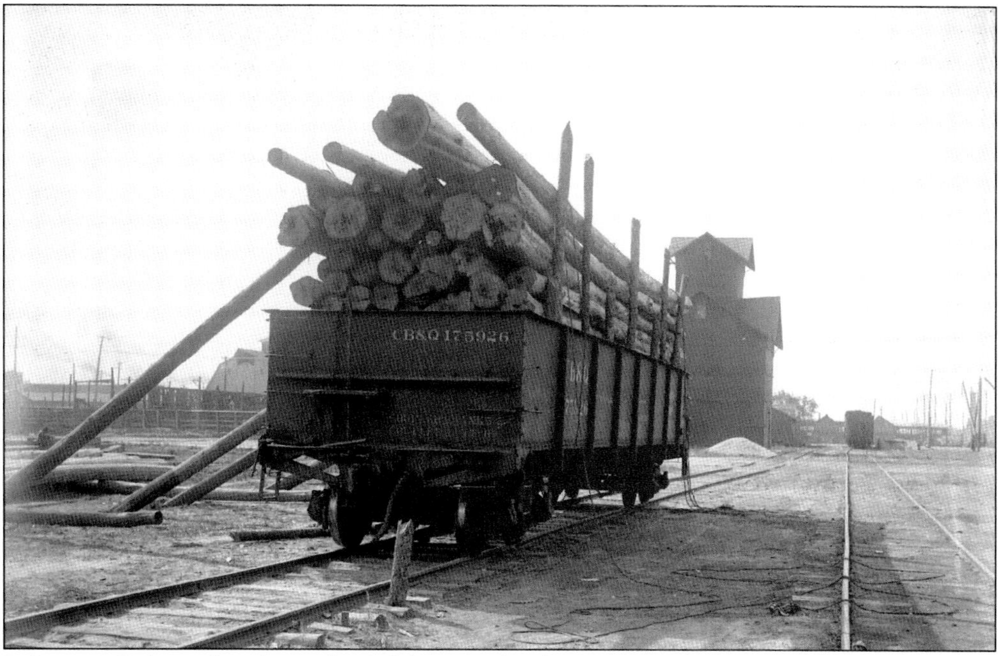

In June 1917, this railroad car is loaded down with a shipment of telephone poles for the Nebraska Telephone Company. The district office for the Nebraska Telephone Company was located in Grand Island at 114 South Walnut Street. By 1920, Grand Island was the toll center for a territory that covered about half the state and had 100 people employed at its office.

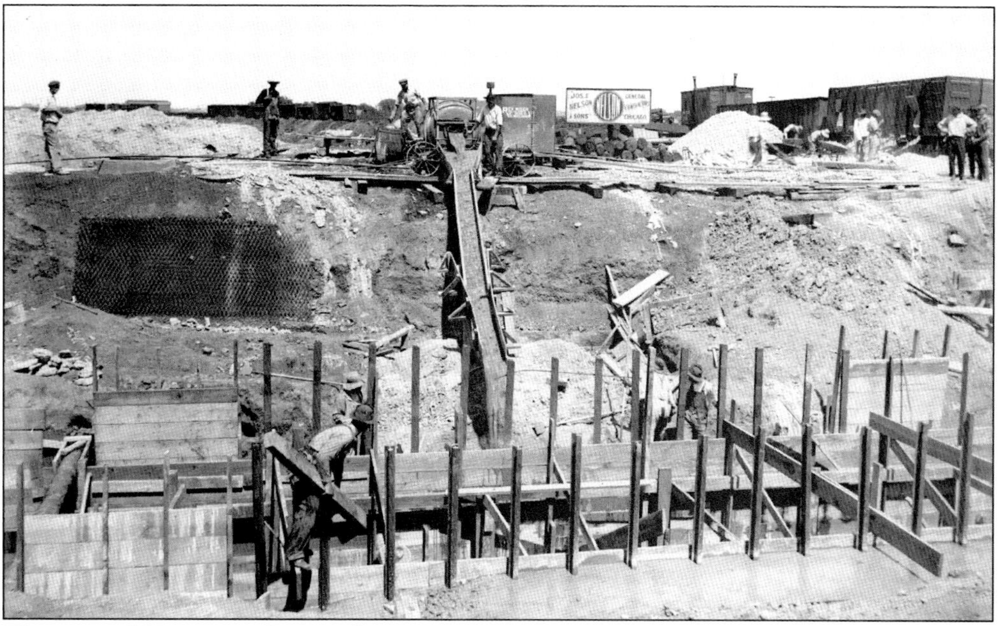

The original Union Pacific roundhouse was built in 1886 and had stalls for 25 locomotives. In this photograph, J. Nelson and Sons General Contractors work on a 15-stall expansion of the roundhouse in July 1917. They appear to be pouring the walls for the drop pit. The drop pit was used to lower the wheels from underneath the engines for servicing. Note the numerous freight and boxcars visible in the background.

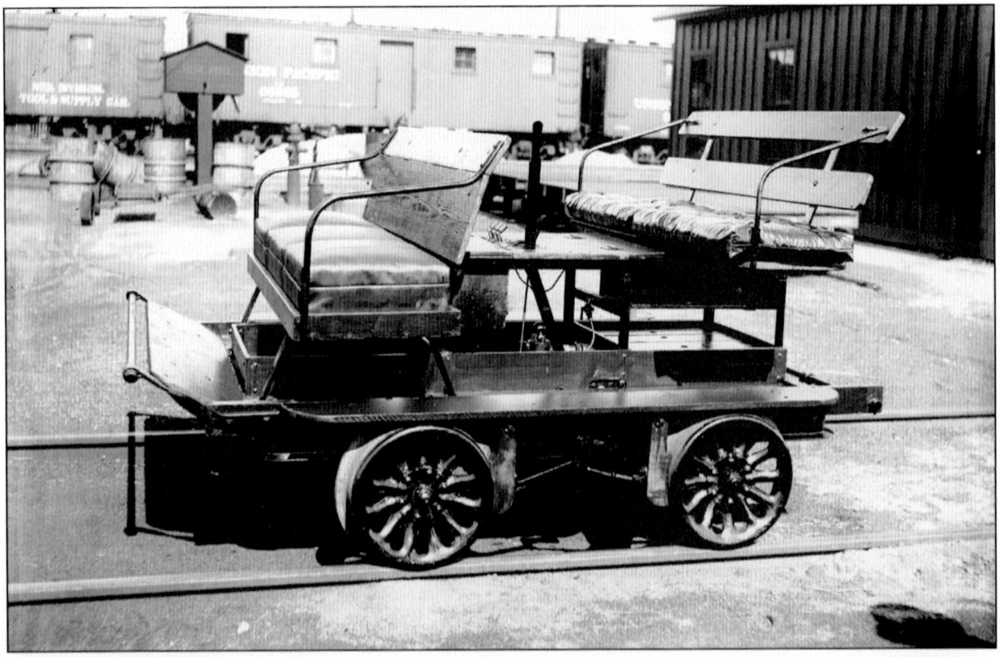

This photograph was commissioned by the Union Pacific Motor Car Department in February 1918. Motorcars, like the one seen here, were used to inspect the railroad line. They came in many different styles but were usually designed to be lightweight enough to be easily moved on and off the track to make way for locomotives.

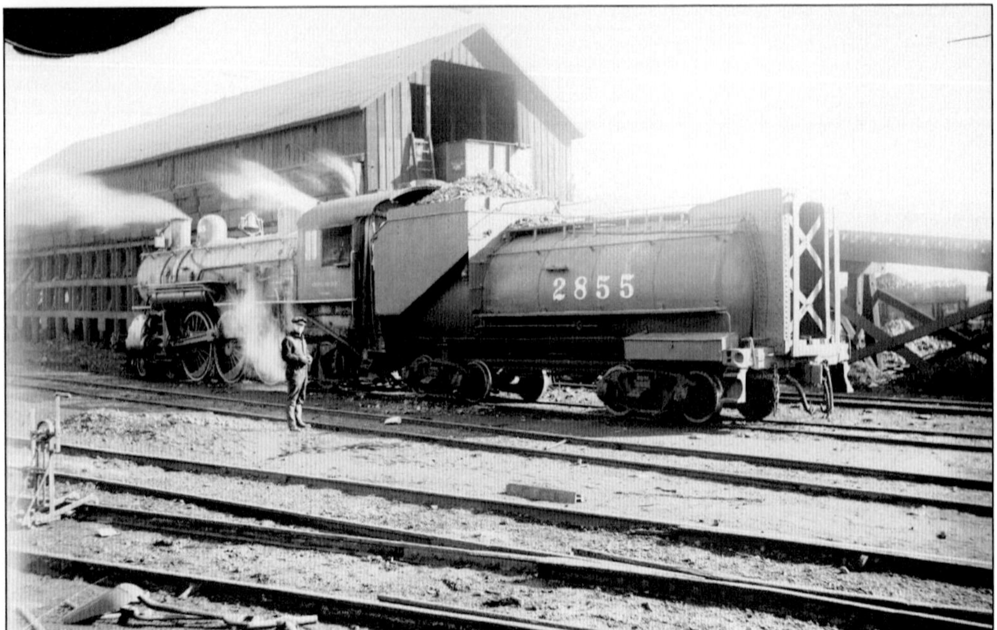

Taken in February 1918, this photograph shows Union Pacific engine 2855 sitting on the ready track after being loaded at the Union Pacific coaling station. It was located in the area of the Union Pacific car and roundhouse on the east edge of Grand Island. Soon after this photograph was taken, the structure seen here was replaced with a new 30-by-95-foot steel station.

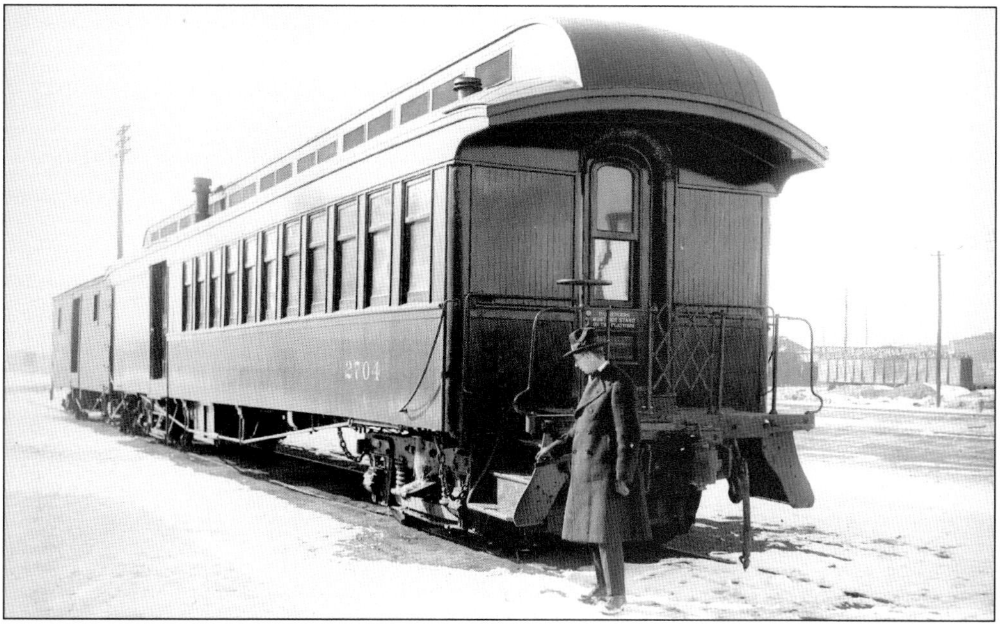

Taken in February 1919, the man in this photograph was likely a railroad official, possibly out of Omaha. During this time period, railroad officials traveled to different locations in a business car, likely the car shown in the image. Car number 2704 was a combination car that would have been used for freight and passengers. Sister car number 2700 currently resides at Stuhr Museum of the Prairie Pioneer.

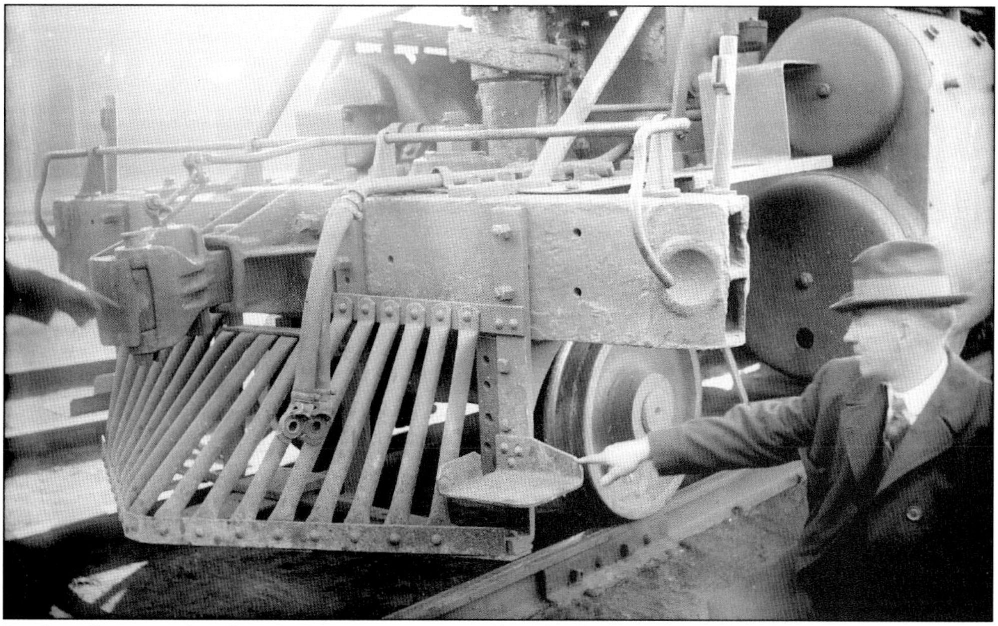

In this photograph taken in January 1919 a railroad official is likely pointing at the footboard. The switchmen rode on the footboard while switching railroad cars. Since the footboards were out of sight of the engineers they were a dangerous location for the switchmen. Switchmen who rode there were called footboard, and later the yardmaster job and footboard were consolidated. The term *footboard yardmaster* is still used by the railroad today.

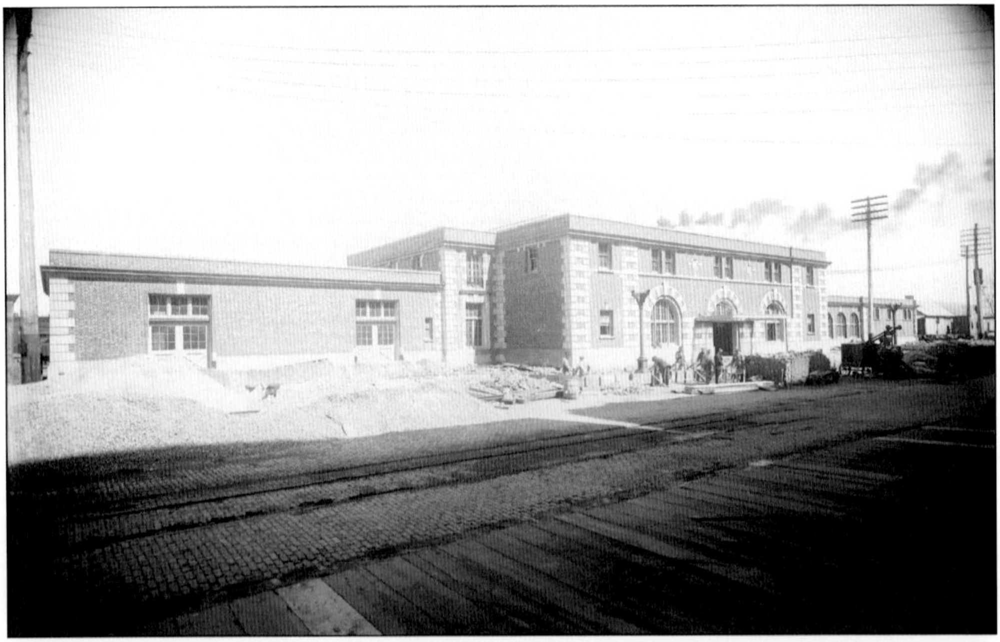

Seen here is the Union Pacific passenger depot under construction in April 1918. The stately redbrick with stone trim depot was opened for service in May 1919. It replaced a smaller passenger depot at the same location on West South Front Street. Designed by the architectural firm Carrere and Hastings of New York City, the depot cost $175,000 to build and stretched nearly an entire city block. For many years it was considered one of the finest small-city depots on the Union Pacific system. The west wing of the depot featured a spacious baggage room while the east wing offered a lunchroom and elegant dining room. In the photograph below, benches for the new depot wait to be removed from their wooden shipping crates in the main lobby.

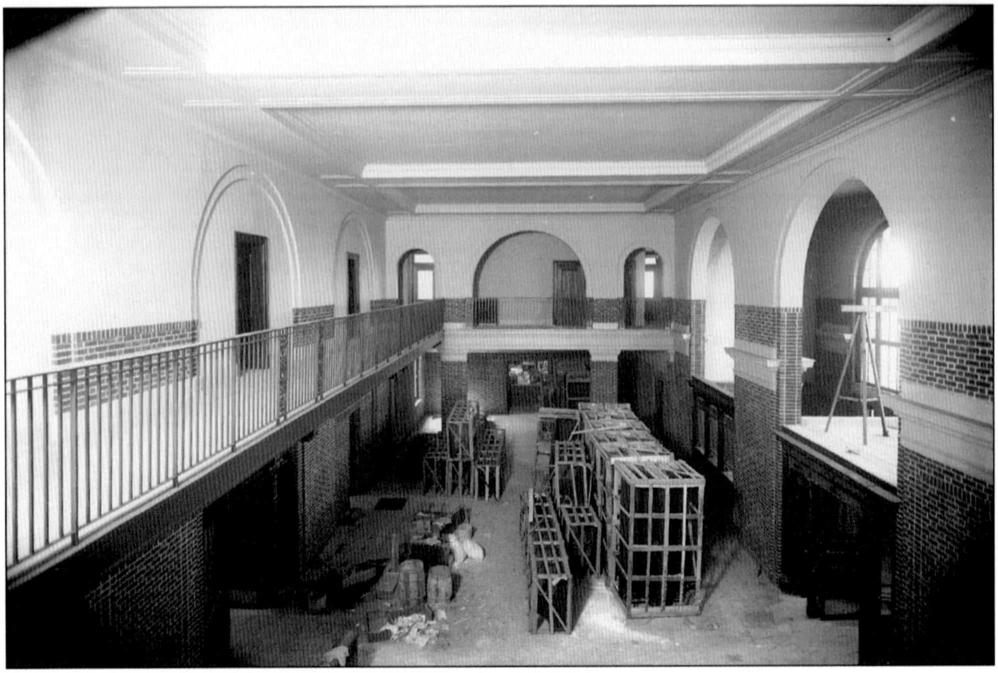

Seven

World War I

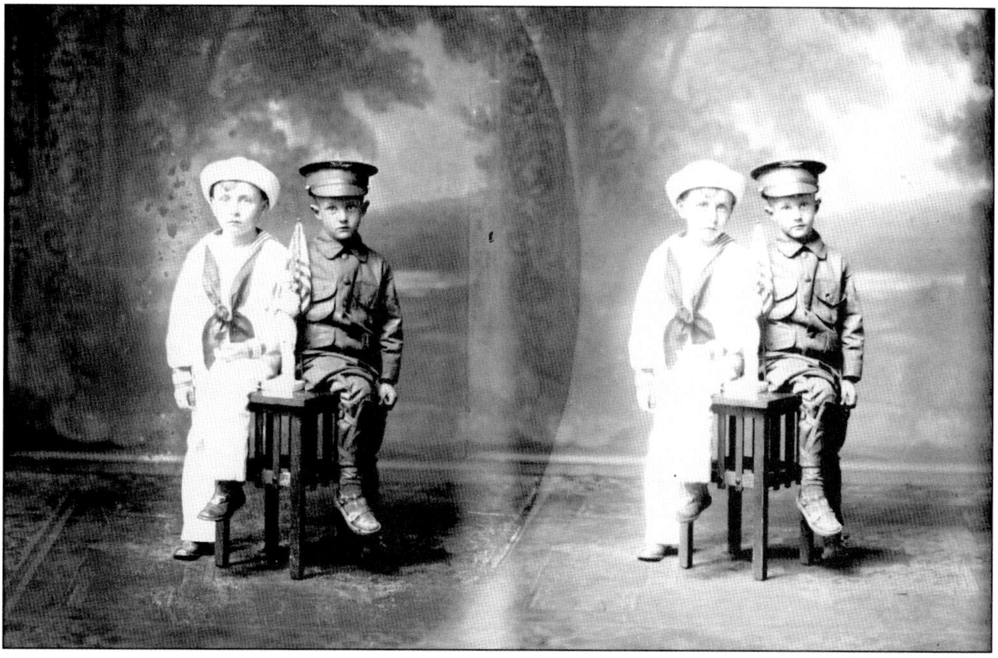

These two patriotic cuties pose for this photograph in May 1918. The boy on the left is wearing a World War I–style naval uniform, while the boy on the right sports an army uniform. On the table between the boys is an Uncle Sam figurine with an American flag. During World War I, Grand Island rallied to support the troops. Displays of patriotism like this were common.

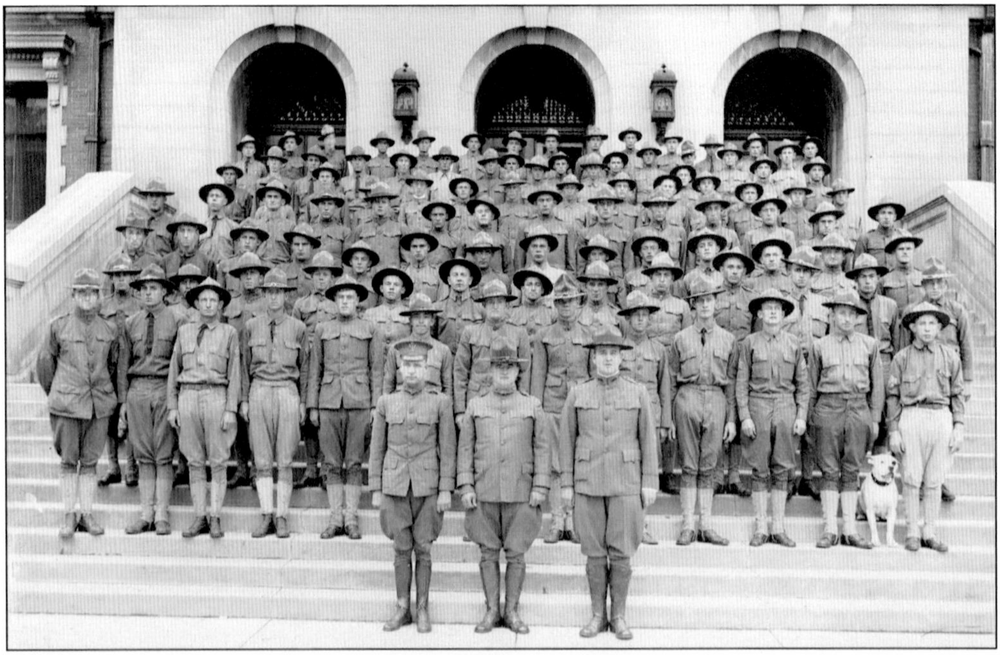

In the image above, members of Grand Island's Company M, 5th Infantry Regiment of the Nebraska National Guard pose on the front steps of the Hall County Courthouse on September 11, 1917. The regiment was called into federal service during World War I on July 14, 1917, and departed for Camp Cody, New Mexico, on September 14, 1917. The regiment's designation was later changed to the 134 Infantry, part of the 34th Division. The company's three commissioned officers are standing in the foreground. They are, from left to right, 1st Lt. William R. Gilchrist, Capt. Leo G. Allan (company commander), and 2nd Lt. Fred H. Schuff. In the lower image, also taken in September 1917, Civil War veterans stand at the top of the stairs behind a group of young men drafted into service during World War I.

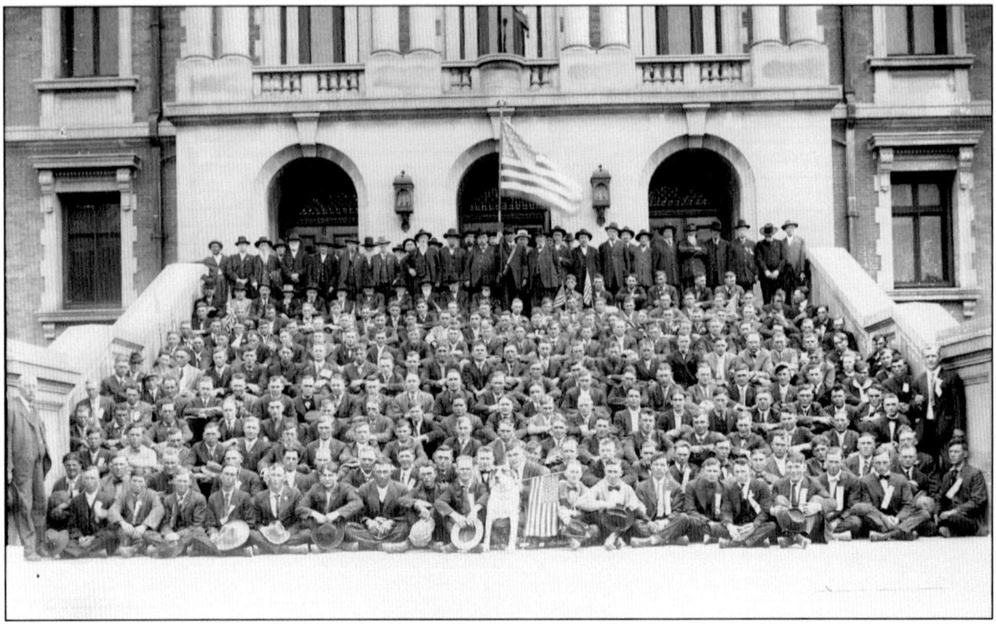

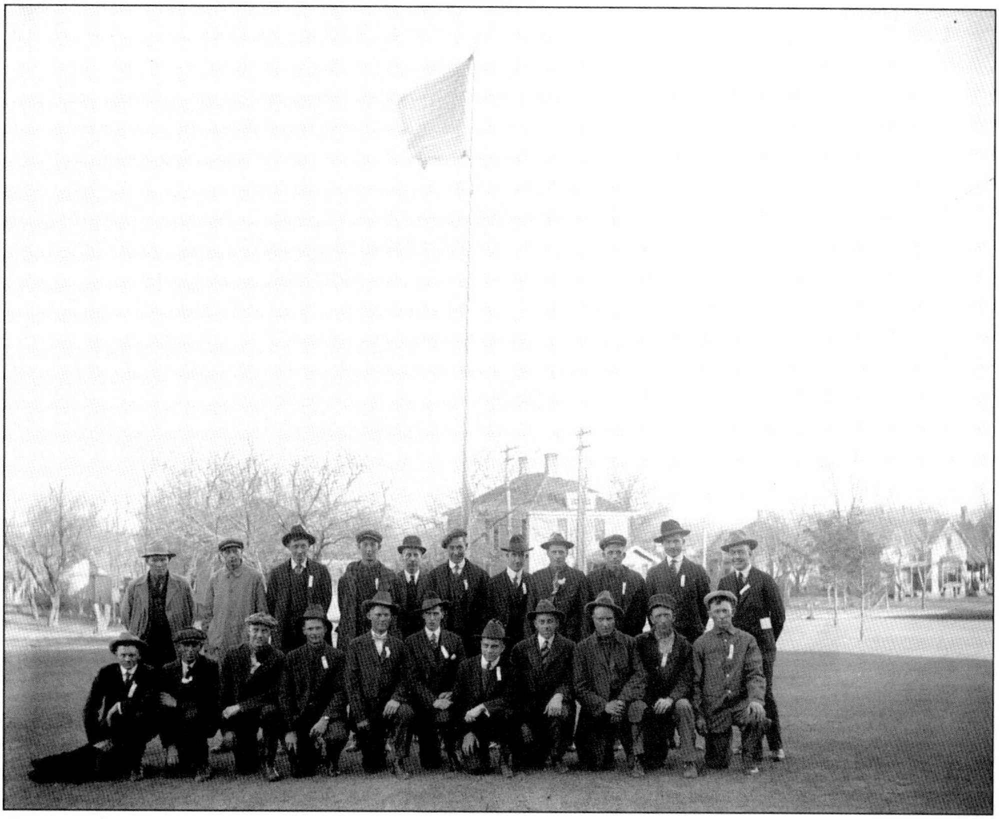

On March 5, 1918, the last 15 percent of Hall County's first quota for the national draft during World War I left Grand Island on a special train on the St. Joseph and Grand Island Railroad at 4:30 a.m. Before they boarded their train, the 22 men posed for this photograph. Despite the early hour, about 125 friends, family, and businessmen gathered at the depot to bid the draftees farewell.

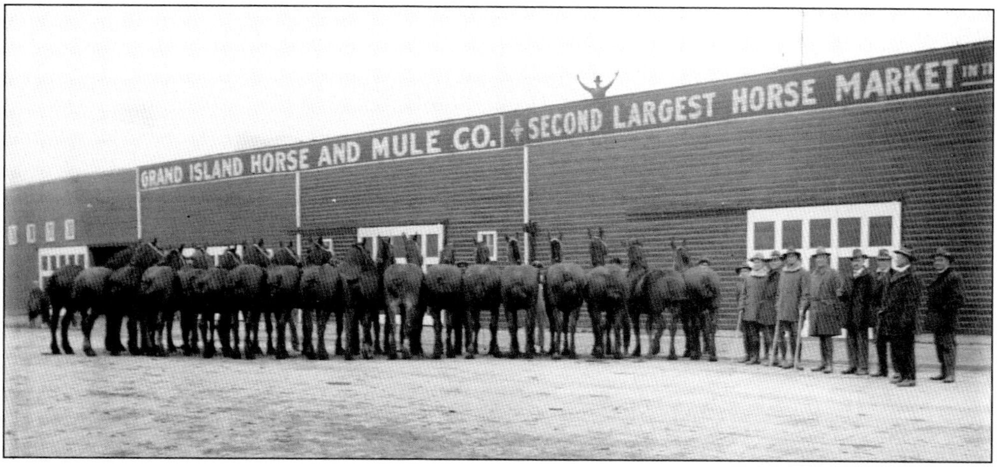

In this photograph, 18 of Grand Island Horse and Mule Company's finest draft horses line up in front of the sale barns in November 1917. According to information found with this image, they were on their way to the war front to become artillery horses for the U.S. Army. To the right of the horses, several men can be seen. Five of the men are wearing military uniforms.

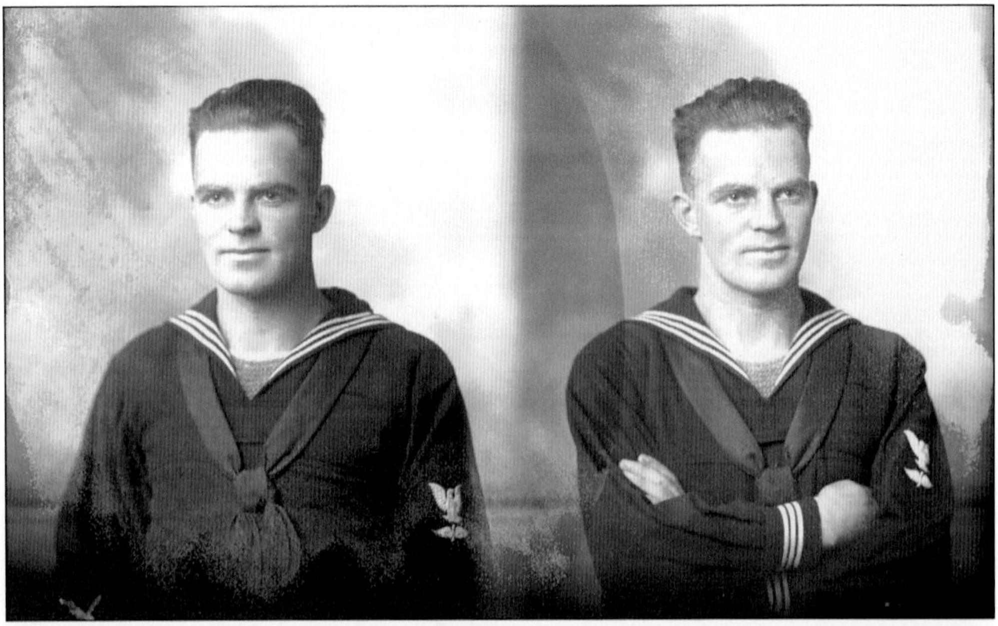

Frank Weiland proudly wears his navy uniform in this series of photographs taken in December 1918. According to his World War I draft registration card, he was 21 years old and working at the Fairmont Creamery when he registered for service. His draft card also says Weiland had blue eyes and red hair. After the war, he attended the Grand Island Baptist College and became a public school teacher.

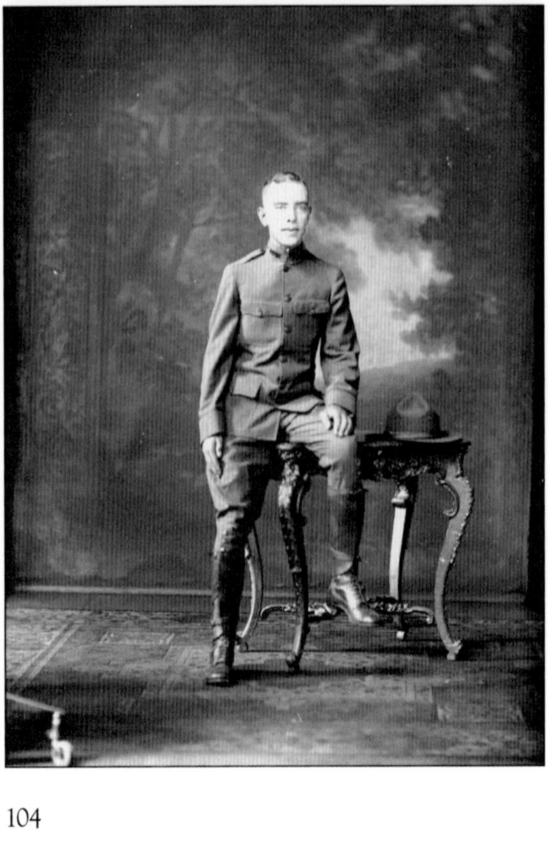

On May 11, 1917, Harold Prince enlisted in the army and entered into officer's training. He received a commission of second lieutenant and sailed for France in August 1917, shortly after this photograph was taken. Prince was promoted to first lieutenant and was part of the army of occupation after the armistice was signed. He mustered out of the service on May 30, 1919, and returned to Grand Island to continue his law practice.

Pvt. Maurice Skeets poses for this portrait in September 1918. Skeets was born in Grand Island on December 5, 1888. He enlisted at Sterling, Colorado, on September 13, 1918. He served with the Ordnance Corp, 6th Supply Arsenal at Rariton. After his discharge in March 1919, he returned to Grand Island to work for the Union Pacific and later as a Hall County sheriff's deputy.

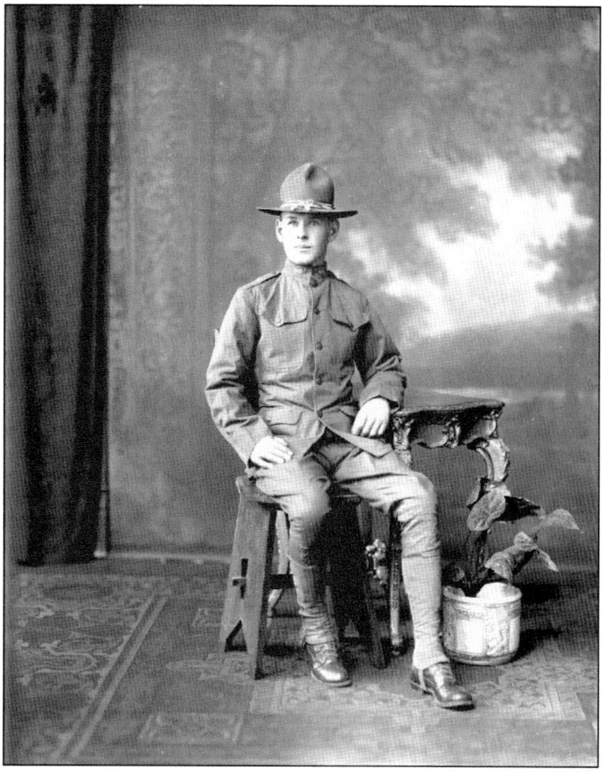

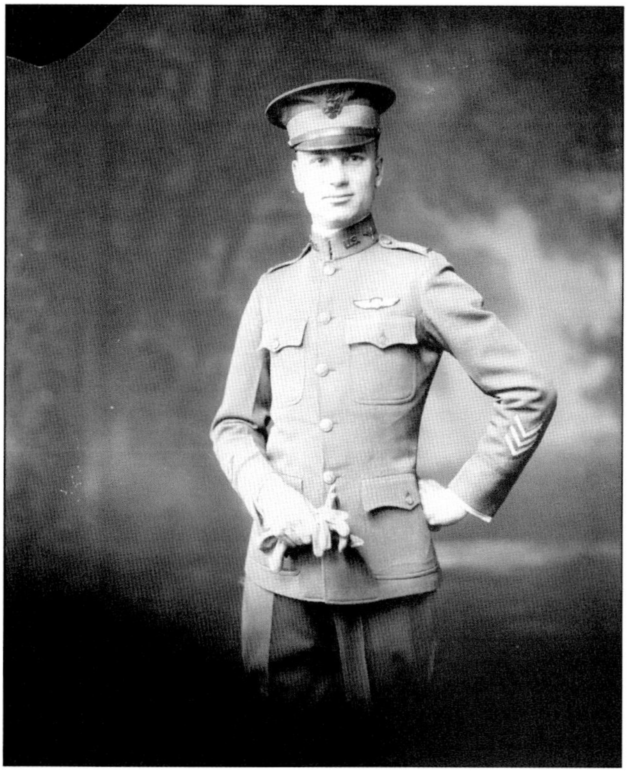

In this photograph, Hubert Wilson has a jaunty stance while wearing his World War I army dress uniform in May 1919. Visible on his uniform is a double-winged insignia above his breast pocket and a collar insignia with two wings and an airplane propeller. This meant that Wilson was a junior aviator or reserve aviator with the Aviation Section of the Signal Corp.

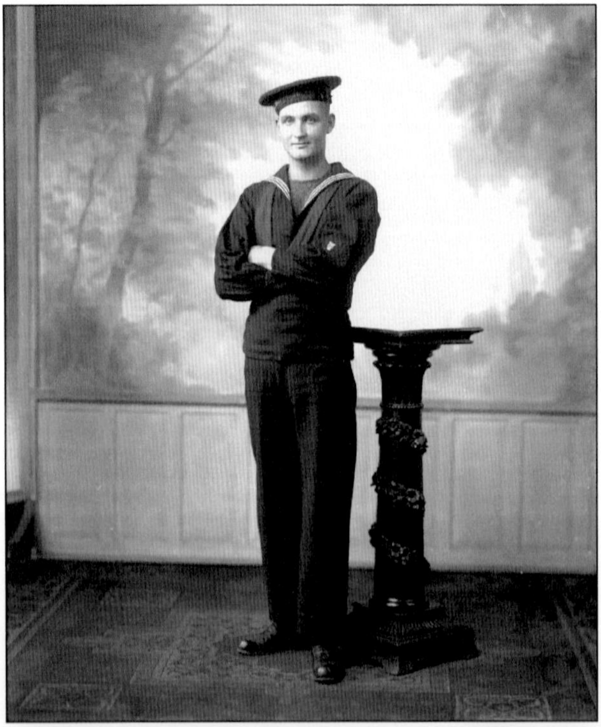

This young man poses for Julius Leschinsky in November 1918. The name in Leschinsky's business records is W. L. or M. L. Henninger of Shelton. This full-length pose allows a look at a typical World War I naval blue dress uniform for enlisted sailors. Note the insignia on his upper left sleeve. It indicates he was a musician first or second class.

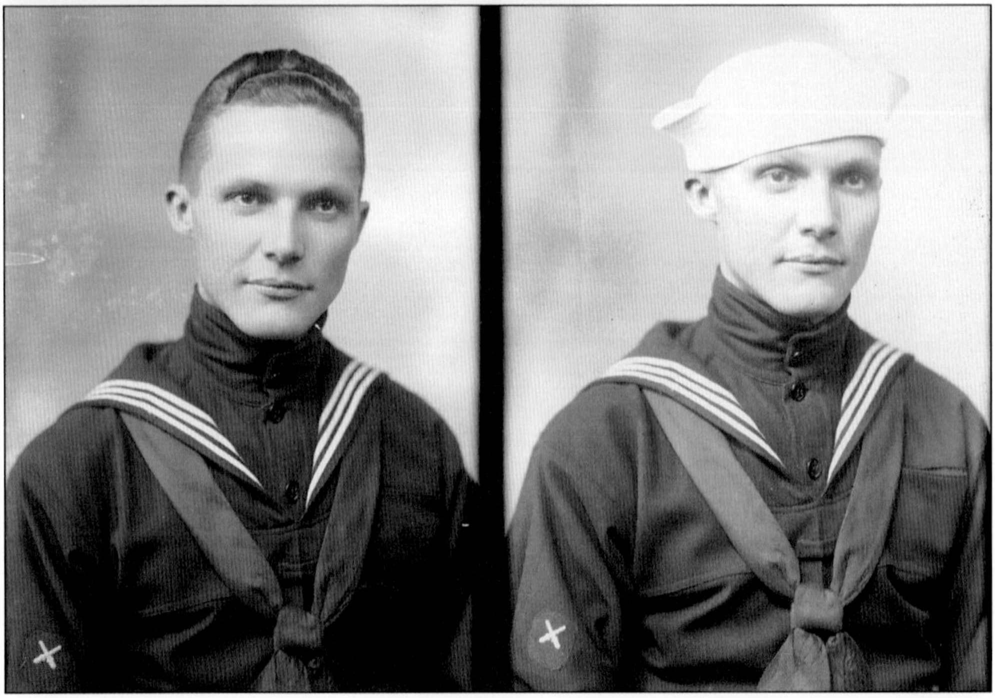

Earl Maddox was born in Aurora on September 11, 1890. He enlisted in the navy on April 27, 1918, in Hall County. The insignia on his sleeve that can be seen in this photograph indicates he was a gunners mate. Maddox was discharged in March 1919 and took up farming in Cheyenne Wells, Colorado.

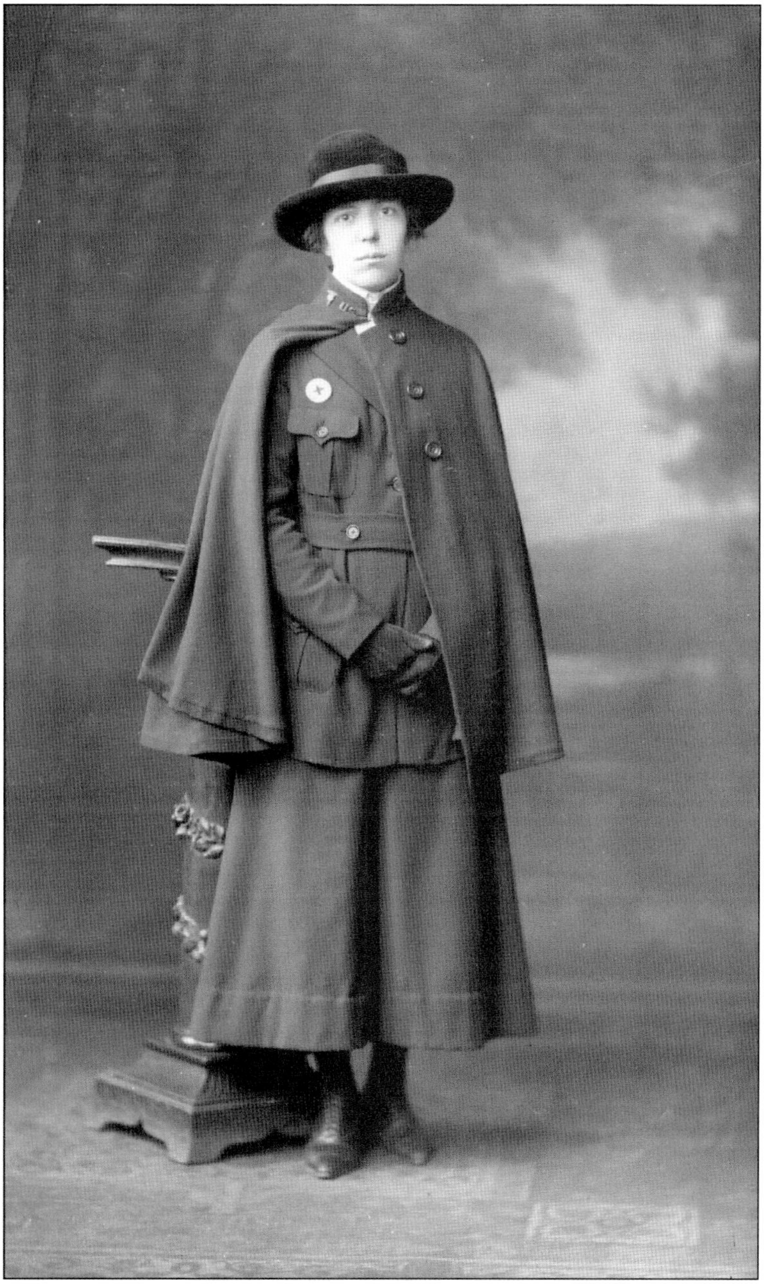

Beulah Marsh poses in her United States Army Nurse's outdoor uniform. Marsh was a Red Cross nurse before enlisting in the Army Nurses Corp. Therefore she was able to retain the Red Cross insignia seen above her breast pocket. She is also wearing the famous red lined cape of dark blue worn by Red Cross nurses. As seen in this photograph, the cape was worn over the shoulder to expose the red lining. On the collar of her cape, the caduceus, the winged staff and serpents of the Medical Corp, and the letters "U.S." can be seen. Marsh was born in Grand Island on August 30, 1899. She enlisted at Grand Island on July 5, 1918, and served at the base hospital at Camp Pike. After her discharge on January 4, 1919, Marsh returned to nursing at the Grand Island General Hospital.

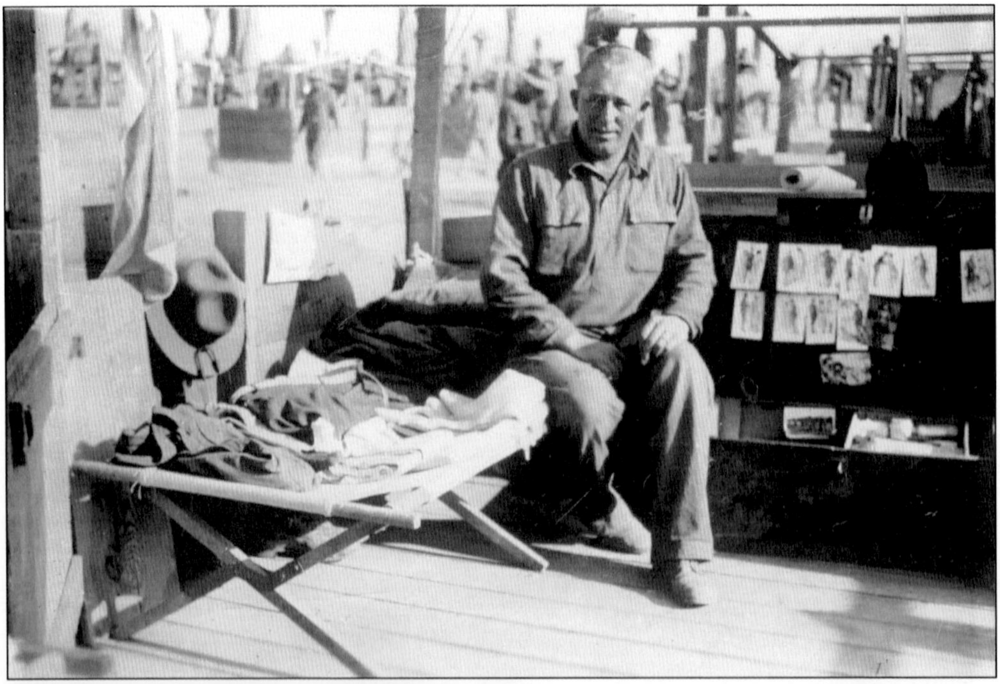

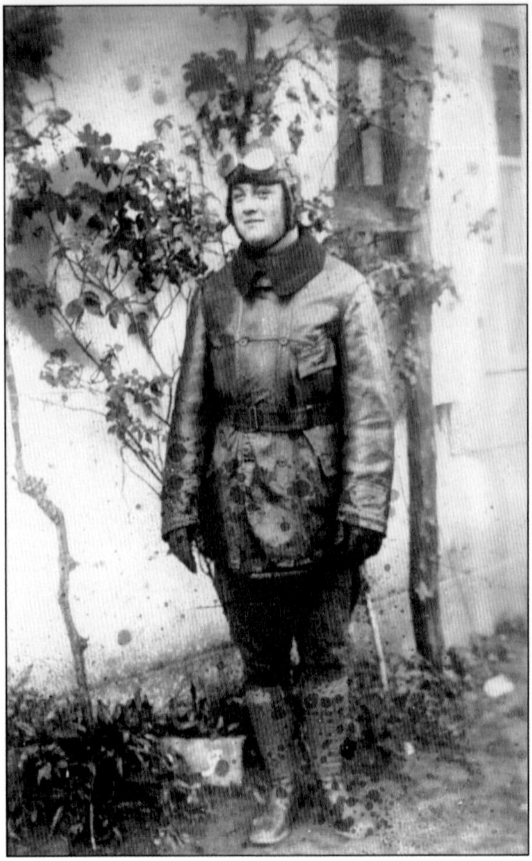

The two images seen here were sent to loved ones living in Grand Island by soldiers serving in World War I. The snapshots were taken to the Leschinsky Studio where they were copied. A photograph copy stand would have been used to minimize distortion and glare. The process created a glass-plate negative, which then could be used to print as many copies as the customer wanted. In the top photograph, a man is seated on a cot in an outdoor barrack. Photographs and postcards have been pinned to the barrack's wooden walls. In the lower photograph, Adolph Betz poses in a leather jacket and helmet with goggles. Betz was a first sergeant with Company M, 134th Infantry, 34th Division. He sent this snapshot home to his sweetheart Ruth Fairbanks, whom he later married.

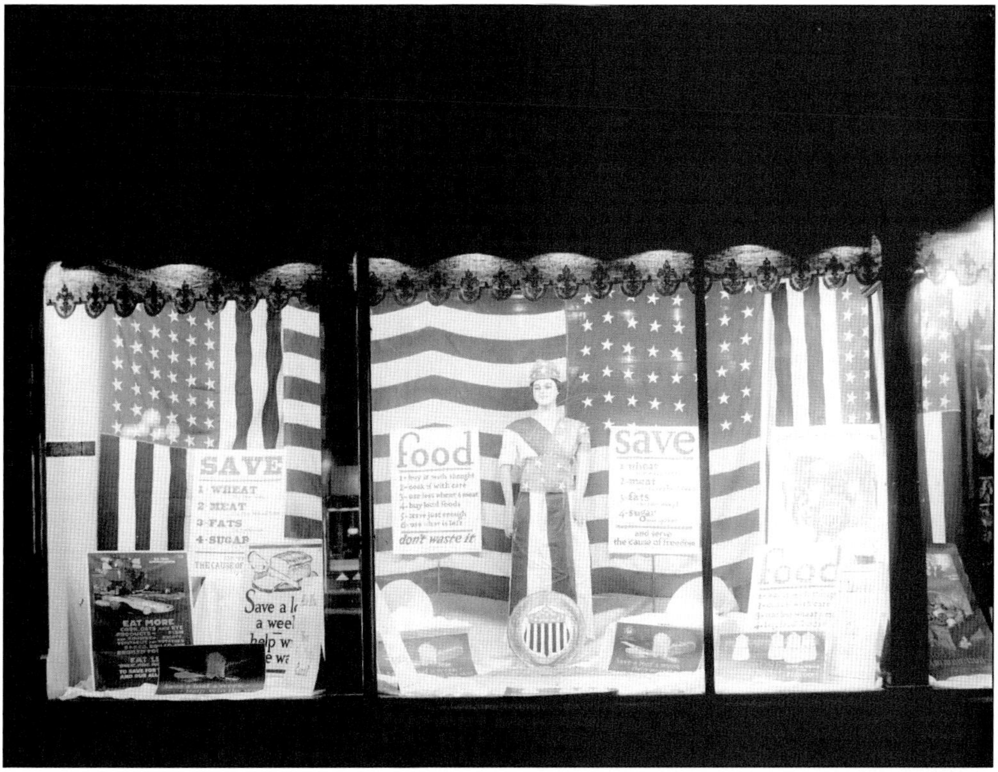

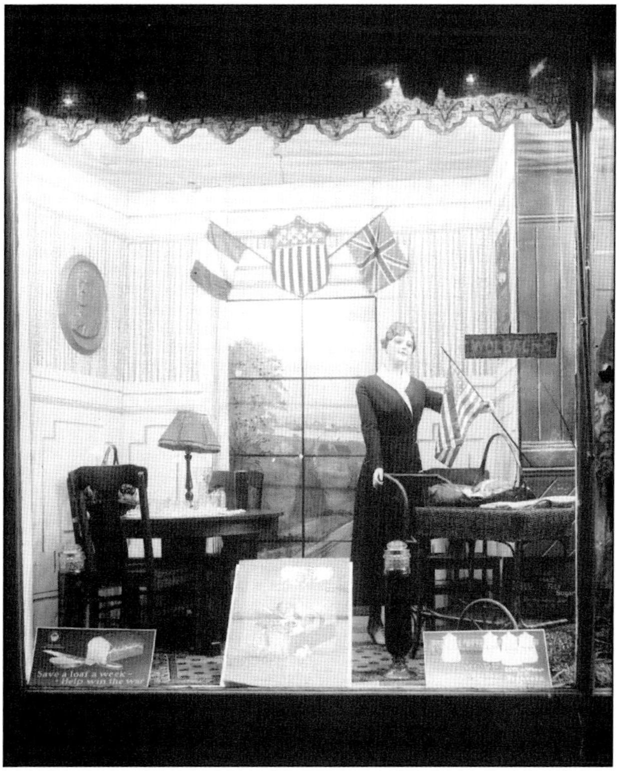

During World War I, the Food Administration encouraged citizens to do their part for the war by rationing certain foods. In these two photographs, the Martin's Dry Goods Store (above) and Wolbach's Department Store (at right) have created elaborate patriotic windows in support of the war effort. The windows display several propaganda posters from the food administration. In the Martin's window, posters claimed that in order to do one's part in the cause of freedom, one should use corn, fish, beans, and syrups as alternatives to wheat, meats, and sugar. In the Wolbach's window, one poster suggests that saving a loaf of bread a week would help win the war. According to the posters, wheat, meat, fats, and sugars should be saved for the needy soldiers.

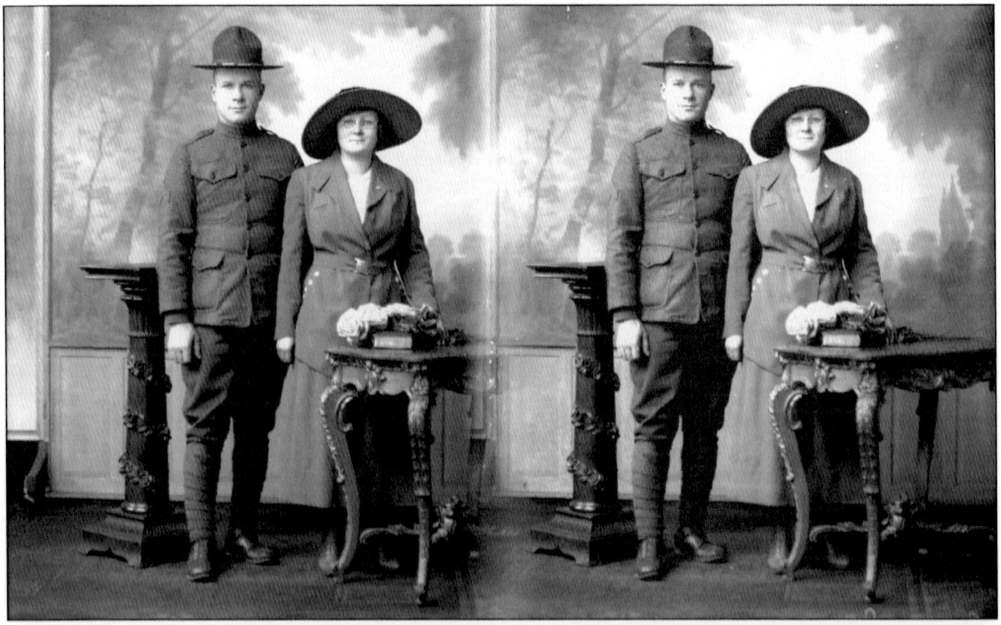

The young couple featured in this photograph taken in January 1919 is Calvin and Jessie Sautter. Calvin enlisted in the army on September 5, 1918, at Grand Island. He served with the machine gun company of the 97th Division. He was discharged from Camp Cody on December 6, 1918, shortly before this photograph was taken. As demonstrated by Jessie's clothing, even civilian fashions during this era took on a military flare.

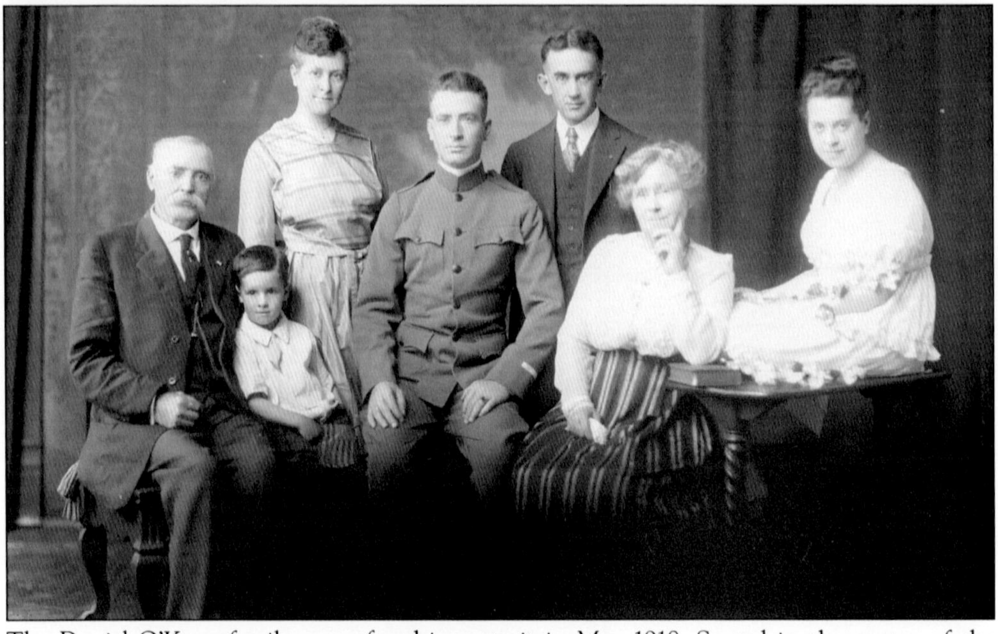

The Daniel O'Kane family poses for this portrait in May 1918. Seated in the center of the photograph, a position usually reserved for the head of the family, is Thomas O'Kane. Thomas enlisted in the army in May 1917. On January 1, 1918, he was sent to officer's school. After receiving his commission, Thomas was assigned to Company F, 143rd Infantry and sent to France, where he was cited for bravery.

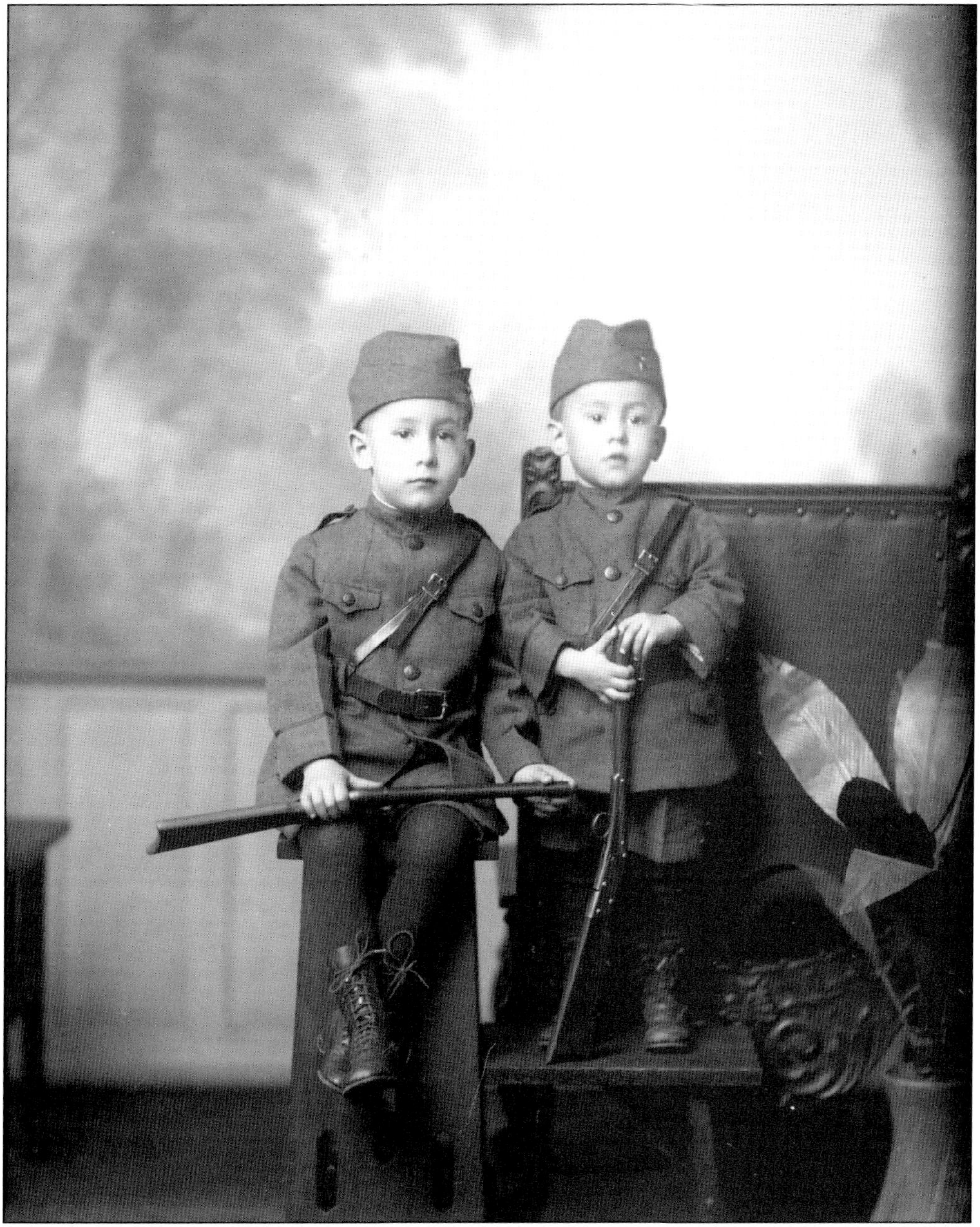

The two precious little boys featured in this photograph are likely Bernard (left) and Harold (right) Mangelsen. They were the sons of Paul and Antoinette Mangelsen. Bernard and Harold are wearing recreations of World War I army uniforms, complete with leather holsters and toy rifles. The boys could be dressed for any number of rallies, parades, or benefits held to support the war efforts on the home front. Taken in December 1918, Bernard would have been about four years old and Harold would have been about three at the time of this photograph. As an adult, Harold became the founder of an Omaha variety store that grew into a large wholesale and retail craft supply operation called Mangelsen's. His son Thomas D. is a well-known wildlife photographer whose photographs have appeared in national publications for National Geographic Society, Smithsonian, and Audubon.

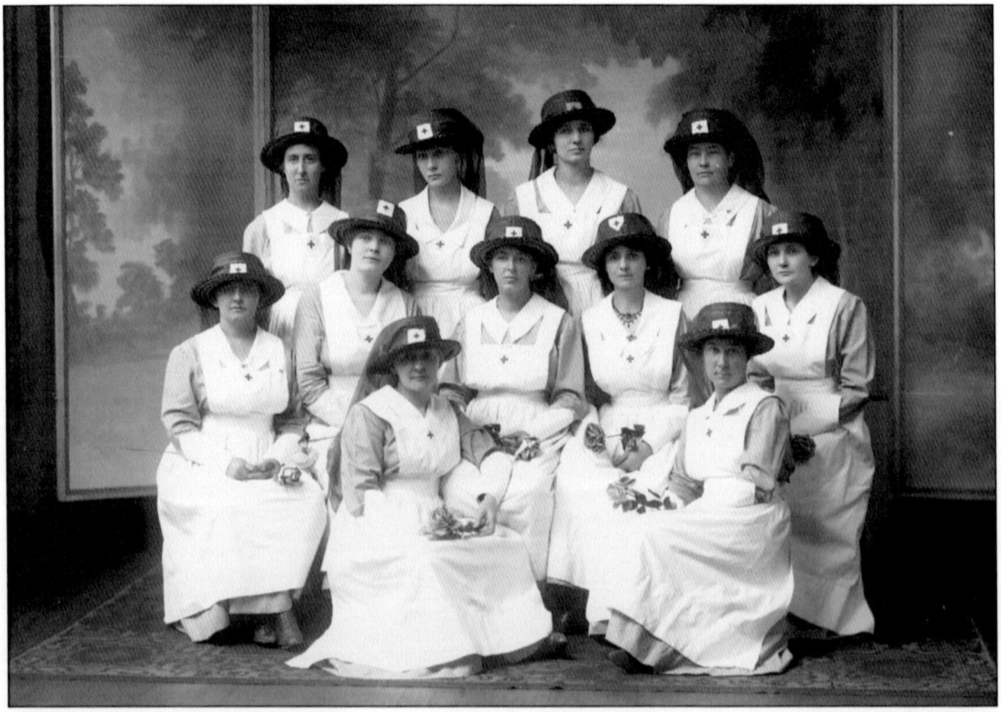

In the summer of 1918, the Hall County Red Cross organized a canteen at the Union Pacific depot. Canteen volunteers, like the ones seen in this April 1919 photograph, served drinks, ice cream, sandwiches, and other delicacies to soldiers on their way to training camps or on their way home from the war. The Grand Island Canteen served 57,890 servicemen from 1918 to 1919.

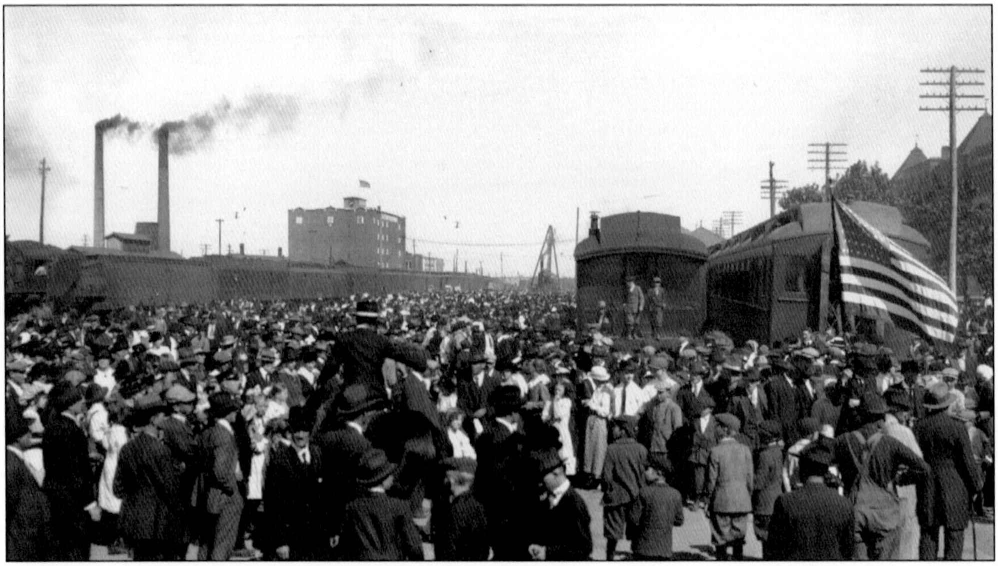

In this photograph a large crowd is gathered at Grand Island's Union Pacific depot. It is unclear if this image captures the send off of the troops as they left for World War I or if the crowd is welcoming the troops home. The distinctive roofline of the Koehler Hotel can be seen at the far right.

Eight

Whimsy, Weird, and Wonderful

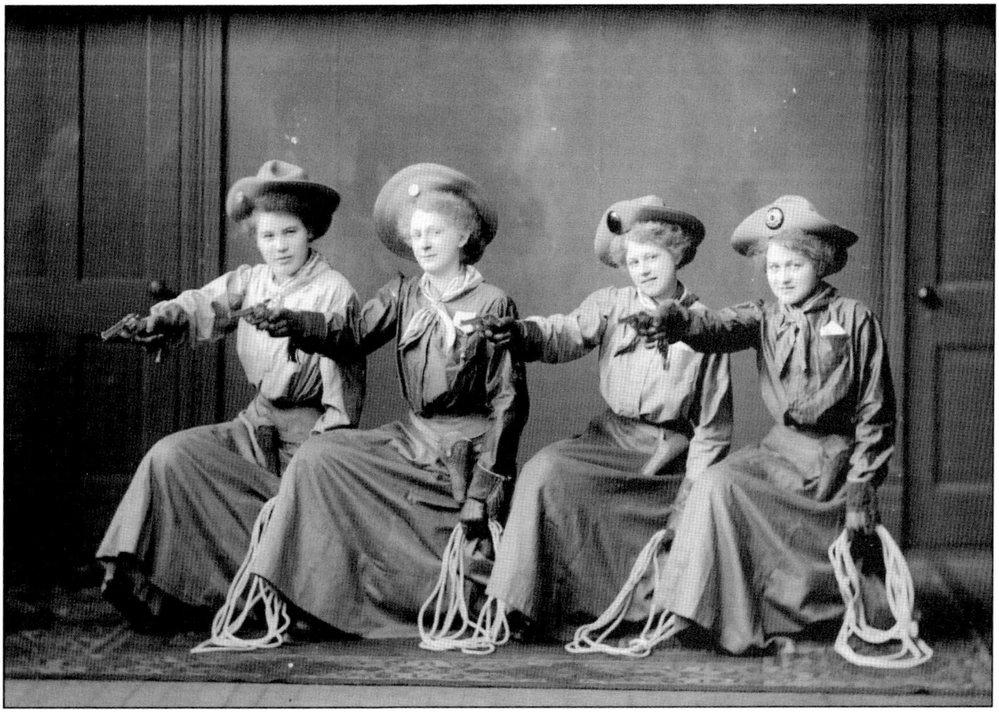

These four young cowgirls appear ready for a rootin' tootin' good time as they pose in costumes complete with lassos and leather holsters for their pistols. Augusta Peters commissioned this photograph in February 1911. Augusta was the daughter of Edward and Amelia (Seier) Peters. Born in 1890, Augusta married Louis Mohr on January 28, 1913.

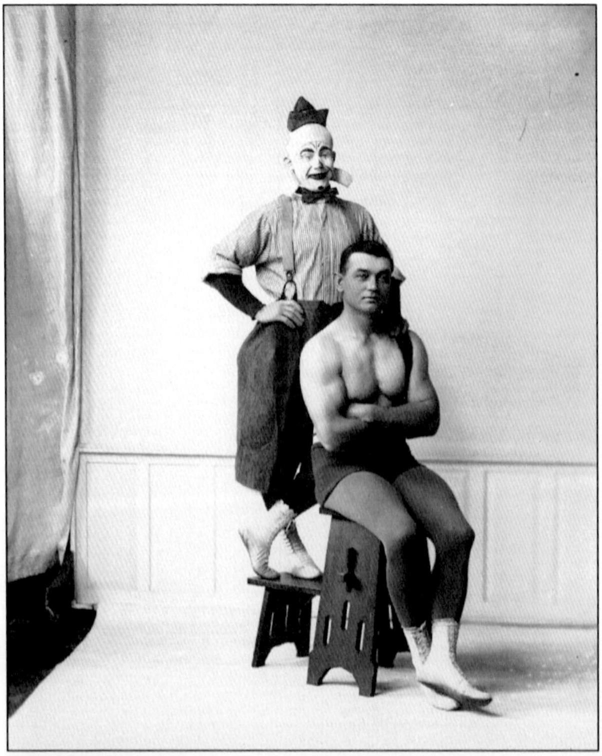

Not much is known about the two men featured in this photograph taken in January 1915. According to Julius Leschinsky's business records, the names associated with this image are "Lade and Smith." They could be the strongman and a clown from a traveling circus or part of a vaudeville act. Both were popular forms of entertainment in 1915. They could also be local boys dressed for a costume party.

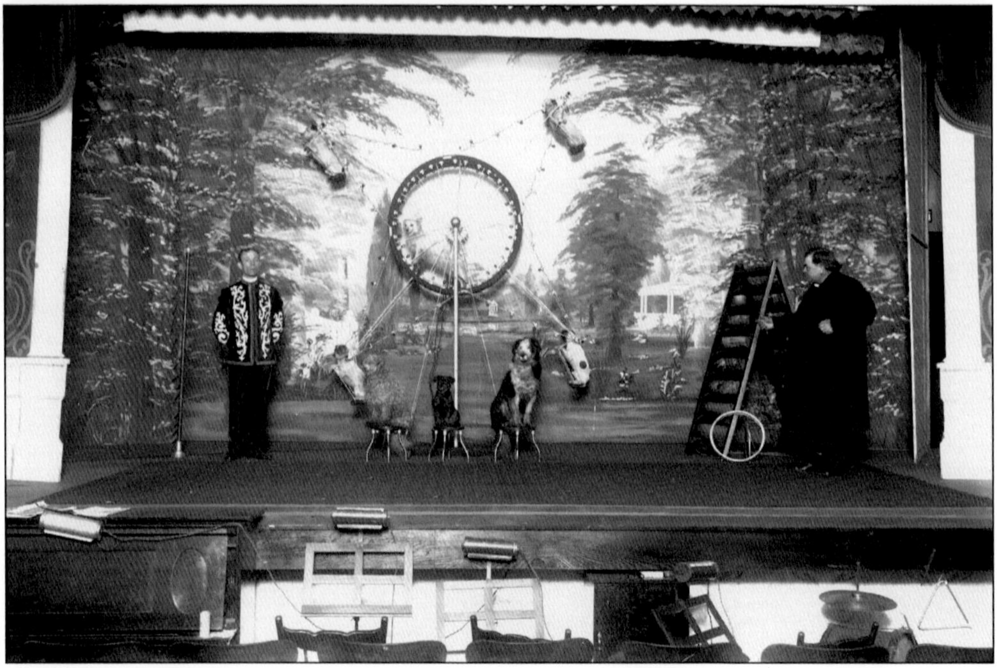

This photograph, taken in September 1915, captures a vaudeville trick dog act on the stage of the Majestic Theater at 214 West Second Street. Three dogs are sitting on stools at center stage. Behind them four smaller dogs ride in baskets attached to a Ferris wheel. Another dog can be seen inside the Ferris wheel. Two men, likely the dogs' handlers, are also onstage.

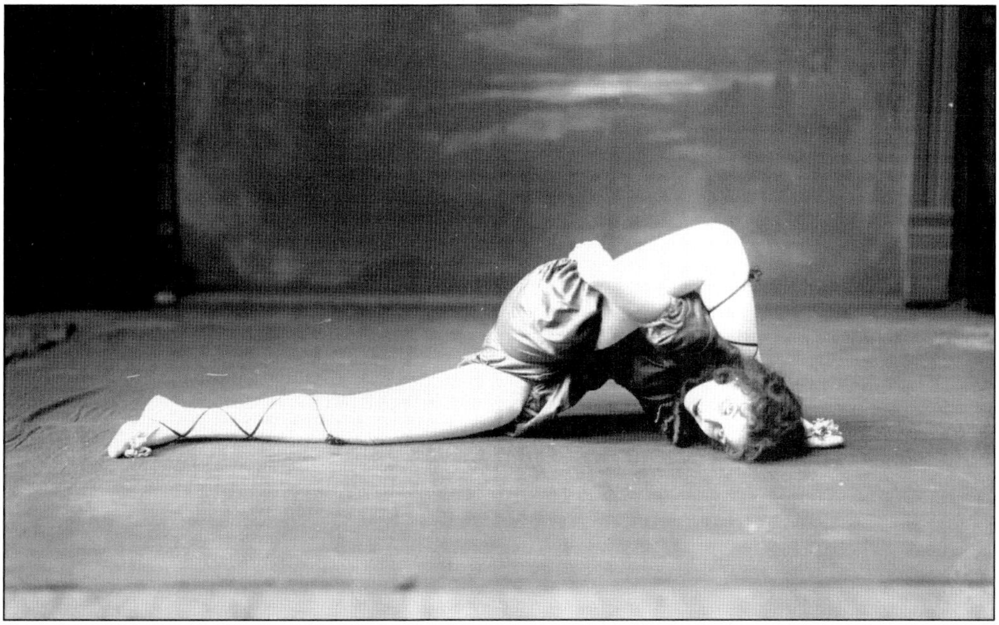

Little is known about this talented young lady. According to Leschinsky's business records, this photograph was commissioned in November 1915 by Miss Roberts. She was likely a traveling vaudevillian who performed at one of Grand Island's theaters. In 1915, the Majestic Theater was known for booking well-known vaudeville acts. The Majestic promised if the show was not worth the price of admission it would refund the money.

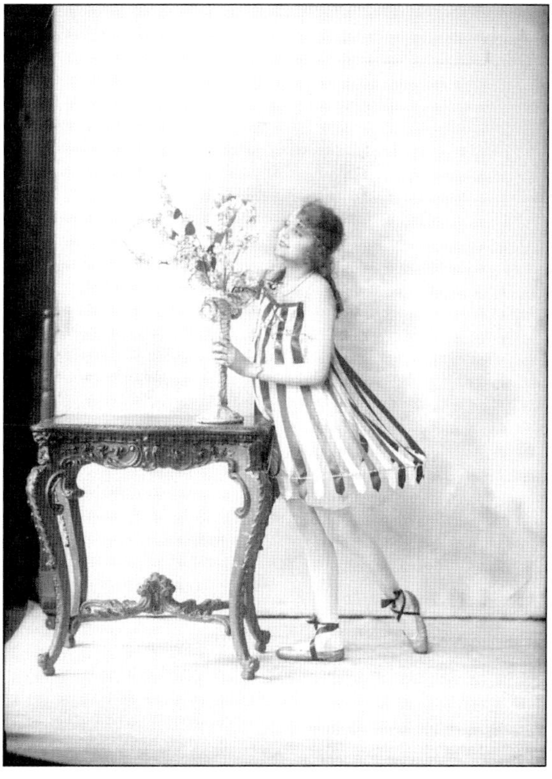

Taken in June 1918, the young girl in this photograph strikes a dramatic pose. Her dress is comprised of ribbons of alternating colors sewn together at the bodice and allowed to flow out at the bottom where they attach to a metal hoop. Her cotton bloomers can be seen through the ribbons. She is also wearing colored silk tights and ballet slippers.

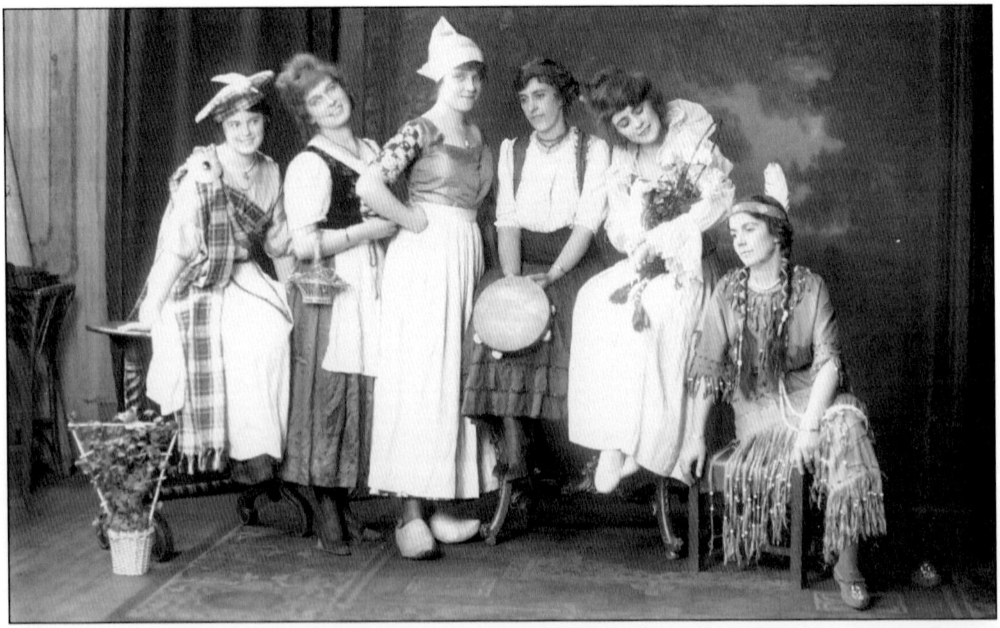

"Miss Gove and her Pioneer Girls" performed as a variety act at the Majestic Theater during the last week of October 1916. They promised a program with good music that was well played, historical, instructive, and fun. In this photograph, the five female performers don costumes from different cultures from around the world. According to the newspaper, matinee performances were 10¢ and evenings were 15¢.

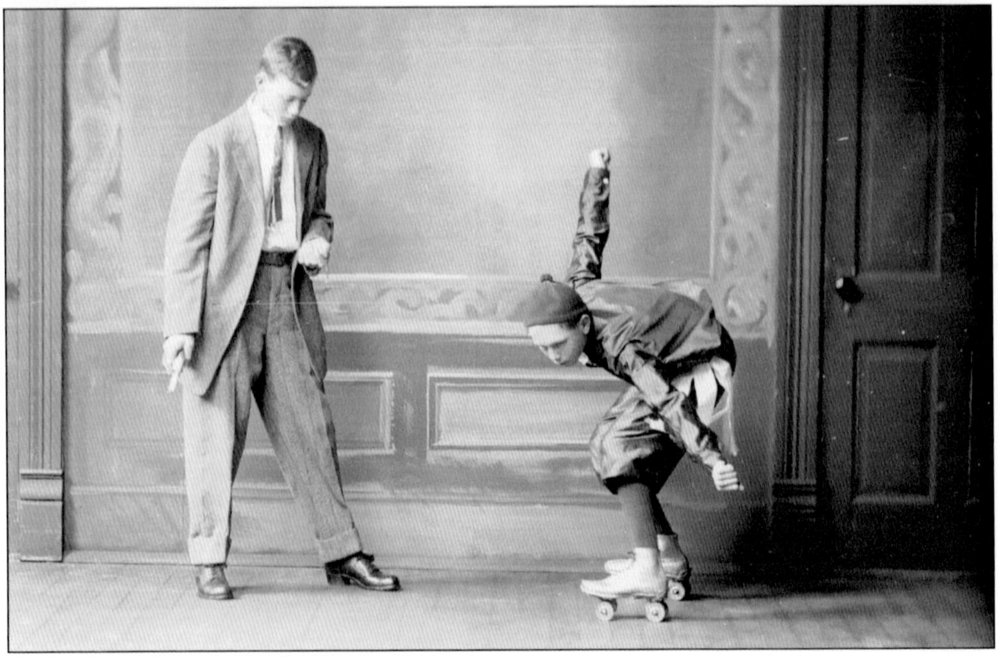

In this photograph, the young man on the left holds a stopwatch and starter pistol. The boy on the right is posing in a racing stance. He is wearing roller skates and what appears to be a silk racing costume. Harris Muhl commissioned the photograph in April 1911. However, it is unclear if Muhl was featured in the photograph.

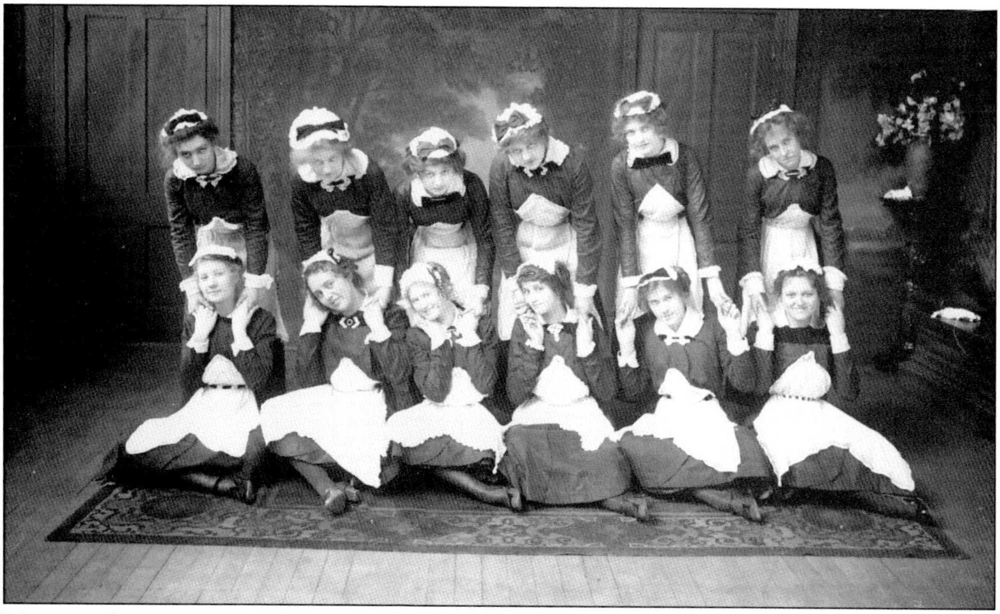

Masquerades were a popular party theme during the early 1900s. The Liederkranz and the Ancient Order of United Workmen both held fancy costume parties, usually in late January or February, near Valentine's Day. As part of the masquerades, many different prizes were awarded, including best group costume. In the photographs seen here, two groups of young ladies pose for Julius Leschinsky in their costumes. Twelve young ladies dressed as French maids pose for the photograph above in February 1913. According to Leschinsky's business records, the ladies in the photograph below were a group of cupids, also known as the Yum-Yum Girls. They pose for their photograph on Valentine's Day in 1911.

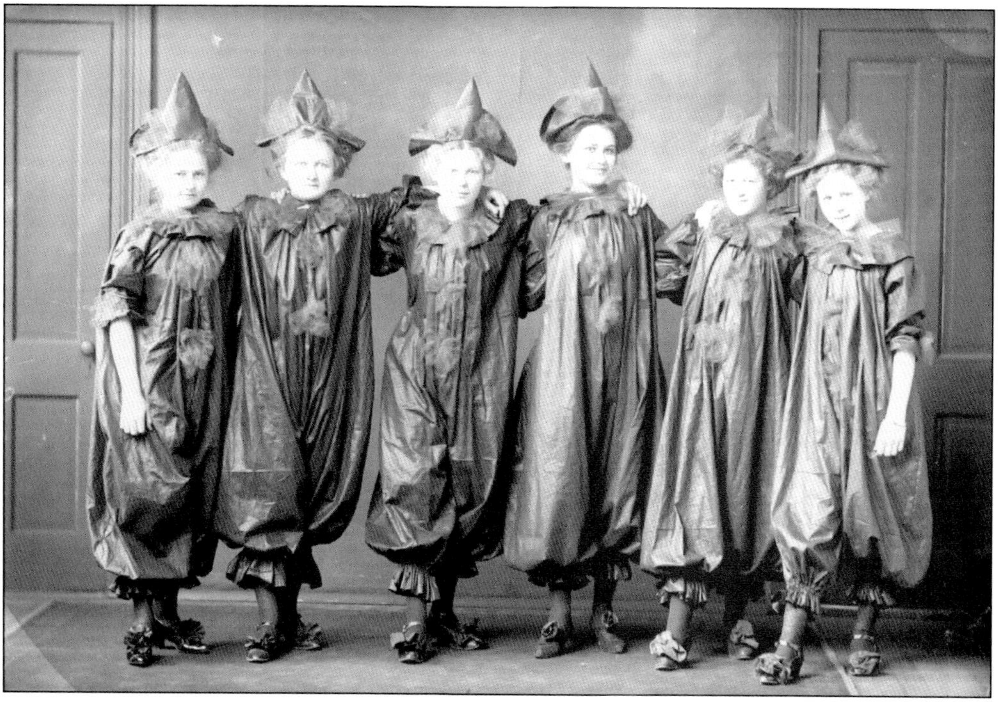

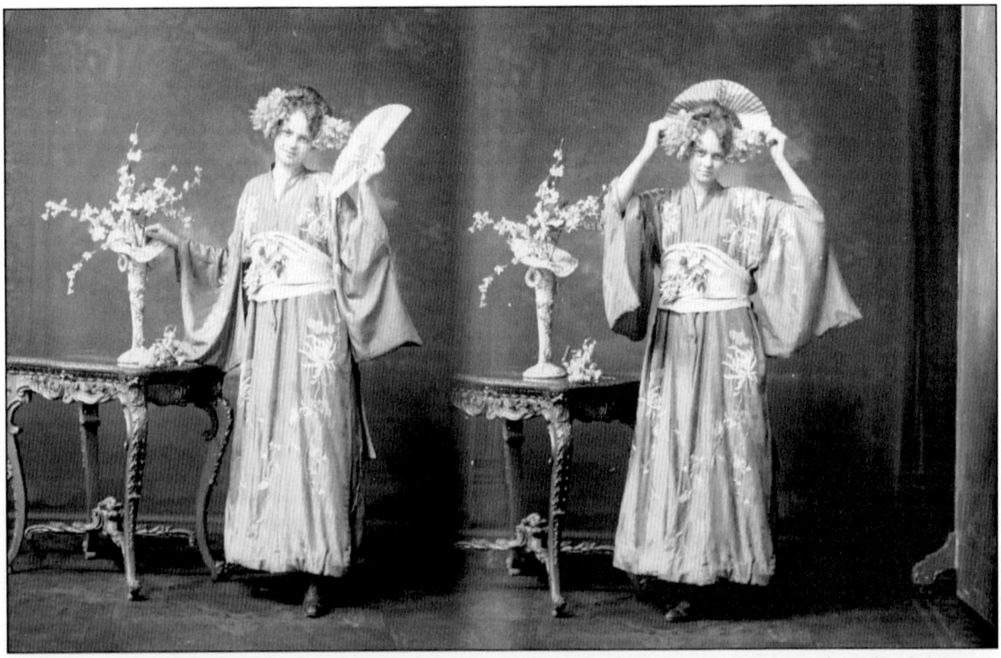

In these photographs, Edith Mehring wears a beautiful silk kimono decorated with elaborate, hand-stitched embroidery. In both images, Mehring is holding a delicate, painted fan. The flowers in her hair add to the innocence of these images. Taken in May 1918, Mehring would have been about 15 years old at the time of these photographs.

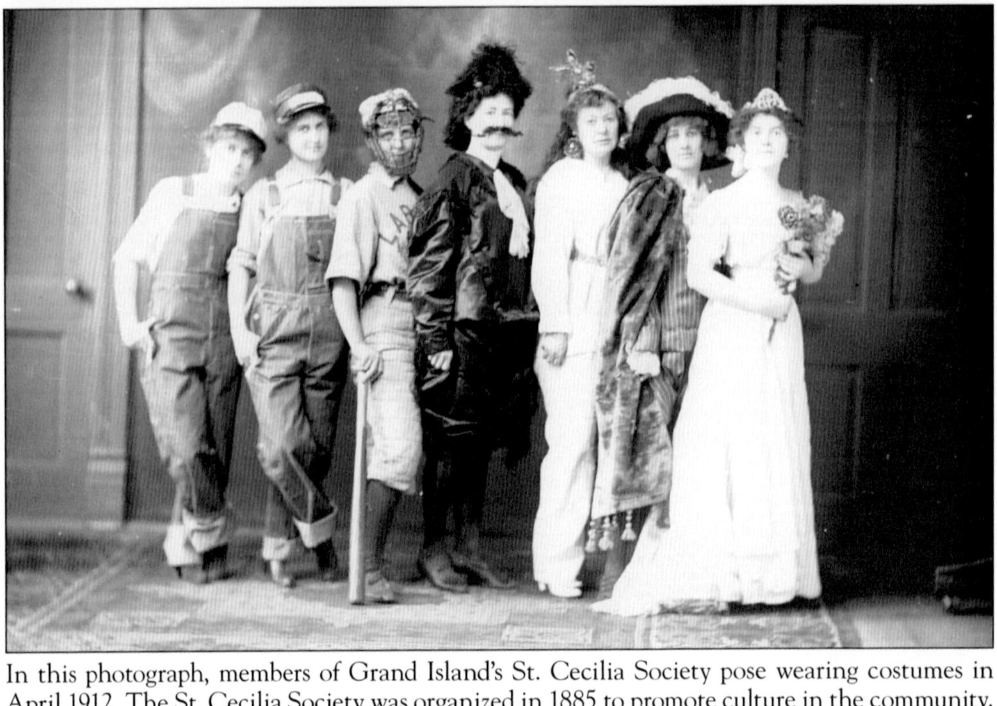

In this photograph, members of Grand Island's St. Cecilia Society pose wearing costumes in April 1912. The St. Cecilia Society was organized in 1885 to promote culture in the community. It was responsible for bringing in distinguished musical artists to Grand Island and held an annual festival of music.

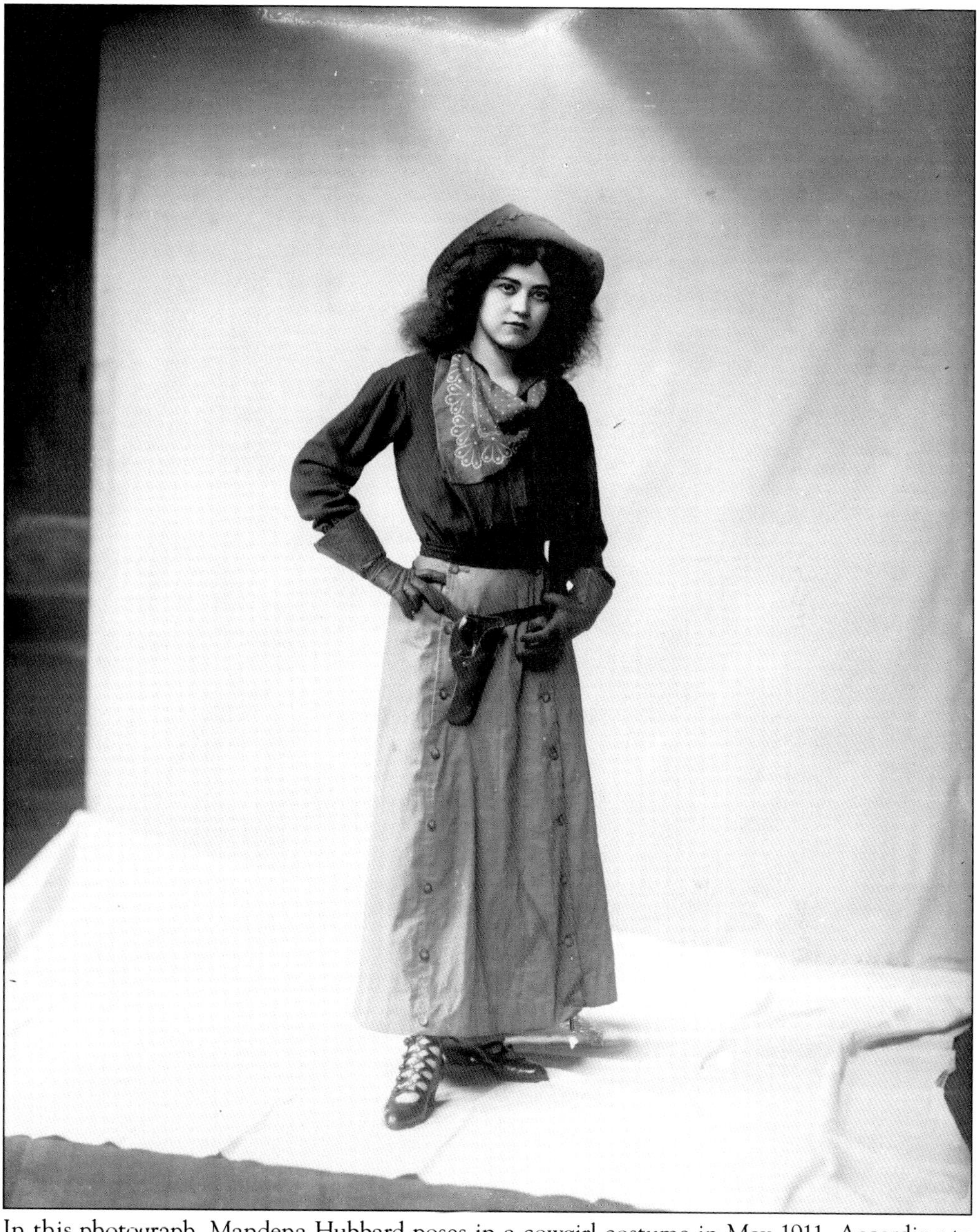

In this photograph, Mandena Hubbard poses in a cowgirl costume in May 1911. According to the 1920 census, Hubbard was an actress and would have been about 20 years old at the time of this photograph. She was likely a member of a touring theatrical company that performed at one of Grand Island's many theaters. Mandena Hubbard is likely a stage name, which would explain why she cannot be found in the 1910 census. This whimsical photograph is one of seven images Julius Leschinsky took of Hubbard in his studio. She also masqueraded as a gypsy, an elegant lady, an innocent girl, and a tomboy, showcasing her diversity as a performer. In this photograph, she is wearing a Western-style hat, leather gauntlet gloves, and a holster with a pistol.

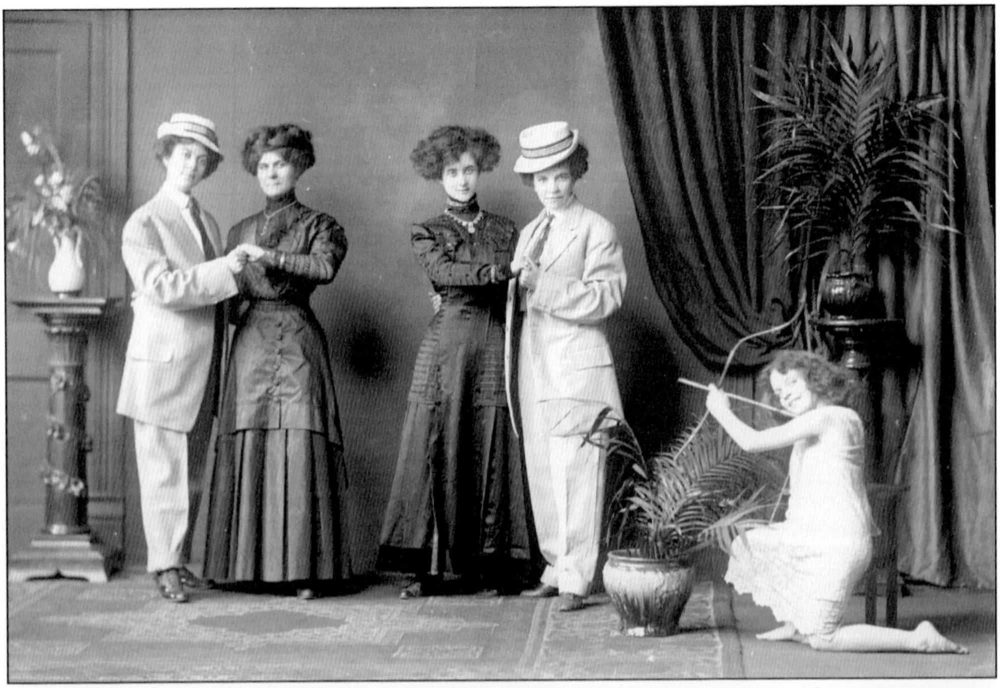

At first glance, this photograph appears to be of two happy couples. However, a closer examination reveals that the two "men" are actually carefully costumed women. They are perhaps acting out a scene from an unknown play with a child playing cupid. The photograph was commissioned in January 1910 by William F. Pierson.

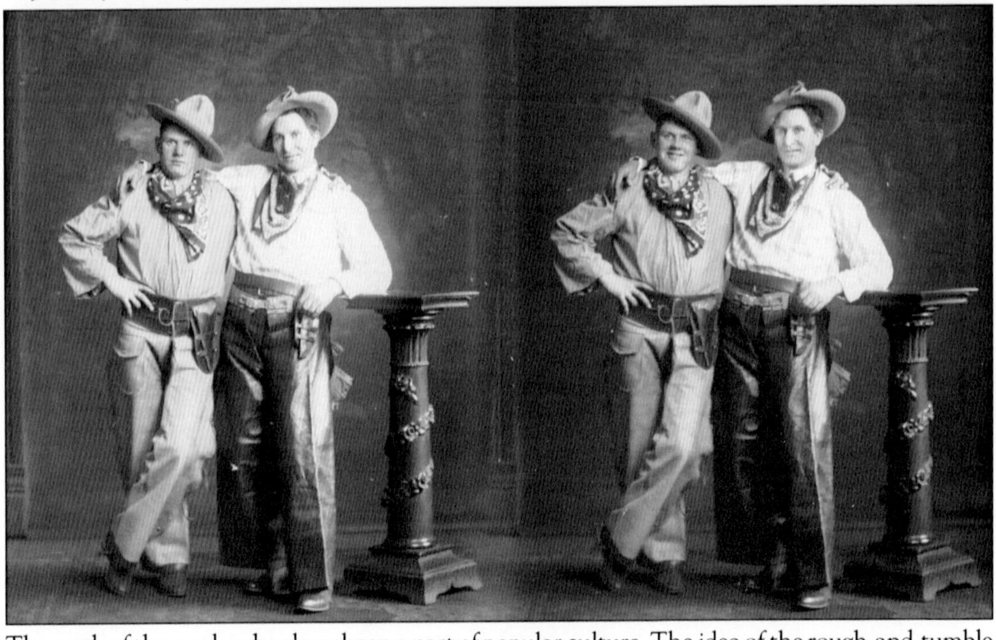

The myth of the cowboy has long been a part of popular culture. The idea of the rough-and-tumble Old West hero was made popular through dime novels and early Hollywood movies. These two young men have put together fine cowboy costumes complete with hats and chaps. The photograph was commissioned by Ray Marsh in February 1918.

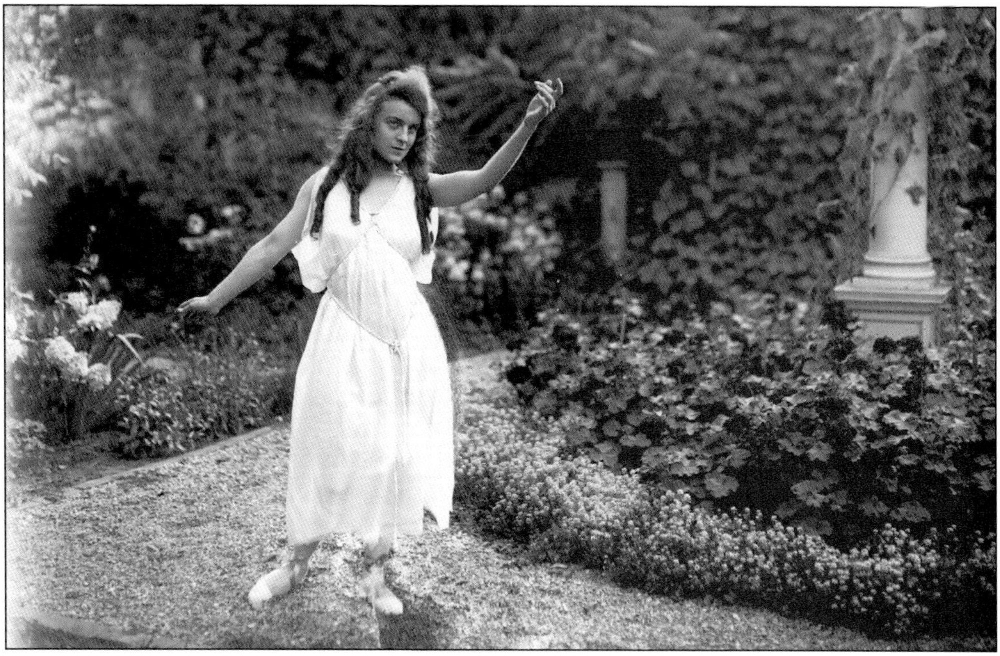

The lovely Vivian Donner poses in the flowing robes of a goddess from Greek mythology in May 1911. This magical garden was in Julius Leschinsky's own backyard at his home at 518 West Koenig Street. Note the many different types of flowers and foliage in Leschinky's garden. A few that are identifiable are hydrangea, white and red geraniums, alyssum, and phlox.

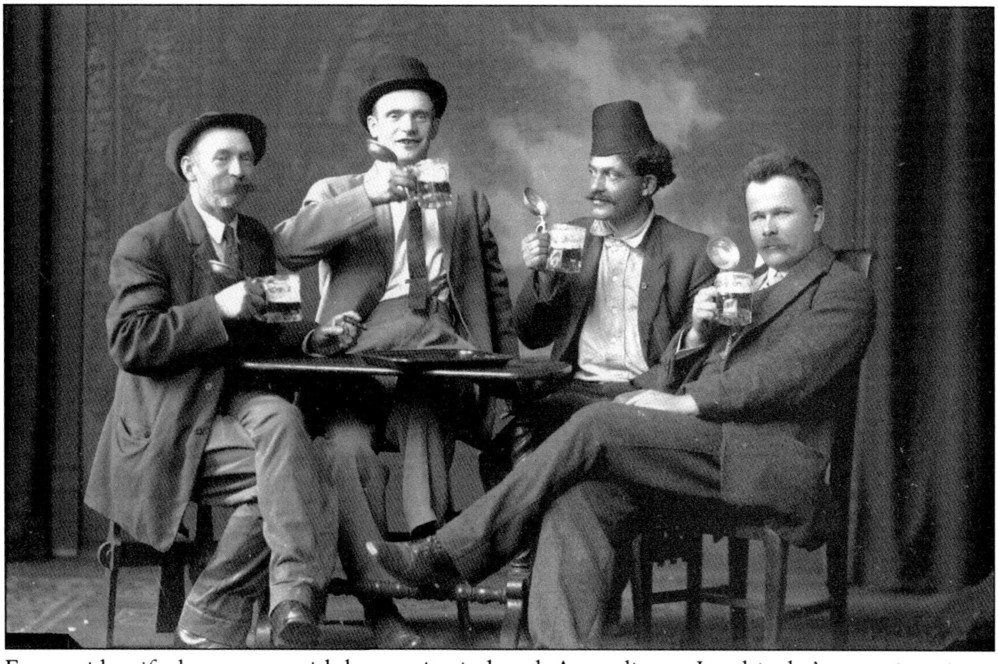

Four unidentified men pose with beer steins in hand. According to Leschinsky's portrait register, Chris Kellner from Deshler commissioned this photograph in June 1915. The man seated at the far left holds a hand-rolled cigar. The third man from the left is wearing a fez, a style of hat that became popular in Turkey during the 19th century.

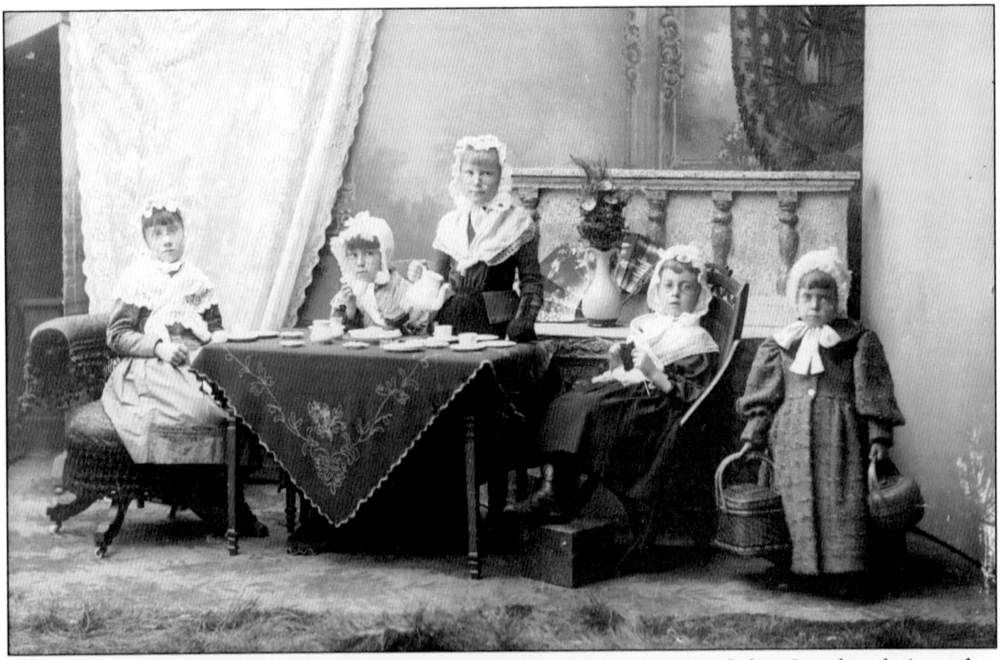

These five little darlings appear to have been holding a tea party in Julius Leschinsky's studio. The girls have dressed themselves in shawls, bonnets, and wire-rimmed glasses to look more adult. One of the girls pretends to knit while seated at the table. The little girl at the far right holds two wicker sewing baskets.

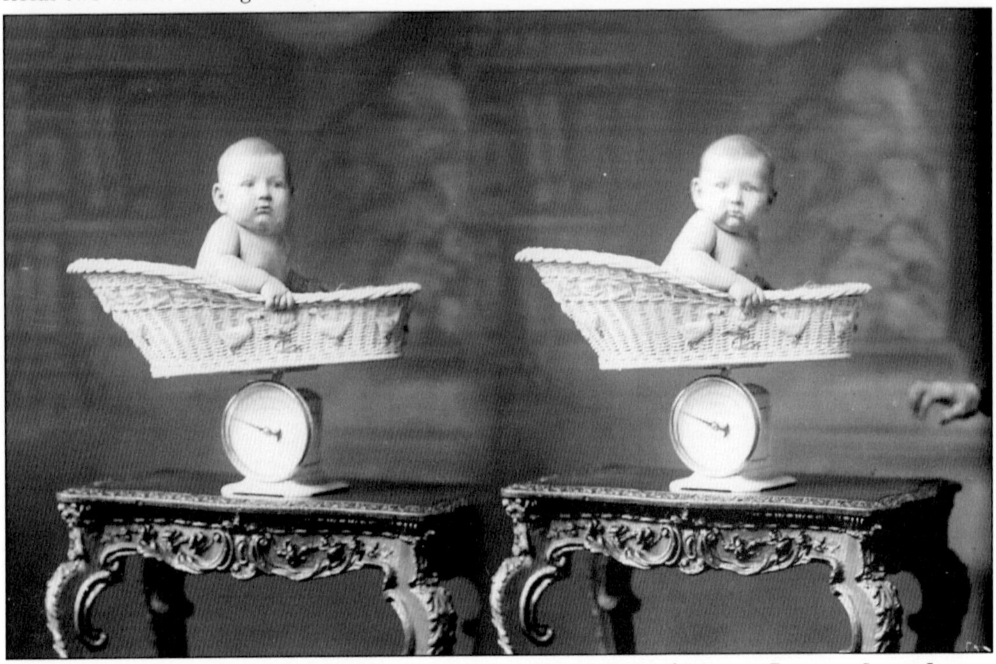

This little cutie is likely Louis R. Burnett Jr., son of Louis R. and Marion Burnett. Louis Jr. was born on May 11, 1917, making him about four months old when he posed for this photograph taken in September 1917. His father worked for the *Grand Island Independent* newspaper as a linotype operator.

This lovely young girl poses with a pair of wooden crutches in June 1914. According to Leschinsky's business records, the photograph was commissioned by Mrs. Fred Roesch. According to the 1910 census, Fred and Wilhelmina Roesch had seven children. Their daughter Olga, 11 years old in 1910, would have been about the right age for this photograph. Unfortunately, it is unknown why she needed the crutches.

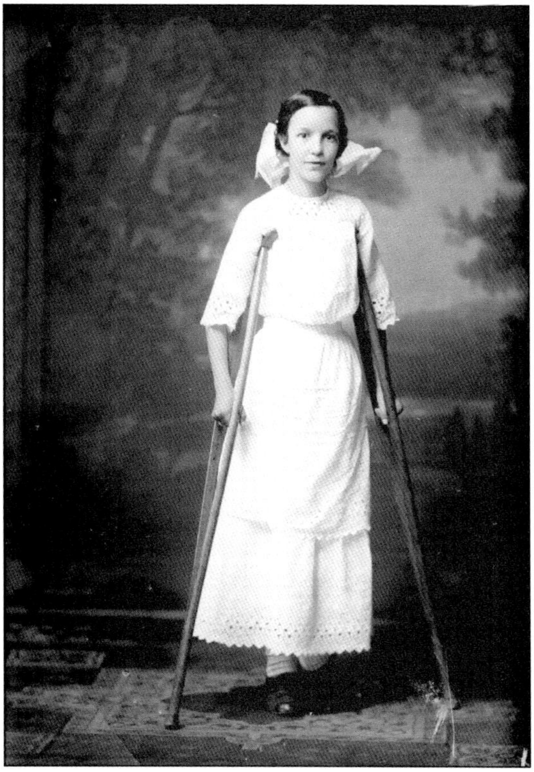

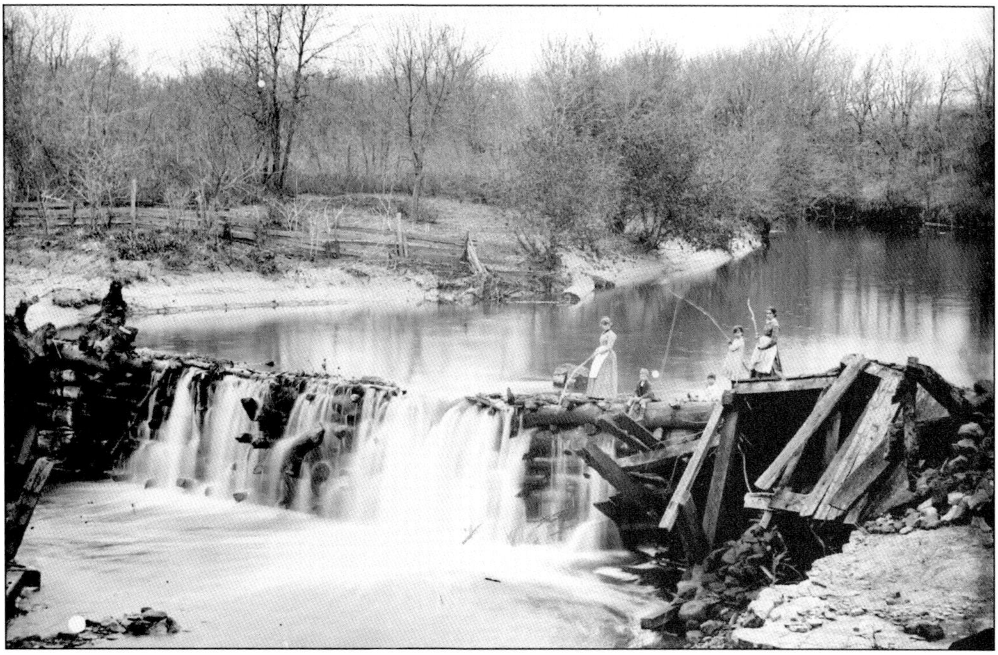

In this image, two women and three children fish off a log dam with homemade fishing poles. The style of the women's dresses suggests this photograph was taken in the early 1890s. Where this photograph was taken is unknown. It could have possibly been taken in Hall County. However, Leschinsky also had family in the Loup City area.

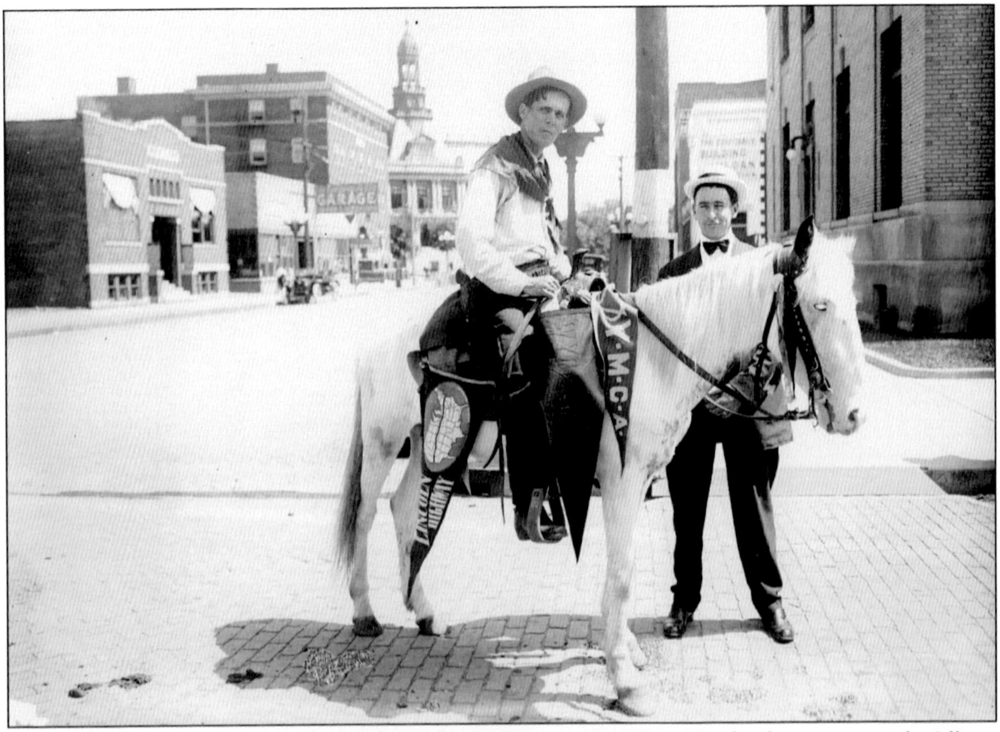

Taken on June 8, 1914, Red Fox James, also known as Red Fox Skiuhushu, poses with Albert Conners (standing), secretary of the Grand Island Commercial Club. Red Fox was a Native American activist who traveled across the country raising awareness on several issues. During his stay, Red Fox spoke at the Grand Island Business College about the importance of the Lincoln Highway, Boy Scouts, and a national holiday for Native Americans.

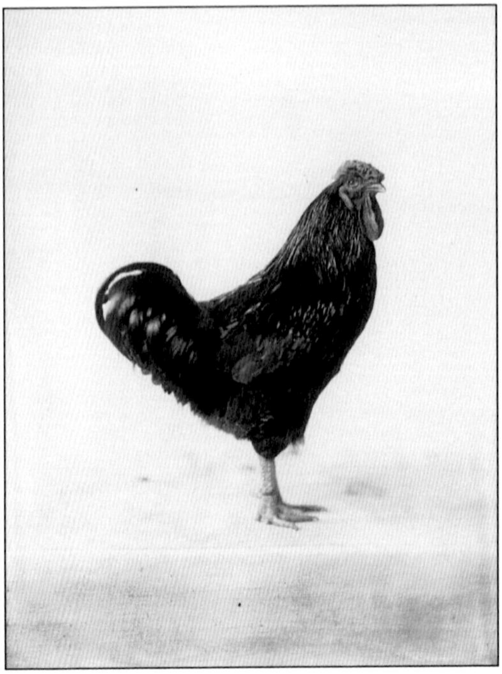

This fine-looking bird belonged to A. M. Johnson of Clarks. Clarks is about 34 miles northeast of Grand Island. Johnson's rooster poses for this photograph in January 1914. Breeding and showing poultry was a popular pastime during the early 20th century, and Grand Island hosted a number of poultry shows.

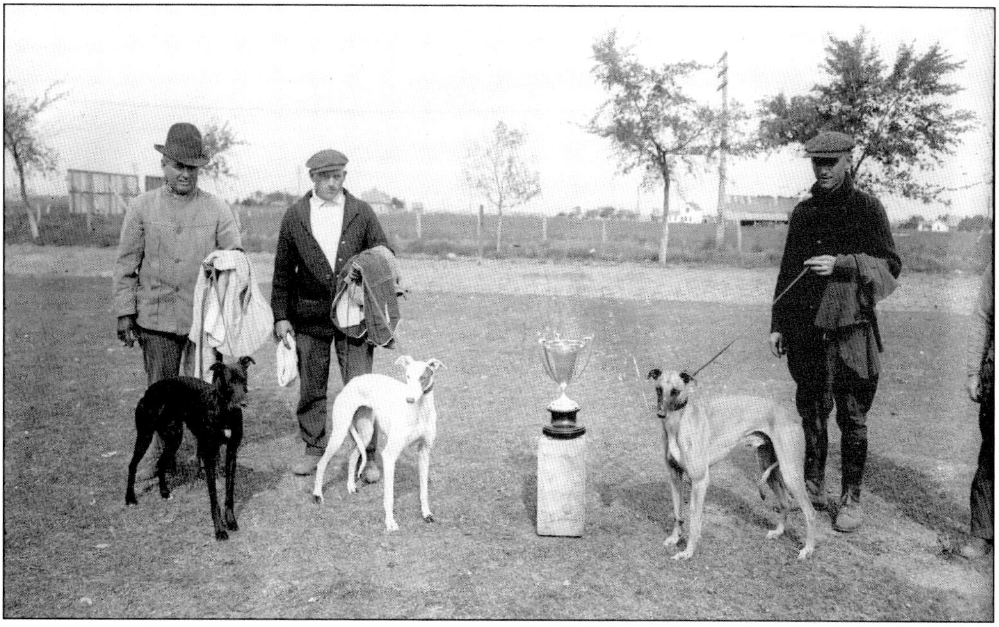

The National Coursing Association held its 10-day national meet in Grand Island from October 1–10, 1917. Coursing at this time referred to greyhound track racing. In this photograph, three hounds and their owners pose with one of the meet's cups. In 1917, the Waterloo Cup was won by Buck owned by Dudley and Obenland of Clay Center, Kansas. Mournful Mose, owned by O. Osterdorf of Wichita, Kansas, took home the Aberdeen Cup.

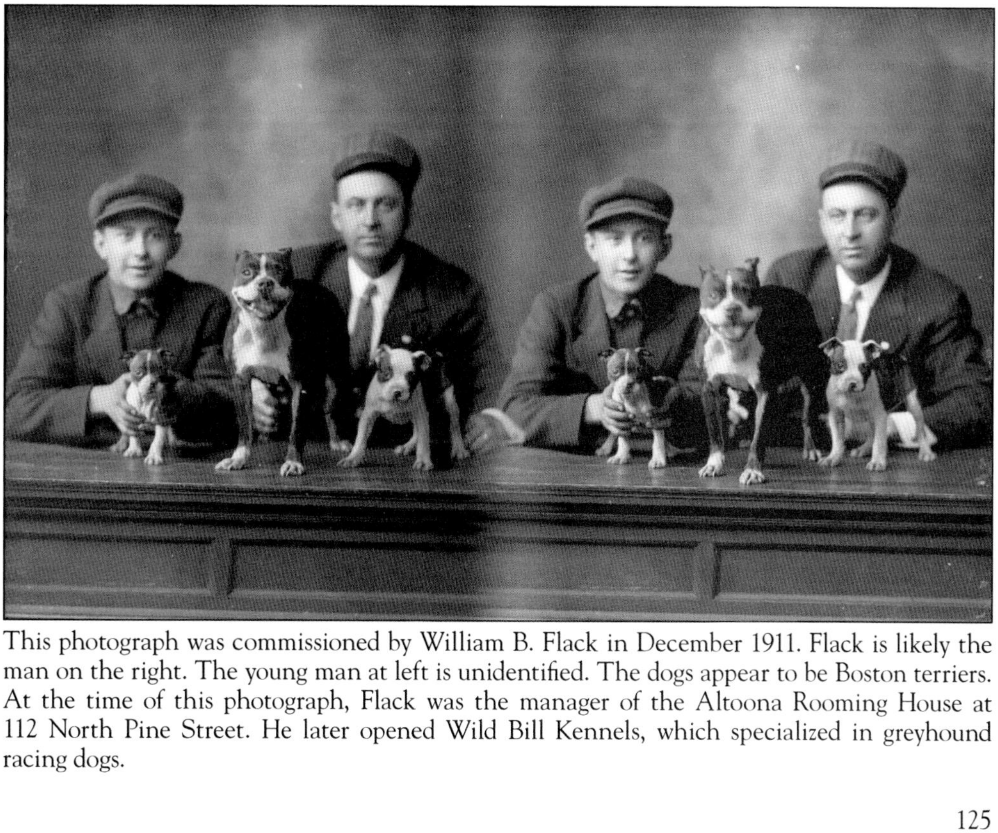

This photograph was commissioned by William B. Flack in December 1911. Flack is likely the man on the right. The young man at left is unidentified. The dogs appear to be Boston terriers. At the time of this photograph, Flack was the manager of the Altoona Rooming House at 112 North Pine Street. He later opened Wild Bill Kennels, which specialized in greyhound racing dogs.

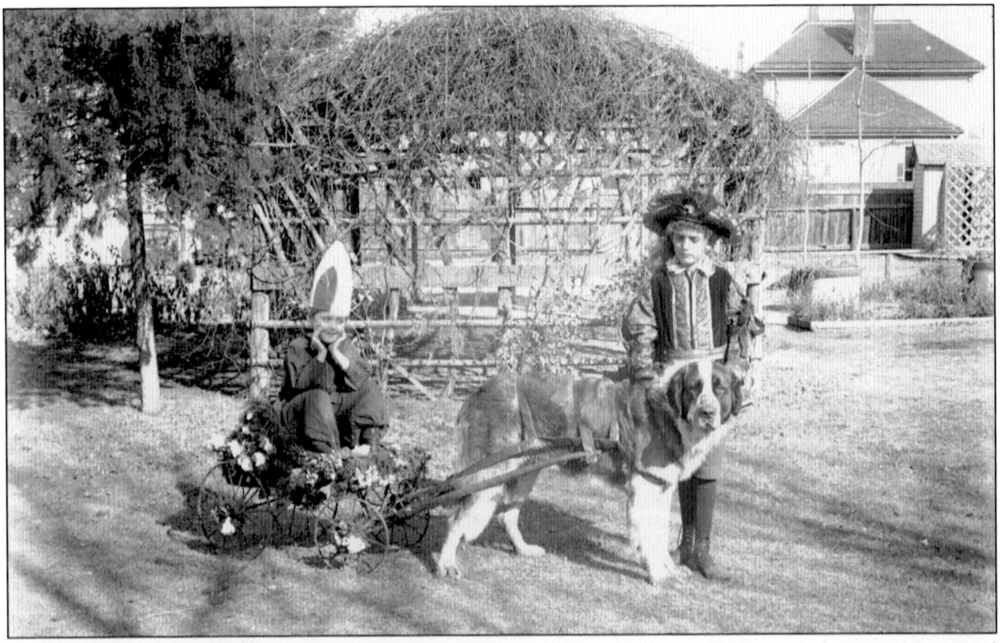

This image was found among Julius Leschinsky's personal collection. It features his sons Armand (left) and Oswald (right) posing in costumes with the family dog. The boys appear to be wearing Renaissance-style costumes. Their dog has been harnessed to a small wagon decorated with flowers. The occasion for this photograph is unknown.

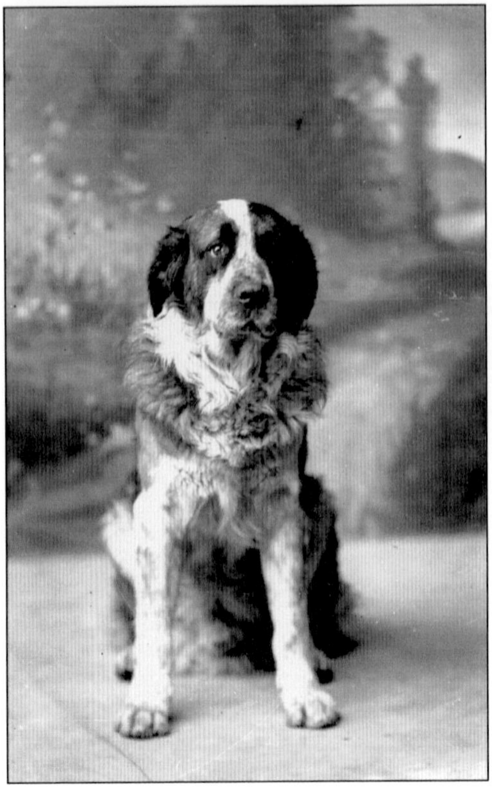

This big dog with gentle eyes is found in several of the Leschinsky family photographs, often with sons Oswald and Armand. During the late 19th and early 20th centuries, few families could afford to have photographs taken of their pets. However, Leschinsky often took his camera home, capturing many unique images of his family and their pets.

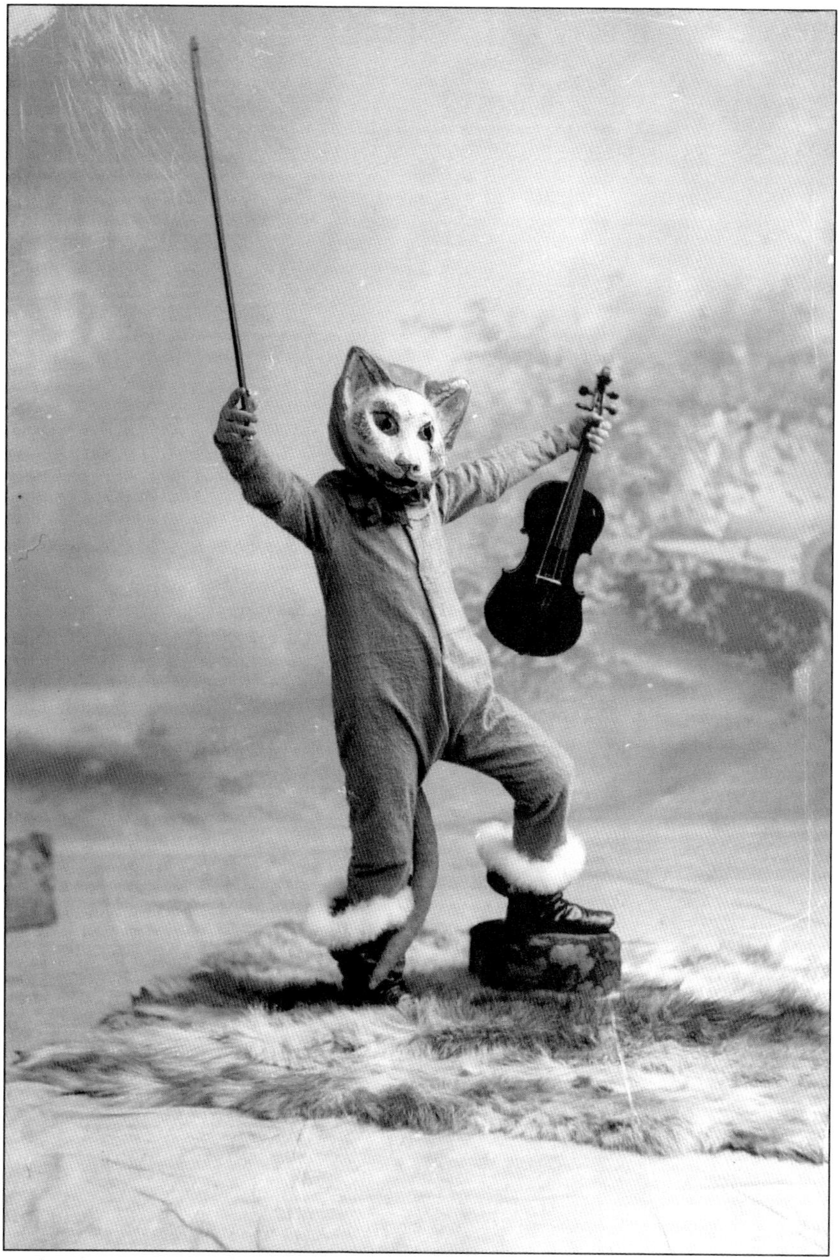

Hidden under this papier-mâché cat mask is Oswald Leschinsky, oldest son of Julius Leschinsky. Oswald's given name was Frederick Charles Oswald Leschinsky. He was born on July 21, 1889, in Grand Island. As an adult, he followed his father into the photography business, only to die suddenly at the age of 37. In this photograph, taken in the late 1890s, Oswald poses in his father's photography studio as a character from the popular nursery rhyme, "Hey Diddle, Diddle." The mask appears to be store-bought and would have been available at several local variety stores. The rest of Oswald's costume, right down to his tail, was likely handmade, possibly by his mother, Minnie. It is likely Oswald's costume was created for the Liederkranz's annual children's masquerade. The Leschinsky family was actively involved in the Liederkranz Society. Julius even served as the organization's president for a number of years.